Dispute Settlement in the World Trade Organization

Dispute Settlement in the World Trade Organization

Practice and Procedure

❖ ❖ ❖ ❖ ❖

by
David Palmeter
and
Petros C. Mavroidis

Springer-Science+
Business Media, B.V.

Library of Congress Cataloging-in-Publication Data

Palmeter, N. David.
Dispute settlement in the World Trade Organization : practice and procedure / by David Palmeter and Petros C. Mavroidis.
p. cm.
Includes index.
ISBN 978-94-011-9793-9 ISBN 978-94-011-9791-5 (eBook)
DOI 10.1007/978-94-011-9791-5
1. General Agreement on Tariffs and Trade (Organization)
2. Tariff--Law and legislation. 3. Foreign trade regulation.
4. Dispute resolution (Law) I. Mavroidis, Petros C. II. Title.
K4602.2 1999
341.7'543--dc21 98-49974

ISBN 978-94-011-9793-9

Originally published by Martinus Nijhoff Publishers 1999

Legal progress is often secreted
in the interstices of legal procedure."

—Oliver Wendell Holmes, Jr.

Table of Contents

CHAPTER 3

Sources of Law 35

CHAPTER 4

The Panel Process 61

CHAPTER 5

Special Rules and Procedures 99

CHAPTER 9
Conclusion 175

Appendices 187

Preface

This is a work for practitioners, for diplomats and government lawyers who prepare and present cases to dispute settlement panels of the World Trade Organization (WTO) and its Appellate Body, and for private practitioners who advise or represent governments and private clients with an interest in the outcomes of these proceedings. It grew from the experience of its authors, a private practitioner who has advised and represented governments and private parties under both the WTO and its predecessor, the General Agreement on Tariffs and Trade (GATT), and a former official of the Legal Affairs Division of GATT and the WTO who advised and assisted numerous panels. We have attempted to address the kinds of procedural questions that confronted us in the very practical world of dispute settlement. We deal with the substantive law of the WTO only incidentally, in connection with procedural issues.

To assist the reader, the appendices contain the texts of the agreements that are the subject of the book, most notably the WTO *Understanding on Rules and Procedures Governing the Settlement of Disputes*. They also contain the provisions of other WTO agreements relevant to dispute settlement. The full texts of these agreements are available from the World Trade Organization and from its page on the World Wide Web, www.wto.org. All footnote numbering in the appendices containing particular provisions of agreements corresponds to the numbering in the full text. Since Articles 31 and 32 of the *Vienna Convention on the Law of Treaties* are central to the interpretation of the WTO texts, these too are included in the appendices.

Chapter 3 is based upon David Palmeter and Petros C. Mavroidis, *The WTO Legal System: Sources of Law*, 92 AJIL 398 (1998), © The American Society of International Law, substantial portions of which are used with permission.

We have benefited from many colleagues and friends who read all or parts of the manuscript and offered helpful comments: Patrick Blatter, Michael P. Daniels, William J. Davey, Paul Demaret, Natalie Erard, Robert E. Howse, Brenda Jacobs, Alexander Koff, Gabrielle Marceau, Ernst-Ulrich Petersmann, Yves Renouf, Andrew W. Shoyer, Randi S. Turner, Deborah Wengel and the Hon. Diane P. Wood. To all of them, our sincere thanks.

CHAPTER 1
Overview

§1.01 THE ITO, THE GATT, AND THE WTO

[1] Bretton Woods and the Havana Charter

Even as World War II was being fought, allied leaders began to plan for the post-war world which, they intended, would not be characterized by the economic isolationism that had marked the pre-war years, particularly the 1930s, and which, many believed, contributed in no small way to the deepening of the Great Depression and the onset of war. In a 1941 speech entitled "Post-War Commercial Policy," United States Undersecretary of State Sumner Wells said:

> Nations have more often than not undertaken economic discriminations and raised up trade barriers with complete disregard for the damaging effects on the trade and livelihood of other peoples, and ironically enough, with similar disregard for the harmful resultant effects upon their own export trade.
>
> The resultant misery, bewilderment, and resentment, together with other equally pernicious contributing causes, paved the way for the rise of those very dictatorships which have plunged almost the entire world into war. [1]

These economic concerns eventually led to the famed July 1944 conference at Bretton Woods, New Hampshire, and the resulting "Bretton

[1] U.S. DEP'T OF STATE, PUB. NO. 1660, Commercial Policy Series 71 (1941), *quoted in* JOHN H. JACKSON, WORLD TRADE AND THE LAW OF GATT 38 (Bobbs-Merrill, 1969).

Woods organizations," the International Bank for Reconstruction and Development (commonly known as the World Bank) and the International Monetary Fund. Probably because Bretton Woods was attended only by representatives of finance ministries and not by representatives of trade ministries, an agreement covering trade was not negotiated there. A trade agreement was very much in the minds of allied economic leaders, however, and in early December 1945, the United States issued a proposal for an International Trade Organization, the ITO. But it was not the time for such an ambitious proposal. To the contrary, almost five years to the day later, on December 6, 1950, the United States Department of State announced that the ITO was dead, killed by the United States Congress which — eerily reminiscent of the United States Senate's treatment of the Treaty of Versailles and the League of Nations — refused to approve it.[2]

Still all was not lost. An odd portion of the ITO, in an odd way, survived. It was known as the General Agreement on Tariffs and Trade, or GATT, and it lasted for nearly half a century, for 47 years. On January 1, 1995, it was replaced by the World Trade Organization, the WTO, an entity broader both in its reach and in its effectiveness, but which is not at all like the ITO was intended to be.

[2] The negotiation of GATT

The ITO was ambitious, certainly too ambitious for the United States Congress and perhaps, with the advantage of hindsight, too ambitious by almost any reasonable standard. It was negotiated over a two year period, from 1946 through 1948, at a series of meetings in London, New York, Geneva, and finally at a United Nations Conference on Trade and Employment in Havana, Cuba, which produced the "Havana Charter for an International Trade Organization." As the conference name suggests, the ITO encompassed not only trade policy, but also employment policy. In addi-

[2]This section draws heavily on RICHARD N. GARDNER, STERLING-DOLLAR DIPLOMACY IN CURRENT PERSPECTIVE: THE ORIGINS AND PROSPECTS OF OUR INTERNATIONAL ECONOMIC ORDER (Columbia Univ. Press ed., 1980); ROBERT E. HUDEC, THE GATT LEGAL SYSTEM AND WORLD TRADE DIPLOMACY (Butterworth 2d ed. 1990); JACKSON, *supra* note 1, and on the WORLD TRADE ORGANIZATION, ANALYTICAL INDEX, GUIDE TO GATT LAW AND PRACTICE (1995). In addition, JOHN JACKSON, THE WORLD TRADING SYSTEM (MIT Press 2d ed.1997) provides an excellent history and description of the world trading system.

tion, it covered commodity agreements, economic development, and restrictive business practices.

While the more ambitious provisions of the ITO were being negotiated, however, governments were interested in relaxing tariffs and other trade restrictions more rapidly. A Drafting Committee, under the sponsorship of the Preparatory Committee charged with drafting the ITO charter, meeting in January and February 1947 at Lake Success, New York, produced a full draft of the GATT. From April through October 1947, the members of the Preparatory Committee conducted a round of tariff negotiations in the course of their ITO work at the European Office of the United Nations in Geneva. This became the first of GATT's eventual eight rounds of negotiations. It produced the "Geneva Final Act," consisting of the Lake Success text of GATT and the schedules of tariff commitments made by the 25 governments taking part.[3] It also included a "Protocol of Provisional Application" or "PPA," a measure intended to be a temporary expedient, which ended up being fundamental to GATT for its 47-year existence.

[3] The Protocol of Provisional Application (PPA)

The broad scope of the ITO called for changes in the laws of many signatory governments and, consequently, eventual legislative approval under their various constitutional systems before it could become effective. Some governments did not want to wait until that process was completed and, accordingly, at the end of October 1947, eight of them agreed to apply GATT provisionally as of January 1, 1948.[4] Under the terms of the PPA, the eight undertook to apply parts I and III of GATT fully, and to apply part II only "to the fullest extent not inconsistent with existing legislation."[5] Part I contained just two articles, dealing with non-discrimination among competing foreign suppliers (most-favored-nation, or MFN) and the schedule of tariff rates just negotiated. Part III contained articles dealing, for the most part,

[3] Final Act Adopted at the Conclusion of the Second Session of the Preparatory Committee of the United Nations Conference on Trade and Employment, UN Sales No. 1947.II/10; 55 UNTS 187 (1947).

[4] The eight were: Australia, Belgium, Canada, France, Luxembourg, the Netherlands, the United Kingdom, and the United States.

[5] 55 U.N.T.S. 308, 1 (a) and (b) (1947).

with administrative matters. The substantive heart of GATT, Part II, consisted of Articles III through XXIII. These included provisions covering national treatment, antidumping and countervailing duties, valuation of imports for customs purposes, marks of origin, import and export quotas and limitations, restrictions on imports for balance of payments purposes, exchange arrangements, subsidies, state trading enterprises, governmental assistance to economic development, emergency action on imports of particular products, exceptions to GATT obligations, including exceptions necessary to protect human, plant, and animal life, health, and safety; and exceptions for national security purposes. Part II thus provides the necessary market access complement to Part I.

Together, Parts I and II set out the basic policy agreed to in GATT for trade liberalization that is based on (i) preference for tariff protection to other forms of protection, such as quantitative restrictions or "quotas"; (ii) following on this, abolition (in principle, but not always in practice) of all quotas; (iii) application of quotas only exceptionally and only with multilateral permission; (iv) most-favored-nation (MFN) treatment, granted in principle to all GATT parties, subject to specific, narrowly-drawn, exceptions; (v) national treatment granted to all products of GATT parties that have lawfully cleared customs.

The application of Part II only to the extent that its articles were consistent with existing legislation created what became known as the "grandfather rights."[6] Consequently, parties with grandfathered rights were allowed to continue applying GATT-inconsistent measures notwithstanding their obligations under the General Agreement. Article XXIX:2 of GATT shows how temporary this was intended to be. It provides, "Part II of this Agreement shall be suspended on the day on which the Havana Charter comes into force." This was expected to occur within a fairly short time, so that inconsistent domestic legislation was not expected to be long-lived. But that day never came, and because the Havana Charter never came into force, GATT, for its entire 47 years, was applied on a "provisional" basis.

[6]An example would be the U.S. countervailing duty law which did not call for a determination of material injury, as called for by Article VI in Part II of GATT, until the United States agreed to include such a requirement for signatories to the so-called 1979 Tokyo Round Subsidies Code or for other countries that entered into comparable bilateral agreements with the United States.

[4] GATT's 47 "provisional" years

Between the October 1947 issuance of the Protocol of Provisional Application and its effectiveness on January 1, 1948, most of the other countries participating in the Geneva tariff negotiations also agreed to apply the Protocol. The 1947 Geneva negotiations were followed by seven additional negotiations, called "rounds," each of which involved more countries as additional countries acceded to the General Agreement:

Round[7]	*Dates*	*Number of Parties*[8]
Geneva	1947	19
Annecy	1949	27
Torquay	1950	33
Geneva	1956	36
Dillon	1960-61	43
Kennedy	1962-67	74
Tokyo	1973-79	85
Uruguay	1986-94	128

All of the rounds through the 1960-61 Dillon Round dealt with tariff cuts. In the Kennedy Round, a first, relatively unsuccessful attempt was made to deal with so-called "non-tariff barriers," or NTBs which, as tariffs were cut progressively, became more prominent as trade barriers. A Kennedy Round Antidumping Code and an agreement dealing with a highly protectionist U.S. method of valuing certain chemicals and footwear for customs purposes were not accepted by the U.S. Congress on the stated

[7] The first four rounds are named for the place where they were held, Geneva; Annecy, France; and Torquay, England. The Dillon Round was named after the United States Under Secretary of State C. Douglas Dillon, and the Kennedy Round after President John F. Kennedy, who were instrumental in starting the rounds. The Tokyo and Uruguay Rounds were named after the city and the country, respectively, where trade ministers agreed to launch the rounds.

[8] Computations of the total number of parties vary from source to source, because some of the original 1947 group subsequently withdrew from GATT (e.g., China, Czechoslovakia) and because countries that acceded to GATT during the course of a round would be counted at the end, but not the beginning. Counts of participants in GATT activities may vary too depending on how the European Union is accounted for — as a single entity or as individual Members.

grounds that in reaching these agreements, the U.S. negotiators had exceeded their mandate.[9]

This experience soured many trading partners of the United States, who found themselves having to negotiate twice: first with the U.S. negotiators and then with the Congress. If NTBs were to be dealt with in future negotiations, another way had to be found. Another way was found that took into account the need of U.S. trading partners to know that a package put together with U.S. negotiators would not be taken apart by the Congress, and the constitutional need of the United States to refer to Congress all agreements requiring statutory change, which was the case with most measures dealing with NTBs. The solution was the so-called "fast-track procedure" first included in the Trade Act of 1974.[10] Under this procedure, the Congress agreed that a bill implementing a negotiated agreement would not be amendable on the floor of either House of Congress, would not be stalled in Committee, and would receive a straight "yes or no" vote within a stated time period.

This provision permitted the Tokyo Round negotiations to go forward, and led to the adoption of a wide variety of side-agreements or "codes" dealing with non-tariff issues:

1. Agreement on Implementation of Article VI of the General Agreement on Tariffs and Trade (Antidumping Code).
2. Agreement on Interpretation and Application of Articles VI, XVI and XXIII of the General Agreement on Tariffs and Trade (Subsidies Code).
3. Agreement on Import Licensing Procedures.
4. Agreement on Trade in Civil Aircraft.
5. Agreement on Technical Barriers to Trade.
6. Agreement on Implementation of Article VII of the General Agreement on Tariffs and Trade and Protocol to the Agreement (Customs Valuation Code).
7. Agreement on Government Procurement.

The Tokyo Round negotiations were the most extensive ever undertaken, but the 1986 - 1994 Uruguay Round was even more extensive in both

[9] *See* Russell Long, *United States Law and the International Antidumping Code*, 3 Int'l Lawyer 464 (1969).

[10] Pub. Law 93-618, 88 Stat. 1978.

its reach and its results. Before turning to a discussion of the Uruguay Round, however, we shall review briefly the evolution of dispute settlement under GATT, particularly as it evolved after the Tokyo Round. As we shall see, dispute settlement was one of the major goals of the Uruguay Round negotiators, and one of their major accomplishments.

[5] GATT dispute settlement[11]

Early dispute settlement in GATT reflected its diplomatic roots. In fact, the process initially was referred to as "conciliation," not as dispute settlement. It all began with a complaint in the summer of 1948 by the Netherlands against Cuba which presented the question, did the most-favored-nation obligation of Article I apply to consular taxes. The matter was referred to the chairman, who ruled that Article I did apply. From these early beginnings of rulings by the chairman, disputes later came to be referred to working parties which consisted of the complaining party, the party complained against, and any others that had an interest. Eventually, the parties directly involved were dropped, and a three or five-member panel process was adopted, using neutral panelists rather than representatives of parties with an interest in the issue.

Most of the advocates before panels and most of the panelists themselves — the "judges" — were diplomats, not lawyers, and as Robert Hudec has observed, "Legal rulings were drafted with an elusive diplomatic vagueness."[12] The goal of the process was more to reach a solution mutually agreeable to the parties than to render a decision in a legal dispute.[13]

GATT dispute settlement was characterized as well by the fact that its procedural rules were very limited, largely because it was anticipated that the ITO rules soon would apply. The ITO Charter contained detailed dispute settlement rules that included a provision for the reference of ques-

---

[11]This section draws heavily on Robert E. Hudec's outstanding two volume history of GATT dispute settlement, The GATT Legal System and World Trade Diplomacy, *supra*, note 2 and Enforcing International Trade Law: The Evolution of the Modern GATT Legal System (Butterworth 1993) (hereafter Enforcing International Trade Law).

[12]Hudec, Enforcing International Trade Law, *supra* note 11, at 12.

[13]*See*, William J. Davey, *Dispute Settlement in GATT*, 11 Fordham International Law Journal 51, 65 (1987).

tions to the International Court of Justice, the ICJ. The limited rules in GATT, based on two of the proposed ITO rules, were GATT Articles XXII and XXIII, dealing, respectively, with consultations and with "nullification and impairment," a phrase that was basic to the jurisprudence of GATT and now is basic to the jurisprudence of the WTO.

By themselves, the consultation provisions of Article XXII have no direct consequences. Article XXII:1 simply requires each contracting party to afford other parties adequate opportunity for consultation with respect to any matter affecting the operation of the Agreement. Article XXII:2 authorizes the CONTRACTING PARTIES acting jointly, at the request of a contracting party, to consult with other parties on matters which were not resolved through Article XXII:1 consultations.[14] Eventually, these consultations became a basis for the generation of GATT's dispute settlement process which was grounded in Article XXIII.

Article XXIII:1 provides that if any contracting party considers that any benefit directly or indirectly accruing to it under the Agreement was being nullified or impaired by another party, it can make written representations or proposals to that other party. If this does not lead to a satisfactory adjustment, the complaining party is authorized by Article XXIII:2 to refer the matter to the CONTRACTING PARTIES, who are required to investigate and make appropriate recommendations. In an appropriate case, Article XXIII:2 permitted the CONTRACTING PARTIES to authorize the complaining party to suspend the application of tariff concessions or other GATT obligations to the party found to be acting inconsistent with its obligations under the Agreement.

Neither article contains any specific procedures.[15] These evolved over time. Some formality was added at the conclusion of the Tokyo Round with the adoption of the *Understanding on Notification, Consultation, Dispute Settlement and Surveillance of 28 November 1979*, which included an annex setting out an *Agreed Description of the Customary Practice of the GATT in the Field of Dispute Settlement.* This *Description* noted, in part, that:

---

[14]The term CONTRACTING PARTIES in upper case letters was the GATT convention for referring to joint action by all of the parties to the Agreement. Since GATT was an agreement, not an organization, GATT itself could not act. In lower case, the term referred to individual signatories.

[15]An early decision by the CONTRACTING PARTIES held that consultations under Article XXII:1 would be considered as fulfilling the consultation requirements of Article XXIII:1. BISD 9S/20.

> Panels set up their own working procedures. The practice for the panels has been to hold two or three formal meetings with the parties concerned. The panel invited the parties to present their views either in writing and/or orally in the presence of each other. The panel can question both parties on any matter which it considers relevant to the dispute. Panels have also heard the views of any contracting party having a substantial interest in the matter, which is not directly party to the dispute, but which has expressed in the Council a desire to present its views. Written memoranda submitted to the panel have been considered confidential, but are made available to the parties to the dispute. Panels often consult with and seek information from any relevant source they deem appropriate and they sometimes consult experts to obtain their technical opinion on certain aspects of the matter. Panels may seek advice or assistance from the secretariat in its capacity as guardian of the General Agreement, especially on historical or procedural aspects. The secretariat provides the secretary and technical services for panels.[16]

Three years later, acting at a Ministerial Conference, the CONTRACTING PARTIES reaffirmed the 1979 Understanding, and added more detail, including a requirement that, "The contracting party to which such a recommendation [i.e., to bring a challenged measure into conformity with GATT] has been addressed, shall report within a reasonable specified period on action taken or on its reasons for not implementing the recommendation or ruling by the CONTRACTING PARTIES."[17] Further minor steps were taken in a *Decision on Dispute Settlement Procedures* on November 30, 1984.[18]

Dispute settlement under GATT was handicapped, however, by the requirement of Article XXIII that all matters be decided, and all action be approved, by the CONTRACTING PARTIES. GATT, in legal form, was a contract — a multi-party contract — and any decision to amend, modify, or interpret that contract required the consent of all of the parties.[19] In practice, this meant that the losing party in a dispute settlement proceeding not only could refuse to agree, and therefore "block" the adoption of an adverse report, it even could refuse to agree to the very establishment of a

[16]*Agreed Description of the Customary Practice of the GATT in the Field of Dispute Settlement (Article XXIII:2),* BISD 26S/215, 217, ¶ 6 (iv).

[17]BISD 29S/13, 15, ¶ (viii).

[18]BISD 31S/9.

[19]In the absence of a specific rule providing otherwise, Article 40 of the *Vienna Convention on the Law of Treaties* requires unanimity among the contracting states.

panel, thereby avoiding the embarrassment of an adopted adverse report altogether.

Adverse GATT panel reports indeed were blocked by losing parties. In fact, parties who anticipated losing sometimes even blocked the establishment of a panel. It is a tribute to the system and the degree to which the parties valued it that blocking of both the establishment of panels and the adoption of their reports did not occur more often than they did. In fact, Prof. Hudec's study shows that from 1947 to 1992, the losing party eventually accepted the results of an adverse panel report in approximately 90 percent of the cases.[20] Still, blocking was a problem, and seemed in the 1980s to be occurring with increasing frequency. A significant step toward alleviating the blockage — at least at the state of establishing a panel — was taken with the adoption of the "Montreal Rules." These grew out of a December 1988 Ministerial meeting in that Canadian city to review the progress of the Uruguay Round and to reap an "early harvest" of any completed results of the Round. Following further consideration in early 1989 in Geneva, the Montreal Rules were adopted by the CONTRACTING PARTIES in April of 1989.[21] They formed the basis of what eventually became the WTO's *Understanding on Rules and Procedures Governing the Settlement of Disputes.*

The CONTRACTING PARTIES agreed to apply the Montreal Rules "on a trial basis from 1 May 1989 to the end of the Uruguay Round in respect of complaints brought during that period under Article XXII or XXIII."[22] The most significant portions of the rules were those that placed time limits on consultations and that provided further for the automatic establishment of a panel. Parties to which a request for consultations had been made under either Article XXII:1 or XXIII:1 would be required to reply to that request within 10 days, and to agree to enter into consultations in good faith in no less than 30 days. In the absence of an agreement to consult and the holding of timely consultations, the complaining party could proceed directly to request the establishment of a panel.[23] If consultations failed to settle the dispute within 60 days of the request, the complaining party then could request the establishment of a panel.[24]

---

[20]HUDEC, ENFORCING INTERNATIONAL TRADE LAW, *supra* note 11 at 278.

[21]*Improvements to the GATT Dispute Settlement Rules and Procedures*, Decision of 12 April 1989, BISD 36S/61 (hereafter "Montreal Rules").

[22]*Id.* ¶ A. 3.

[23]*Id.* ¶ C.1.

[24]*Id.* ¶ C.2.

Most significantly, in GATT's all-too-typically indirect language, the Montreal Rules provided that, "If the complaining party so requests, a decision to establish a panel or a working party shall be taken at the latest at the Council meeting following that at which the request first appeared as an item on the Council's regular agenda, unless at that meeting the Council decides otherwise."[25] What this meant was that a panel would be established, without fail, at the second meeting of the GATT Council after the request was put on the agenda, unless the Council decided otherwise. For the Council to decide "otherwise" under GATT's process of decision by consensus, however, all parties — including the complaining party — would have to decide "otherwise." In other words, the system had changed from one that required consensus — "positive consensus" — to establish a panel to a system of "negative consensus" — a system that required consensus *not* to establish a panel.

These changes were adopted on a permanent basis in the WTO. Other significant provisions of the Montreal Rules that eventually found their way into the WTO, in identical or similar form, dealt with the terms of reference for panels, the composition of panels, procedures for multiple complaints and for third party participation, and time limits. Specific rules were included, too, on the sensitive topic of adoption of panel reports, which made blocking somewhat more embarrassing diplomatically, but did not eliminate it. Elimination of the power of the losing party unilaterally to block adoption of a report had to await the completion of the Uruguay Round and the establishment of the World Trade Organization.

§1.02 THE URUGUAY ROUND

The Uruguay Round was the largest, most far-reaching, longest, and most contentious round of multilateral trade negotiations ever undertaken. It began in September of 1986, the end of the Southern Hemisphere's winter, in a driving wind, under a gray sky, with an off-season meeting of GATT Ministers in the Uruguayan resort city of Punta del Este. It concluded nearly eight years later, in the warm April sunshine of Marrakesh, Morocco. "Few trading caravans can have viewed this beautiful city with as much pleasure — and as much relief — as ours does," GATT Director-General

[25] *Id.* ¶ F.(a).

Peter Sutherland told the representatives of 124 Uruguay Round participants assembled to sign the *Marrakesh Agreement Establishing the World Trade Organization*. "But then very few trading caravans were on the road for more than seven years, and none carried such a priceless cargo."[26]

The Uruguay Round grew largely out of the unfinished business of the Tokyo Round which, despite its achievements, was viewed by many as incomplete. The Tokyo Round had largely solved the structural problems of dealing with non-tariff barriers, but parties were not required to agree to its codes dealing with dumping, subsidies, government procurement and the like. These agreements bound only those parties that adhered to them, creating what many called "GATT *a la carte.*" Agriculture, the perennial problem of international trade, had been left all but untouched, and nothing had been done about trade in counterfeit goods, a new concern of the industrialized countries, particularly of the United States.

These and other concerns led to a November 1982 meeting of GATT Ministers in Geneva, called primarily by the United States in the hope of launching a new round of multilateral negotiations. The effort failed, but not completely. Efforts to find a basis for further negotiations continued through the early 1980s, and these led eventually to the decision to meet in September 1986 in Punta del Este.

The Punta del Este Declaration, issued by the Ministers at the close of the conference, outlined the agenda for the negotiations and stated with undue optimism that they would be concluded within four years. The negotiations, as noted, took nearly twice as long. In the process, the negotiating agenda, not surprisingly, changed in important ways. As it was, however, the Punta del Este agenda was far-reaching.

The major portion of the agenda concerned trade in goods, GATT's traditional subject. In addition to tariff liberalization, the Punta del Este agenda called for negotiations on non-tariff measures, tropical and natural resource-based products, textiles and clothing, agriculture, safeguards (provisions that allow countries temporarily to protect domestic industries injured by import competition), subsidies, and dispute settlement. Particularly noteworthy was the inclusion on the agenda of a broadened version of the counterfeit goods item: "Trade-related aspects of intellectual property rights, including trade in counterfeit goods," and a further item covering trade-related investment measures. These led eventually to WTO agreements in each area, the Agreement on Trade-Related Aspects of Intellectual

[26]GATT Focus, May 1994, No. 107 *Special Issue* at 2.

Property Rights (TRIPS) and the Agreement on Trade-Related Investment Measures (TRIMS). Finally, Part II of the agenda called for negotiations on trade in services, leading to the WTO's General Agreement on Trade in Services (GATS).

The course of the Uruguay Round negotiations, as Peter Sutherland's Marrakesh remarks suggest, was long and tortuous.[27] Deadlines were set, missed, set again, and missed again. The most likely Round-breaker, as the headlines of the times suggested, was agriculture, but it was not alone. Industries interested in the use of antidumping laws against imported goods had their own demands, which almost sank the round at the last minute.[28] But success finally came, and on December 15, 1993, negotiations were formally ended. The world's press congratulated the negotiators, but beyond a cleaning up of loose ends, much work remained, including the monumental clerical and administrative task of putting the agreements into consistent form, and preparing for Marrakesh and the formal signing. When it all was done, the world had a new World Trade Organization.

§1.03 THE WORLD TRADE ORGANIZATION

The World Trade Organization officially was established on January 1, 1995, as the successor to GATT and as the legal and institutional foundation of the international trading system. It was formally created by the *Marrakesh Agreement Establishing the World Trade Organization,* ("*WTO Agreement*") signed by the Ministers the previous April. Unlike GATT, the WTO is an organization, not just an agreement. It is on an official par with the

[27]The history of the Uruguay Round has been told in a number of works. John Croome, Reshaping the World Trading System: A History of the Uruguay Round (World Trade Organization 1995), is the most comprehensive of the histories published to date; Hugo Paemen & Alexandra Bensch, From the GATT to the WTO: The European Community in the Uruguay Round (Leuven University Press 1995) offers a European perspective; Ernest H. Preeg, Traders in a Brave New World: The Uruguay Round and the Future of the International Trading System (Chicago 1995) offers a United States perspective; and Jeffrey J. Schott, The Uruguay Round: An Assessment (Institute for International Economics 1994), is an early evaluation of the results from an economic and policy perspective.

[28]Ernst-Ulrich Petersmann, *The Dispute Settlement System of the World Trade Organization and the Evolution of the GATT Dispute Settlement System Since 1948*, 31 Common Market Law Review 1157, 1204, 1224 (1994).

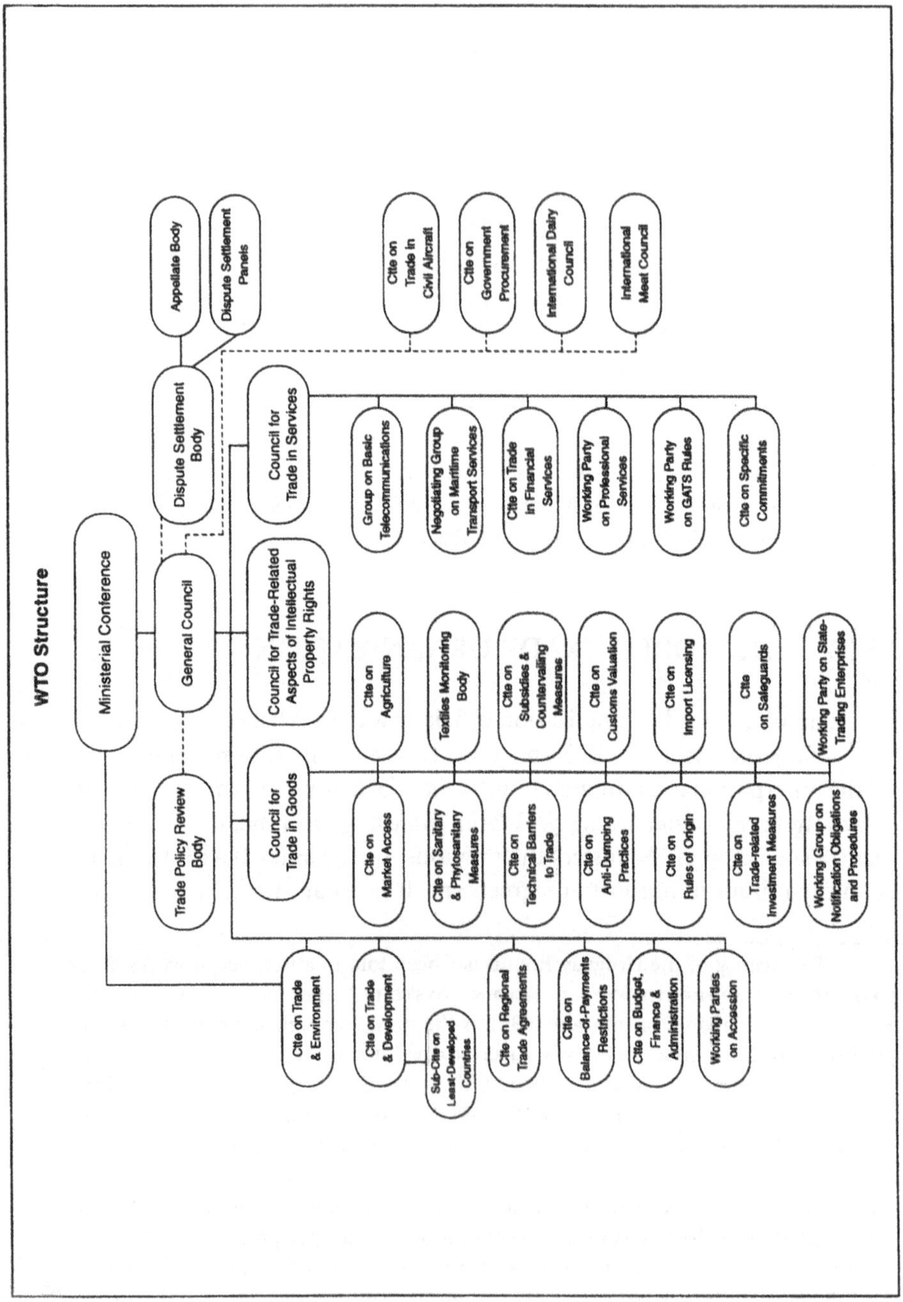
WTO Structure
Ministerial Conference
General Council
Trade Policy Review Body
Dispute Settlement Body
Appellate Body
Dispute Settlement Panels
Council for Trade in Goods
Council for Trade-Related Aspects of Intellectual Property Rights
Council for Trade in Services
Cttee on Trade in Civil Aircraft
Cttee on Government Procurement
International Dairy Council
International Meat Council
Group on Basic Telecommunications
Negotiating Group on Maritime Transport Services
Cttee on Trade in Financial Services
Working Party on Professional Services
Working Party on GATS Rules
Cttee on Specific Commitments
Cttee on Market Access
Cttee on Agriculture
Cttee on Sanitary & Phytosanitary Measures
Textiles Monitoring Body
Cttee on Technical Barriers to Trade
Cttee on Subsidies & Countervailing Measures
Cttee on Anti-Dumping Practices
Cttee on Customs Valuation
Cttee on Rules of Origin
Cttee on Import Licensing
Cttee on Trade-related Investment Measures
Cttee on Safeguards
Working Group on Notification Obligations and Procedures
Working Party on State-Trading Enterprises
Cttee on Trade & Environment
Cttee on Trade & Development
Sub-Cttee on Least-Developed Countries
Cttee on Regional Trade Agreements
Cttee on Balance-of-Payments Restrictions
Cttee on Budget, Finance & Administration
Working Parties on Accession

Bretton Woods organizations, the World Bank and the International Monetary Fund.[29]

Attached to the WTO Agreement are four annexes which contain the substance of the organization. Annex 1, with three subparts, is its substantive core. The first subpart, Annex 1A, contains 13 separate agreements covering trade in goods:

1. General Agreement on Tariffs and Trade 1994
2. Agreement on Agriculture
3. Agreement on the Application of Sanitary and Phytosanitary Measures
4. Agreement on Textiles and Clothing
5. Agreement on Technical Barriers to Trade
6. Agreement on Trade-Related Investment Measures
7. Agreement on Implementation of Articles VI of the General Agreement on Tariffs and Trade 1994 (Antidumping Agreement)
8. Agreement on Implementation of Article VII of the General Agreement on Tariffs and Trade 1994 (Customs Valuation Agreement)
9. Agreement on Preshipment Inspection
10. Agreement on Rules of Origin
11. Agreement on Import Licensing Procedures
12. Agreement on Subsidies and Countervailing Measures
13. Agreement on Safeguards

The first of the 13 agreements, General Agreement on Tariffs and Trade 1994, known as GATT 1994, contains the text of the original GATT, now known as GATT 1947, its "aquis" or the decisions of the GATT CONTRACTING PARTIES, six separate interpretative Understandings, and an implementing protocol signed at Marrakesh. Along with its annexes, GATT 1994 comprises the WTO's rules governing trade in goods. The next two subparts of Annex 1 cover the important new trade areas: *GATS*, in Annex 1B, and *TRIPS* in Annex 1C.

Annex 2 to the *WTO Agreement* consists of the *Understanding on Rules and Procedures Governing the Settlement of Disputes*, which is the subject of

[29] The WTO is described in detail in BERNARD HOEKMAN & MICHEL KOSTECKI, THE POLITICAL ECONOMY OF THE WORLD TRADING SYSTEM: FROM GATT TO THE WTO (Oxford 1995); *see also*, PATRICK MESSERLIN, LA NOUVELLE OMC (Dunod 1995).

this volume. Annex 3 contains the Trade Policy Review Mechanism, by which the WTO Secretariat conducts regular studies of the trade policies of its Members, while Annex 4 contains the text of two plurilateral agreements, the only *a la carte* aspects of the WTO that Members may join or not, as they wish. These are the *Agreement on Trade in Civil Aircraft*, and the *Agreement on Government Procurement*.[30]

The WTO is governed by a Ministerial Conference which meets at least every two years to review its performance and establish policy. On a day-to-day basis, the WTO is governed by its General Council and several subsidiary bodies, principally by separate Councils for Goods, for Services, and for TRIPS. In addition, there are committees for 12 of the 13 multilateral goods agreements and for the two plurilateral agreements. (The *Agreement on Preshipment Inspection* does not provide for a committee.)

The WTO has established a number of other committees dealing with areas of substantive and negotiating interest, such as trade and the environment, trade and development, and regional trade agreements. In addition, a number of substantive and negotiation groups, dealing with such topics as telecommunications, financial services, and maritime services, were established by the GATS Council. Of particular relevance to this study is one of the most important of the new bodies created by the *WTO Agreement* — the Dispute Settlement Body.

§1.04 THE DISPUTE SETTLEMENT BODY

The Dispute Settlement Body (DSB), consists of representatives of every WTO Member. It was created during the Uruguay Round to deal with disputes arising under any of the WTO agreements; it does so in accordance with the provisions of the *Understanding on Rules and Procedures Governing the Settlement of Disputes*, the "Dispute Settlement Understanding" or "DSU." The DSB has the authority to establish dispute settlement panels, to adopt panel and Appellate Body reports, to maintain surveillance of the implementation of the rulings and recommendations it adopts, and to authorize the suspension of concessions and other obligations under the covered

[30]Two other plurilateral agreements, the *International Dairy Agreement*, and the *International Bovine Meat Agreement*, were terminated as of 1 January 1998. WT/L/251, 17 December 1997, and WT/L/252, 16 December 1997.

WTO agreements, if its rulings and recommendations are not acted upon by Members in a timely fashion.

The DSB meets "as often as necessary to carry out its functions,"[31] normally monthly, but it may also meet at special sessions at the request of a Member. Its decisions are taken by consensus, which is deemed to have resulted if no Member present at the DSB meeting when a decision is taken formally objects.[32] It is presided over by a chairman, usually the head of one of the permanent missions to Geneva of one of its Members.

The DSB is more than the vehicle by which panels are established and reports adopted and implemented; it also serves as the forum where matters of dispute are discussed. While it has the legal authority not to establish a panel or not to adopt a report, this power is more illusory than real because the DSB operates on the "negative" consensus principle, the opposite of GATT's positive consensus principle. Under the WTO, as under GATT after the Montreal Rules became effective, panels will be established, automatically, *unless* there is consensus to the contrary. Unlike under GATT, however, under the WTO reports also will be adopted automatically *unless* there is consensus to the contrary. Since consensus requires the approval of the complaining party and the prevailing party, those parties, not the DSB, normally will have the effective last word on these crucial topics.

§1.05 THE DISPUTE SETTLEMENT UNDERSTANDING

The Dispute Settlement Understanding or DSU, with 27 sections totalling 143 paragraphs plus four appendices, is perhaps the most significant achievement of the Uruguay Round negotiations. Unique in public international law, the DSU confers compulsory jurisdiction on the DSB for purposes of resolving disputes. In the words of Article 3.2 of the DSU, "The dispute settlement system of the WTO is a central element in providing security and predictability to the multilateral trading system."

The DSU, which sets out the basic institutional and jurisdictional scope of WTO dispute settlement, also contains the rules of procedure for

[31] DSU Article 2.3.

[32] A WTO body "shall be deemed to have decided by consensus on a matter submitted for its consideration, if no Member, present at the meeting when the decision is taken, formally objects to the proposed decision." *WTO Agreement* Article IX, note 1.

Chairman of the DSB, in consultation with the parties, shall determine the rules and procedures to be followed within 10 days of a request to do so by either party. The DSB Chairman should be guided by the principle that special or additional rules and procedures should be used where possible, with the DSU rules and procedures being used where necessary to avoid conflict.[4]

[2] Simultaneous application of different agreements

Obligations can and do exist simultaneously under different WTO agreements, including GATT 1995 and the General Agreement on Trade in Services.[5] As one panel stated;

> [I]f we were to find the scope of the GATS and that of GATT to be mutually exclusive, in other words, if we were to find that a measure considered to fall within the scope of one agreement could not at the same time fall within the scope of the other, the value of members' obligations and commitments would be undermined and the object and purpose of both agreements would be frustrated. Obligations could be circumvented by the adoption of measures under one agreement with indirect effects on trade covered by the other without the possibility of any legal recourse.[6]

[3] Non-application between particular Members

The *WTO Agreement* provides that the DSU, the 13 multilateral agreements on trade in goods, *GATS*, and *TRIPS* "shall not apply as between any

[4]DSU Art. 1.2.

[5]*European Communities — Regime for the Importation, Sale and Distribution of Bananas*, AB-1997-3, WT/DS27/AB/R (9 September 1997) (Adopted 25 September 1997), ¶222; *Canada — Certain Measures Concerning Periodicals*, WT/DS31/R (14 March 1997) (Adopted as Modified by the Appellate Body 30 July 1997) ¶5.17; *Canada — Certain Measures Concerning Periodicals*, WT/DS31/AB/R (30 June 1997) (Adopted 30 July 1997), §IV, at 20.

[6]*European Communities — Regime for the Importation, Sale and Distribution of Bananas*, WT/DS27/R (22 May 1997) (Adopted as Modified by the Appellate Body 25 September 1997), ¶ 7.283.

Member and any other Member if either of the Members, at the time either becomes a Member, does not consent to such application."[7]

This provision conforms to Article XXXV of GATT 1947 which was widely invoked, particularly against Japan when it acceded to GATT in 1955. By mid-1997, only Botswana, Guinea and Lesotho continued to apply Article XXXV treatment against Japan, while Morocco and Tunisia applied Article XXXV against Israel. The only developed country maintaining Article XXXV treatment against other contracting parties as of mid-1995 was the United States with respect to Hungary and Mongolia.

§ 2.02 NON-MEMBER COUNTRIES OR TERRITORIES

The WTO's obligations extend only to Member governments, those that have acceded to the *WTO Agreement*. Non-members may neither take advantage of the WTO, nor are they subject to its requirements. In this regard, the WTO's judicial organs differ from the International Court of Justice where non-members of the United Nations may be parties as applicant, respondent, and perhaps as intervenor.[8] GATT contracting parties, however, have brought disputes on behalf of non-member territories for which they had international responsibility at the time. For example, the United Kingdom initiated dispute settlement proceedings against Norway on behalf of Hong Kong, while the Netherlands did so against the United States on behalf of the Netherlands Antilles.[9]

Issues of WTO applicability may arise when political developments call into question the continued existence of a Member government. Under GATT, for example, the European Community refused to proceed with a panel established at the request of Yugoslavia on the ground that the succession of the Socialist Federal Republic of Yugoslavia by the Federal Republic of Yugoslavia, consisting of Serbia and Montenegro, called into question Yugoslavia's status as a contracting party.[10]

---

[7]Art. XIII:1.

[8]SHABTAI ROSENNE, THE WORLD COURT 31 (5th ed. 1995, Martinus Nijhoff).

[9]*Norway — Restrictions on Imports of Certain Textile Products*, BISD 27S/119 (Adopted 18 June 1980) (hereafter Certain Textile Products); and *United States — Restrictions on Imports of Tuna*, DS33/1, 10 June 1994 (hereafter "Tuna II") 33 I.L.M. 839 (1994) (Unadopted). Hong Kong subsequently became a GATT contracting party and is now a Member of the WTO.

[10]GATT Council Minutes 256, at 32.

interest and its interest in a determination of its WTO rights and obligations are each sufficient to obtain the establishment of a dispute settlement panel.[18] It is not necessary that a Member have a "legal" or trade interest as a prerequisite.[19]

§ 2.05 MEASURES AS APPLIED VS. MEASURES AS SUCH

The *WTO Agreement* provides that, "Each Member shall ensure the conformity of its laws, regulations and administrative procedures with its obligations as provided in the annexed [WTO] Agreements."[20] This is consistent with the conclusion of a GATT panel that "legislation *mandatorily* requiring the executive authority to impose a measure inconsistent with that Agreement, as such, whether or not an occasion for the actual application of the legislation had arisen."[21] Consequently, "these provisions as such, not merely their application in concrete cases, have to be consistent with Article I:1."[22]

Thus, in *United States — Section 337 of the Tariff Act of 1930*, the panel's terms of reference encompassed both the law itself and its application in a particular instance. When the private parties involved in the underlying dispute reached agreement, the complainant, the European Economic Community, withdrew that portion of its request that applied to the application of the law in the particular case, and the panel went on to consider the mandatory aspects of Section 337 as such.[23]

---

[18]*European Communities — Regime for the Importation, Sale and Distribution of Bananas*, WT/DS27/R (22 May 1997) (Adopted as modified by the Appellate Body 25 September 1997), ¶ 7.50.

[19]*Id.* at ¶ 7.49.

[20]Art. XVI:4.

[21]*United States — Denial of Most-Favoured-Nation Treatment as to Non-Rubber Footwear from Brazil*, BISD 39S/128 (Adopted 19 June 1992) at ¶ 6.13 (*emphasis added*) *citing United States — Taxes on Petroleum and Certain Imported Substances*, ("Superfund Taxes") BISD 34S/136 (Adopted 17 June 1987), and *European Economic Community — Regulation on Imports of Parts and Components*, BISD 37S/132 (Adopted 16 May 1990).

[22]*Id.*

[23]BISD 36S/345 (Adopted 7 November 1989). For a comment on this report, *see* David Palmeter, *Section 337 and the WTO Agreements: Still in Violation?*, 20 World Competition No. 1, p. 27 (Sept. 1996).

§ 2.06 DISCRETIONARY MEASURES

While legislation mandatorily requiring action inconsistent with GATT was itself held to be inconsistent even if not applied, GATT panels also determined that legislation merely giving authorities discretionary power to act inconsistently with GATT was not, in itself, inconsistent with GATT. The last GATT panel to consider the question said:

> . . . the Panel recalled that panels had consistently ruled that legislation which mandated action inconsistent with the General Agreement could be challenged as such, whereas legislation which merely gave the discretion to the executive authority of a contracting party to act inconsistently with the General Agreement could not be challenged as such; only the actual application of such legislation inconsistent with the General Agreement could be subject to challenge.[24]

An earlier panel observed:

> From the perspective of the overall objectives of the General Agreement it is regrettable that the Superfund Act explicitly directs the United States tax authorities to impose a tax inconsistent with the national treatment principle, but since the Superfund Act also gives them the possibility to avoid the need to impose that tax by issuing regulations, the existence of the penalty rate provisions as such does not constitute a violation of the United States obligations under the General Agreement.[25]

Similarly, the panel that considered Japan's challenge to an anticircumvention provision in the European Economic Community's antidumping regulation, implicitly agreed with Japan that the imposition of antidumping duties pursuant to the regulation would be inconsistent with the EEC's obligations, but

> found that the mere existence of the anti-circumvention provision in the EEC's anti-dumping Regulation is not inconsistent with the EEC's obligations under the General Agreement. Although it would, from the perspective

[24] *United States — Measures Affecting the Importation, Internal Sale and Use of Tobacco*, BISD 41S/131 (Adopted 4 October 1994), ¶ 118.

[25] *United States — Taxes on Petroleum and Certain Imported Substances* ("Superfund Taxes"), *supra* note 21, ¶ 5.2.9.

the course of the proceedings, the restrictions were lifted, but the provision of law under which they were imposed remained in effect. At a meeting of the panel held to determine the appropriate course of action, Canada argued that the panel should go forward because the law requiring restrictions remained in place and, accordingly, the possibility of further embargoes remained. The United States stated that it doubted the necessity of proceeding since the restriction had been eliminated, but said that it would cooperate should the panel decide to continue. The proceeding went forward.[31]

The panel concluded that the temporary embargo was inconsistent with GATT Article XI, even though it had expired, but the panel made no finding with regard to the underlying, mandatory law which was its legal basis.[32] Presumably the panel reasoned that even if the law was consistent with GATT requirements, specific action requiring particular findings could be inconsistent, and that this phenomenon could recur. In these circumstances, if the panel had declined to consider the measure because it was no longer in effect, it might be re-imposed in a process that could continue *ad infinitum*. The same reasoning may have motivated the panels in two cases involving five month-long restrictions imposed on imports of apples, which expired after the panels were established, but before they issued their reports. In both cases, the panels found in favor of the complainant, and in neither case was the issue of the termination of the measures discussed.[33]

In the first WTO report, *United States — Standards for Reformulated and Conventional Gasoline*, the panel declined to consider a measure that had ceased to have any effect prior to the establishment of the panel's terms of reference when the measure was not specifically mentioned in the terms of reference. The panel added that there was no indication that the measure was likely to be renewed.[34] In *United States — Measure Affecting Imports of*

---

[31]BISD 29S/91 (Adopted 22 February 1982) at 92, 94, and 106, ¶¶ 2.2, 2.8, and 4.8. In *EEC — Measures on Animal Feed Proteins*, the challenged restriction came into effect in April 1976 and was terminated the following October. BISD 25S/49 (Adopted 14 March 1978) at 51, ¶ 2.4. The panel issued a complete report on the merits. It does not appear that the question of the measure's termination was argued.

[32]*Id.* at 109, ¶ 4.15.

[33]*EEC — Restrictions on Imports of Apples from Chile*, BISD 27S/98 (Adopted 10 November 1980); *European Economic Community — Restrictions on Imports of Dessert Apples, Complaint by Chile*, BISD 36S/93 (Adopted 22 June 1989).

Woven Wool Shirts and Blouses from India, on the other hand, the import restriction that was the object of the dispute was withdrawn after the panel had submitted its interim report to the parties, but before the final report was issued. The panel decided to continue to consider the matter:

> In the absence of an agreement between the parties to terminate the proceedings, we think it is appropriate to issue our final report regarding the matter set out in the terms of reference of this Panel in order to comply with our mandate . . . notwithstanding the withdrawal of the US restraint.[35]

In *Argentina — Measures Affecting Imports of Footwear, Textiles, Apparel and Other Items*, the measure on footwear was revoked after the circulation of the request for the establishment of a panel, but before the panel was established by the DSB.[36] On the day the measure was revoked, a provisional safeguard was imposed.[37] Even though the measure was referred to in its terms of reference, the panel followed the reasoning of the *Gasoline* panel and declined to consider the revoked measure, quoting from the Appellate Body's opinion in *Shirts and Blouses*:

> The aim of dispute settlement is not to encourage either panels or the Appellate Body to "make law" by clarifying existing provisions of the *WTO Agreement* outside the context of resolving a particular dispute. A panel need only address those claims which must be addressed in order to resolve the matter in issue in the dispute.[38]

It will be apparent from this doctrine that the WTO—like GATT before it—does not make complaining parties whole for damage suffered as a result of measures which violate commitments and accordingly restrict trade. This is dealt with in greater detail in Chapter 8.

---

[34]WT/DS2/R (29 January 1996) (Adopted as Modified by the Appellate Body 20 May 1996).

[35]WT/DS33/R (6 January 1997) (Adopted as Affirmed by the Appellate Body 23 May 1997) ¶ 6.2.

[36]WT/DS56/R (25 November 1997) (Adopted as Modified by the Appellate Body 22 April 1998).¶6.4.

[37]*Id.* at ¶6.5.

[38]*Id.* ¶6.13, quoting *United States — Measures Affecting Imports of Woven Wool Shirts and Blouses from India, supra* note 35 at 19.

put forward by a party as factual evidence with relevance to the question of a reasonable interpretation of a WTO requirement. This might occur, for example, with regard to antidumping legislation implementing the *Agreement on Implementation of Article VI of GATT 1994*, or with regard to legislation implementing some aspect of *GATS* or *TRIPS*.

Panels are required to consider everything within their terms of reference. Thus, also in *Japan — Taxes on Alcoholic Beverages*, the panel was directed to consider whether a wide variety of specifically named alcoholic beverages were "like products" or "directly competitive or substitutable" products within the meaning of Article III of GATT 1994. Included in one of the requests for the establishment of a panel was the category "all other distilled spirits and liquers falling within HS heading 2208." The panel's conclusions did not explicitly incorporate this "all other" category, an omission the Appellate Body considered to be an error of law.[47]

However, when a complaining party fails to raise at any point in the proceedings specific arguments against a measure, or submit any factual or scientific evidence against the measure, the panel may consider the measure outside the scope of the dispute, even though "technically" within the terms of reference.[48]

§ 2.12 PARTICIPATION BY *AMICUS CURIAE*

Two environmental organizations filed briefs *amicus curiae* with the panel in *United States – Import Prohibition of Certain Shrimp and Shrimp Products*.[49] Although these briefs were served upon the parties and acknowledged by the panel, the panel declined to take them into consideration.[50]

The panel noted that under Article 13 of the DSU it had the au-

[47]*Japan — Taxes on Alcoholic Beverages*, AB-1996-2, WT/DSI/AB/R; WT/DS10/AB/R; WT/DS22/AB/4, (Adopted 1 November 1996) at 29.

[48]*EC - Measures Concerning Meat and Meat Products (Hormones), Complaint by the United States*, WT/DS26/R/USA (18 August 1997) (Adopted as Modified by the Appellate Body, 13 February 1998) at ¶ 8.17.

[49]WT/DS58/R (15 May 1998).

[50]*Id.* ¶ 3.129.

thority to seek information from any source, but that it had not sought information from the organizations submitting the briefs. The panel stated, "Accepting non-requested information from non-governmental sources, would be, in our opinion, incompatible with the provisions of the DSU as currently applied."[51] However, the panel noted that if any of the parties wished to put forward all or parts of the *amicus* briefs as their own documents, the panel would be willing to accept them as such. The United States, accordingly, designation a portion of one of the briefs as an annex to its second submission to the panel.[52]

[51] *Id.* ¶ 7.8.
[52] *Id.*

The *Marrakesh Agreement Establishing the World Trade Organization* — the WTO Agreement — is a "particular" international convention, within the meaning of Article 38(1)(a), as are the additional agreements and legal instruments dealing with trade in goods and services as well as intellectual property rights, referred to in the Dispute Settlement Understanding as "covered agreements." Resolution of disputes concerning the substantive rights and obligations of Members of the WTO under the covered agreements, of course, is governed by the DSU. Thus, in the words of Article 38(1)(a), the rules of the DSU "are expressly recognized by the contesting states" that are parties to WTO dispute settlement procedures. The same is true of the special rules and procedures contained in several of the covered agreements.[2]

The fundamental source of law in the WTO is, therefore, the text of the relevant agreements themselves. All legal analysis begins there. In the words of the Appellate Body, "The proper interpretation of the Article is, first of all, a textual interpretation."[3]

The texts, however, are only "first of all." They do not exhaust the sources of potentially relevant law. To the contrary, all of the subparagraphs of Article 38(1) are potential sources of law to be drawn on in WTO dispute settlement. More specifically, prior practice under GATT, including reports of GATT dispute settlement panels; WTO practice, particularly reports of dispute settlement panels and the Appellate Body; custom; the teachings of highly qualified publicists; general principles of law; and other international agreements, all contribute to the rapidly growing and increasingly important body of law known as "WTO Law."

While there is no explicit equivalent to Article 38(1) in the Dispute Settlement Understanding or any other of the WTO Agreements, its terms effectively are brought into WTO dispute settlement by Articles 3.2 and 7 of the DSU. Article 3.2 specifies that the purpose of dispute settlement is to clarify the provisions of the WTO Agreements "in accordance with customary rules of interpretation of public international law." Article 7 specifies that the terms of reference for panels shall be, "To examine, in the light of *the relevant provisions in . . . the covered agreement(s)* cited by the parties to the

[2]These are discussed in Chapter 5.

[3]*Japan – Taxes on Alcoholic Beverages,* AB-1996-2, WT/DS8/AB/R; WT/DS10/AB/R; WT/DS22/AB/R (Adopted 1 November 1996) at 19.

dispute the matter referred to the DSB" and to "*address the relevant provisions in any covered agreement or agreements* cited by the parties to the dispute."[4]

§ 3.02 COVERED AGREEMENTS

The term "covered agreements" in Article 7 of the Disipute Settlement Understanding means all of the multilateral *WTO Agreements* annexed to the *Marrakesh WTO Agreement*. The DSU also is applicable to disputes between the parties to the two plurilateral agreements that also are part of the WTO.[5] These texts, as noted, are the starting point for dispute settlement proceedings, since Article 6.2 of the DSU requires that a request for the establishment of a panel identify the legal basis for the request. The legal basis for a request would be the specific provisions of a particular agreement or agreements. Implicit in this requirement is a due process consideration of fair notice which has led the Appellate Body to observe, "it is incumbent upon a panel to examine the request for the establishment of the panel very carefully to ensure its compliance with both the letter and the spirit of Article 6.2 of the DSU."[6] The texts of several covered agreements explicitly refer to other international agreements which, in this sense, may be considered to be "covered agreements."[7]

§ 3.03 REPORTS OF PRIOR PANELS AND THE APPELLATE BODY

Other than the texts of the covered agreements themselves, no source of law is as important in WTO dispute settlement as the reported decisions

---

[4]*Emphasis added.*

[5]*See* §§ 5.13 and 5.14.

[6]*European Communities – Regime for the Importation, Sale and Distribution of Bananas*, AB-1997-3 WT/DS27/AB/R (9 September 1997) (Adopted 25 September 1997), ¶ 142.

[7]*See* § 3.07.

WTO Members, and, therefore, should be taken into account where they are relevant to any dispute. However, they are not binding, except with respect to resolving the particular dispute between the parties to that dispute."[20]

This statement reads very much like Article 38(1)(d) of the Statute of the ICJ and its reference to "subsidiary" sources of international law. Indeed, in a footnote to this passage, the Appellate Body went on to draw a parallel to the practice of the World Court:

> It is worth noting that the Statute of the International Court of Justice has an explicit provision, Article 59, to the same effect. This has not inhibited the development by that Court (and its predecessor) of a body of case law in which considerable reliance on the value of previous decisions is readily discernible.[21]

All of this discussion took place in the context of adopted GATT reports. However, the same reasoning, *mutatis mutandis*, would apply to adopted WTO reports themselves, not only under GATT 1994 but also reports concerned with the *GATS*, *TRIPS*, and the plurilateral trade agreements. In the end, the result seems to be that adopted reports are not binding precedent and do not control subsequent panels; neither may they "add to or diminish the rights and obligations provided in the covered agreements."[22] Nevertheless, panels "should" take them into account. Adopted reports have strong persuasive power and may be viewed as a form of non-binding precedent, comparable to the role played by *la jurisprudence* in the contemporary Civil Law of many countries, such as France, and comparable to the role played by decisions of courts at the same level in the United States. As a practical matter, parties will continue to cite prior reports to panels, and panels will continue to take them into account by adopting their reasoning — in effect, following precedent — unless panels conclude, for good and articulated reasons, that they should do otherwise.

The role of unadopted panel reports is something less, but they remain relevant. The Appellate Body agreed with the panel in *Japan – Alcoholic Beverages* that unadopted reports "have no legal status in either the GATT

---

[20] *Id.*

[21] *Id.*, n. 30.

[22] DSU Art. 3.2.

or the WTO system since they have not been endorsed through decisions by the CONTRACTING PARTIES to GATT or WTO Members."[23] However, the Appellate Body also agreed with the panel that "a panel could nevertheless find useful guidance in the reasoning of an unadopted panel report that it considered to be relevant."[24]

The persuasive power of the prior reports rests not only on the reasoning they contain, important as this is, but also on the mere fact that once a dispute has been decided a certain way, subsequent panels are likely to follow even if they believe they might have decided the case otherwise had they been viewing the question in the first instance. Continuity and consistency are valuable attributes in any legal system: application of the same rules to the same factual issues, independent of the parties involved — treating like cases alike — is an important source of legitimacy for any adjudicator. It is particularly important for international adjudicators, who, unlike their municipal counterparts, lack a monopoly of enforcement power, and have only the power to persuade the addressees of their decisions that those decisions are correct.[25] Thus, if a panel decides not to treat like causes alike by not following a prior report, the panel most certainly "should" — to use the words of the Appellate Body — address that report, which "create[d] legitimate expectations among WTO Members." To do otherwise would call into serious question the very legitimacy of the process.

Tribunals choose to follow previous cases not only for reasons of fairness and legitimacy, but also for reasons of efficiency: today's tribunal benefits from the work done yesterday on the same legal question; the wheel does not have to be re-invented. Finally, following precedent tends to make the law more certain and more clear, which also is of benefit to the legal system and those that take part in it.

The practical impact of the status of prior panel reports as persuasive but not binding is to put the burden on the party seeking a different interpretation to show the panel why it should depart from the reasoning and conclusions of its predecessor. Because, as the Appellate Body has said,

---

[23] *See supra* note 3 at 15, citing and quoting from *Japan – Taxes on Alcoholic Beverages, supra* note 11, ¶ 6.10.

[24] *Id.* at 16.

[25] *See*, THOMAS FRANCK, FAIRNESS IN INTERNATIONAL LAW AND INSTITUTIONS 26-46 (Clarendon Press 1995).

Nevertheless, panels do not always seem to be treating past reports in the [illegible] might be indicated by two reports which set out the [illegible] and Clothing that were faced with the question of the appropriate standard of review [illegible] and Underwear [illegible] [illegible] in a report [illegible] found [illegible] a standard of [illegible] panel. Two months later the second panel [illegible] [illegible] a report [illegible] [illegible] the [illegible] with other reports [illegible] the panel.

[illegible] consider that the reports cited by the parties [illegible] to the [illegible] [illegible] many passages [illegible] and they [illegible] different agreements in different contexts [illegible] has indicated a [illegible] [illegible] panels.

The [illegible] panel not only [illegible] the [illegible] report [illegible] did not even refer to the [illegible] [illegible] [illegible] panel report [illegible] consideration of the [illegible] [illegible] [illegible] [illegible] the [illegible] of the [illegible] [illegible] [illegible] [illegible] [illegible] [illegible] [illegible] [illegible] [illegible] [illegible] [illegible] [illegible] [illegible] [illegible] [illegible]

Nevertheless, panels sometimes can seem to be trains passing in the night, as indicated by two reports arising out of the *Agreement on Textiles and Clothing* that were faced at the outset with the question of the appropriate standard of review. The first panel, *Cotton and Man-Made Fibre Underwear*, in a report dated 8 November 1996, found "great force" in the argument of a 1985 panel.[34] Two months later, the second panel, *Woven Wool Shirts and Blouses*, in a report dated 6 January 1997, dismissed the 1985 report together with other reports cited by the parties:

> We do not consider that the reports cited by the parties are relevant to the present dispute . . . [they] were adopted many years ago . . . and they interpreted different agreements in different contexts . . . the ATC has instituted a new regime for textile products and the DSU has instituted new rules for panels.[35]

The *Woven Wool Shirts and Blouses* panel not only saw the prior reports very differently, it did not even refer to the *Cotton and Man-Made Fibre Underwear* panel report and its consideration of the same question. Given the sizeable records in both cases, the fact that the nearly-contemporaneous proceedings overlapped to a considerable degree, and the time constraints on panels, this is not surprising. It is more than likely that the *Woven Wool Shirts and Blouses* panel was not even aware of the *Cotton and Man-Made Fibre Underwear* report at the time it prepared its own report.

Finally, the question of the degree to which facts found by a previous panel may be relevant to a later panel has not arisen often. Nevertheless, one of the early WTO panels had occasion to consider a purely factual conclusion of an earlier GATT panel. After quoting the factual finding of the previous panel, the WTO panel said, "Following its independent consideration of the factors mentioned in the 1987 Panel Report, the Panel agreed with

---

risdiction case . . ." (¶ 104); "The Court will *recall* in this context that, as it said in the *North Sea Continental Shelf* case . . . (¶ 141); but more authoritatively, "The Permanent Court of International Justice *stated* in its Judgment of 13 September 1928 in the case concerning the *Factory at Chorzow* . . . (¶ 149) (*emphasis added*).

[34] *United States – Restrictions on Imports of Cotton and Man-Made Fibre Underwear*, *supra* note 32, ¶¶ 7.11-12.

[35] *United States – Measure Affecting Imports of Woven Wool Shirts and Blouses from India*, WT/DS33/R (6 January 1997) (Adopted as Affirmed by the Appellate Body 23 May 1997), ¶ 7.15.

this statement."[36] It went on to observe that the responding Member "offered no further convincing evidence that the conclusion reached by the 1987 Panel Report was wrong," thus clearly stating the otherwise always implicit burden on the party challenging a prior report, as to law or fact, to demonstrate its error.[37]

[2] Appellate Body Reports

As a formal matter, Appellate Body reports, like panel reports, bind only the parties to the particular dispute, and do not create binding precedent. Indeed, the text of any agreement is open to legal challenge regardless of what a panel or the Appellate Body has said about it by virtue of the last sentence of Article 3.2 of the DSU which provides that, "Recommendations and rulings of the DSB cannot add to or diminish the rights and obligations provided in the covered agreements." If the recommendations and rulings of the DSB — which has the authority to adopt or reject reports of panels or the Appellate Body — cannot add to or diminish the rights of Members under the agreements, a *fortiori*, those of panels or the Appellate Body cannot.

This having been said, however, it is clear that not very much has been said. The DSB cannot refuse to adopt a report absent consensus, and consensus requires at a minimum that the prevailing party not object.[38] Rarely will a party join in opposing the adoption of a report in its favor. The real question, therefore, is the extent to which panels and the Appellate Body itself will treat Appellate Body reports as authoritative.

The answers to these questions must await more experience; however, it is reasonable to presume that, absent unusual circumstances, panels will follow the decisions of the Appellate Body in much the same way that a lower court follows the decisions of a higher court. This is a mandatory practice in some legal systems. In others it occurs as a practical matter.[39]

---

[36] *Japan—Taxes on Alcoholic Beverages, supra* note 11, ¶6.22.

[37] *Id.*

[38] DSU Art. 16.

[39] *See, e.g.*, RENE DAVID, FRENCH LAW: ITS STRUCTURE, SOURCES, AND METHODOLOGY 186 (Michael Kindred, trans.) (Louisiana State University Press 1972).

§ 3.04 CUSTOM

Customary international law plays a specific role in WTO dispute settlement by virtue of Article 3.2 of the Dispute Settlement Understanding, which specifies that the purpose of dispute settlement is to clarify the provisions of the *WTO Agreements* "in accordance with customary rules of interpretation of public international law." In practice, Article 3.2 has led panels and the Appellate Body to Articles 31 and 32 of the *Vienna Convention on the Law of Treaties*, which have been held to codify customary international law on the subject.[48] The customary rules of interpretation of public international law are, so far, the only portions of customary international law to have found their way meaningfully into WTO dispute settlement.

The issue of substantive — as opposed to procedural — custom did arise in one important WTO proceeding. This was the question of whether the precautionary princple is part of customary international law.[49] In *EC – Measures Concerning Meat and Meat Products (Hormones)*, the panel stated that "even if" the precautionary principle is considered customary international law, it would not override explicit provisions of the WTO Agreements.[50] This conclusion was affirmed by the Appellate Body, which noted that the status of the precautionary principle in international law is the subject of debate.[51] The Appellate Body also stated that while the precautionary

---

> sonnel comprising different courts. However, reversal by a higher court is not proof that justice is thereby better done. . . We are not final because we are infallible, but we are infallible only because we are final."

Brown v. Allen, 344 U.S. 443, 540 (1953) (concurring).

[48]*See, e.g., United States – Standards for Reformulated and Conventional Gasoline*, AB-1996-1, WT/DS2/AB/R (29 April 1996) (Adopted 20 May 1996) at 17.

[49]The "precautionary principle" holds generally that "Where there are threats of serious or irreversible damage, lack of full scientific certainty shall not be used as a reason for postponing cost-effective measures to prevent environmental degradation." *Rio Declaration on Environment and Development* Article 15. *See, also*, FRANCK, *supra* note 25, at 370; PHILLIPE SANDS, PRINCIPLES OF INTERNATIONAL ENVIRONMENTAL LAW, Vol. I at 208-13 (Manchester Univ. Press 1995).

[50] *Complaint by the United States*, WT/DS26/R/USA (18 August 1997) at ¶ 8.157 and *Complaint by Canada*, WT/DS48/R/C (18 August 1997) at ¶ 8.160 (Adopted as Modified by the Appellate Body 13 February 1998).

[51]*EC Measures Concerning Meat and Meat Products (Hormones)*, AB-1997-4, WT/DS26/AB/R, WT/DS48/AB/R (16 January 1998) (Adopted 13 February 1998) ¶ 123.

principle might have crystallized into a general principle of customary international environmental law, it is less than clear whether it has been widely accepted as a principle of general or customary international law.[52] It is not clear from the opinion what the consequences would be if, in the view of the Appellate Body, the principle had been accepted as part of customary international environmental law but not of international law generally.

But the WTO, like GATT before it, is grounded in agreement, not in custom, and questions of custom, therefore, are likely to be rare. Even GATT's first and most basic provision, the most-favored-nation clause (MFN), was not a codification of customary international law, nor did it establish a custom. To the contrary, GATT's MFN obligation extended only to other contracting parties, and contracting parties frequently denied MFN to non-parties, as the United States did, for example, with China. This remains true of the covered WTO agreements.

Article XVI:1 of the *WTO Agreement*, as stated earlier, specifies that "the WTO shall be guided by the decisions, procedures and *customary practices* followed by the CONTRACTING PARTIES to GATT 1947." It is doubtful that the "customary practices" referred to would be recognized as customary international law. Although the customary practices of GATT might meet some of the requirements of custom, it is doubtful that they were accepted by the parties to GATT or are viewed by the Members of the WTO "as law."[53]

§ 3.05 TEACHINGS OF THE MOST HIGHLY QUALIFIED PUBLICISTS

Sporadic references can be found in panel reports to the teachings and writings of highly qualified publicists in GATT law, but these references were rare.[54] In large part, this reticence may stem from GATT's diplomatic heritage. What is now essentially a juridical system of dispute settlement

[52] *Id.*

[53] This is the *opinio juris* requirement, set out in Article 38(1)(b) of the Statute of the International Court of Justice.

[54] *See, e.g., United States – Measures Affecting Alcoholic and Malt Beverages*, BISD 39S/206 (Adopted 19 June 1992) at 285, citing the works of Profs. John H. Jackson and Robert E. Hudec.

began as a diplomatic system of "conciliation". Not only were diplomats less likely than lawyers even to be aware of, let alone to be influenced by, the writings of legal scholars, GATT diplomats for many years were decidedly averse to the very notion of turning conciliation into a legal proceeding.[55] The views of legal publicists, however qualified, impressed few "old GATT hands."[56]

If legal scholars are more likely than diplomats to cite the writings of other legal scholars, one of the reasons for the relative absence of citation to scholarly writings thus far is the relative absence of scholars among the panelists. While some academics have served as panelists, particularly in recent years, for most of GATT's history the practice was not widespread.

The authors of WTO reports, on the other hand, seem to be far more willing to refer to the teachings of highly qualified publicists in justifying their positions.[57] This development no doubt reflects recognition of the increasing importance of law to the trading system, made clear by the very establishment of the Appellate Body. The Appellate Body, confined to considering issues of law and legal interpretations of panel reports,[58] of necessity brings a legal perspective to the process; and panels, advised by lawyers (as was not the case for the first few decades of GATT), increasingly deal with complex issues of law, such as standing, adequacy of notice and admissibility of evidence.

---

[55]The history is recounted in R.E. Hudec's two volumes, The GATT Legal System and World Trade Diplomacy (2d ed., Butterworth, 1990) and Enforcing International Trade Law: The Evolution of the Modern GATT Legal System (Butterworth 1993).

[56]This skeptical attitude toward law is apparent from the very title of a work by GATT's second Director General, Olivier Long: Law and Its *Limitations* in the GATT Multilateral Trade System (Martinus Nijhoff, 1985) (emphasis added).

[57]*See, e.g., Argentina – Measures Affecting Imports of Footwear, Textiles, Apparel and other Items*, notes 176 (John H. Jackson), 184 (Keith Highet), and 185 (Mojtaba Kazazi), WT/DS56/R (25 November 1997) (Adopted as Modified by the Appellate Body 22 April 1998); *India – Patent Protection for Pharmaceutical and Agricultural Chemical Products*, note 26 (F. Roessler and E.-U. Petersmann), note 28 (E.-U. Petersmann) and note 52 (I. Brownlie), AB-1997-5, WT/DS50/AB/R (19 December 1997) (Adopted 16 January 1998); *EC Measures Concerning Meat and Meat Products (Hormones)*, note 92 (P. Sands, J. Cameron, J. Abouchar, P. Birnie, A. Boyle, L. Gündling, A. deMestral, and D. Bodansky), AB-1997-4, WT/DS26/AB/R, WT/DS48/AB/R (16 January 1998).

[58] DSU Art. 17.6

§ 3.06 GENERAL PRINCIPLES OF LAW

On occasion GATT panels have invoked general principles of law in support of their reasoning, as have WTO panels and the Appellate Body. The principle that an exception to a general rule should be interpreted narrowly has been utilized several times. The WTO panel on *United States – Restrictions on Imports of Cotton and Man-Made Fibre Underwear*, for example, concluded that the transitional safeguard mechanism of the Agreement on Textiles and Clothing is an exceptional measure and "should be interpreted narrowly."[59] In *United States – Measures Affecting Imports of Softwood Lumber from Canada*, the panel effectively invoked the equitable principle of estoppel in a proceeding involving subsidies and countervailing measures.[60] The interpretive principle that readings which would result in reducing whole clauses or paragraphs of a text to "redundancy or inutility" must be avoided has been recognized several times by the Appellate Body.[61]

Articles 22.4 and 22.6 of the Dispute Settlement Understanding, confining the level of suspension of concessions to the level of the nullification and impairment, are, of course more than principle. They are the law of the agreement itself. It is worth noting, however, that these provisions conform to the principle of proportionality recognized by the World Court.[62]

---

[59]*Supra* note 32, ¶ 7.21 (citing several additional cases). *See also, Canada – Import Restrictions on Ice Cream and Yoghurt*, BISD 36S/68 (Adopted 5 December 1989) at 84, ¶ 59, "The Panel recalled that . . . exceptions were to be treated narrowly," citing *Japan – Restrictions on Imports of Certain Agricultural Products*, BISD 35S/163 (Adopted 22 March 1988) and *EEC – Restrictions on Imports of Apples – Complaint by the United States*, BISD 36S/135 (Adopted 22 June 1989). This principle may no longer be applicable. *See* § 4.13.

[60]BISD 40S/358 (Adopted 27 October 1993) at 480-486, ¶¶ 308-325.

[61]*United States – Standards for Reformulated and Conventional Gasoline, supra* note 42, (III.B, p.23); *Japan – Taxes on Alcoholic Beverages, supra* note 3, at 12; *United States – Restrictions on Imports of Cotton and Man-made Cotton Fibre Underwear*, AB-1996-3, WT/DS24/AB/R (10 February 1997) (Adopted 25 February 1997) at 16.

[62]"[A]n important consideration is that the effects of a countermeasure must be commensurate with the injury suffered;" this is "the proportionality which is required by international law." *Case Concerning the Gabcíkovo-Nagymaros Project (Hungary/Slovakia), supra* note 33, ¶ 85. *See* § 8.06[1].

§ 3.07 OTHER INTERNATIONAL AGREEMENTS

Other international agreements, may become sources of WTO law either because they are referred to specifically in the covered agreements or because the parties to a WTO dispute are also parties to another agreement.

[1] Agreements referred to in the WTO Agreements

The texts of several WTO agreements explicitly refer to other international agreements which may therefore serve as direct sources of law in WTO dispute settlement proceedings. These include the major international intellectual property conventions, the *Paris Convention* (1967), the *Berne Convention* (1971), the *Rome Convention*, and the *Treaty on Intellectual Property in Respect of Integrated Circuits*, as provided for the in the TRIPS agreement.[63] The *WTO Agreement on Subsidies and Countervailing Measures* provides, somewhat indirectly, that the grant by governments of export credits in conformity with the provisions of the *Arrangement on Guidelines for Officially Supported Export Credits* of the Organization for Economic Cooperation and Development shall not be considered an export subsidy.[64] As noted above, the reference in Article 3.2 of the DSU to the "customary rules of interpretation of public international law" has been held by the Appellate Body to refer to Articles 31 and 32 of the *Vienna Convention*, whose provisions become a source of law in so far as they reflect customary international law.[65] Other provisions of the *Vienna Convention*

---

[63]TRIPS Art. I:3.

[64]*Agreement on Subsidies and Countervailing Measures*, Annex I (k):

> . . . if a Member is a party to an international undertaking on official export credits to which at least twelve original Members to this Agreement are parties as of 1 January 1979 (or a successor undertaking which has been adopted by those original Members), or if in practice a Member applies the interest rates provisions of the relevant undertaking, an export credit practice which is in conformity with those provisions shall not be considered an export subsidy prohibited by this Agreement.

The "international undertaking" described is the OECD *Arrangement on Guidelines for Officially Supported Export Credits.*

[65]*See United States – Standards for Reformulated and Conventional Gasoline, supra* note 48.

may also provide law in WTO proceedings. For example, a WTO panel considered Article 28 of the *Vienna Convention* concerning non-retroactivity of treaties before concluding that it did not apply to the facts of the case.[66] Parties also have cited other articles of the *Convention* to panels, including Articles 18 (Obligation not to defeat the object and purpose of a treaty prior to its entry into force); 26 (*Pacta sunt servanda*: "Every treaty in force is binding upon the parties to it and must be performed by them in good faith"); and 30 (Application of successive treaties relating to the same subject matter), although the panels have not yet found it necessary to address them.[67]

An as yet unresolved question is whether the rights and obligations brought into the WTO by these other agreements are only those that were in effect at the time the *WTO Agreements* became effective, or whether WTO rights and obligations change as these agreements change. Footnote 2 to the *TRIPS Agreement* states that references to the intellectual property conventions are to specific versions of those conventions.[68] Presumably, therefore, any rights and obligations negotiated later by the parties to the intellectual property conventions would not affect WTO rights and obligations and would not, therefore, be sources of WTO law. However, a panel

---

[66] *EC-Measures Concerning Meat and Meat Products (Hormones) supra,* note 50, *Complaint by the United States* ¶¶ 8.24, 8.21 and *Complaint by Canada* ¶¶ 8.27, 8.28. Article 28 states that the provisions of a treaty normally do not bind a party in relation to any situation which ceased to exist before entry into force of the treaty.

[67] *See, e.g., Brazil – Measures Affecting Desiccated Coconut,* WT/DS22/R (17 October 1996) (Adopted as Modified by the Appellate Body 20 March 1997), ¶¶ 23-36 and 37-39; *United States – Restrictions on Imports of Cotton and Man-Made Fibre Underwear supra* note 32, ¶¶ 5.224 and 7.63.

[68] The text of footnote 2 to the *TRIPS Agreement* in relevant *part* specifies:

> In this Agreement, "Paris Convention" refers to the Paris Convention for the Protection of Industrial Property: "Paris Convention (1967)" refers to the Stockholm Act of this Convention of 14 July 1967. "Berne Convention" refers to the Berne Convention for the Protection of Literary and Artistic Works: "Berne Convention (1971)" refers to the Paris Act of this Convention of 24 July1971. "Rome Convention" refers to the International Convention for the Protection of Performers, Producers of Phonograms and Broadcasting Organizations, adopted at Rome on 26 October 1961. "Treaty on Intellectual Property in Respect of Integrated Circuits" (IPIC Treaty) refers to the Treaty on Intellectual Property in Respect of Integrated Circuits, adopted at Washington on 26 May 1989.

established under the North American Free Trade Agreement, in considering a provision of NAFTA preserving the rights of the parties under GATT and agreements negotiated under GATT, concluded that the particular reference at issue was not simply to GATT as it existed when the NAFTA provision came into effect, but to the GATT regime as it evolved, eventually, into the WTO.[69] The NAFTA panel also noted that a reference in that agreement to customary international law was "a reference to an evolving system."[70]

[2] Agreements between the parties

The *WTO Agreement* and its subsidiary agreements are among the many international regulatory agreements entered into by governments, particularly in the post-World War II era, to address economic, environmental, and social problems.[71] Many WTO Members are signatories to these agreements. Moreover, it seems likely that the number of regulatory agreements is likely to grow, particularly in the environmental field. This raises the question of the extent to which these agreements affect the rights and obligations of signatory WTO Members *vis a vis* other signatory WTO Members.

The issue began to appear in the early 1990s. One instance involved not a multilateral treaty, but a bilateral agreement between Canada and the European Community. In connection with negotiations in the early 1960s concerning Canada's exports of wheat to the Community under the Common Agricultural Policy, the parties entered into an agreement that would have extended the time limits within which Canada could challenge the Community's treatment of its wheat exports under Article XXVIII of GATT. Before an arbitrator agreed to by the parties to resolve a dispute as to whether Canada's Article XXVIII complaint had been made too late, the Community challenged Canada's right to bring a claim based on a bilateral

---

[69] *In the Matter of Tariffs Applied by Canada to Certain U.S.-Origin Agricultural Products*, Final Report of the Arbitral Panel Established Pursuant to Article 2008 of the North American Free Trade Agreement, December 2, 1996.

[70] *Id.* at ¶ 134.

[71] The apt phrase "international regulatory agreements" is taken from the subtitle of Abram Chayes & Antonia Handler Chayes, The New Sovereignty: Compliance With International Regulatory Agreements (Harvard 1995).

agreement under the multilateral procedures of GATT. The arbitrator disagreed:

> In principle a claim based on a bilateral agreement cannot be brought under the multilateral dispute settlement procedures of the GATT. An exception is warranted in this case given the close connection of this particular bilateral agreement with the GATT, the fact that the Agreement is consistent with the objectives of the GATT, and that both parties joined in requesting recourse to the GATT Arbitration procedures.[72]

A similar issue arose in a WTO panel's consideration of a dispute between Brazil and the Community involving exports of poultry products from Brazil to Europe.[73] Brazil argued that a bilateral "Oilseeds Agreement" between it and the Community applied to the resolution of the dispute. Although the United States, as third party, argued that the Oilseeds Agreement was not within the terms of reference of the panel, the Community did not explicitly object to its consideration by the panel.[74] Noting that the Oilseeds Agreement had been negotiated within the framework of GATT Article XXVIII, and citing the *Canada/EC Wheat* arbitration, the panel decided to consider the Oilseeds Agreement "to the extent relevant to the determination of the EC's obligations under the WTO agreements vis-à -vis Brazil."[75]

The Appellate Body found "no reversible error in the Panel's treatment" of the Oilseeds Agreement.[76] The Appellate Body described at length what the Oilseeds Agreement is *not*: as a bilateral agreement between Brazil and the European Communities, it is not a "covered agreement" within the meaning of Articles 1 and 2 of the DSU; it is not cited in an annex to the *WTO Agreement*; it is not among the legal instruments that entered into

---

[72] *Canada/European Communities Article XXVIII Rights, Award by the Arbitrator*, BISD 37S/80 at 84.

[73] *European Communities – Measures Affecting the Importation of Certain Poultry Products*, WT/DS69/R (12 March 1998) (Adopted as Modified by the Appellate Body 23 July 1998).

[74] *Id.*, ¶ 197.

[75] *Id.*, ¶ 2.02. The panel also referred to the *Banana* panel's consideration of the Lomé Convention. *See infra* note 88.

[76] *European Communities – Measures Affecting the Importation of Certain Poultry Products*, AB-1998-3, WT/DS69/AB/R (13 July 1998) (Adopted 23 July 1998) ¶ 85.

force under GATT 1947 that were made a part of GATT 1994; it does not constitute part of the "decisions, procedures and customary practices followed by the CONTRACTING PARTIES to GATT 1947" which, under Article XVI:1 of the *WTO Agreement*, are to guide the WTO. [77]

In the end, however, the Appellate Body reached a result not perceptibly different from that reached by the panel. It recognized that the Oilseeds Agreement was negotiated within the framework of Article XXVIII of GATT and provided the basis for the tariff-rate quota that was at issue in the dispute. Accordingly, the Appellate Body stated, "the Oilseeds Agreement may serve as a *supplementary means* of interpretation."[78]

United States – Restrictions on Imports of Tuna is illustrative of the tendency of GATT panels to disregard public international law when it came to interpreting the General Agreement.[79] The United States argued in *Tuna, inter alia*, that the Convention on International Trade in Endangered Species ("CITES"), and a number of other bilateral and plurilateral agreements, were relevant to the dispute between GATT parties who were parties to those agreements.[80] After noting, with a tone suggestive of less than whole-hearted approval, that "the parties based many of their arguments . . . on environmental and trade treaties," the panel said that "it was first of all necessary to determine the extent to which these treaties were relevant to the interpretation of the text of the General Agreement."[81] The panel concluded that they were not relevant, stating that, "the agreements cited by the parties to the dispute were bilateral or plurilateral agreements that were not concluded among the contracting parties to the General Agreement, and that they did not apply to the interpretation of the General Agreement or the application of its provisions."[82]

The Panel's conclusion that another international treaty would be relevant to the interpretation of a GATT obligation only to the extent that the treaty was accepted by all GATT parties does not appear to be consistent with Article 31(3)(c) of the *Vienna Convention* which specifies that "any relevant rules of international law applicable in the relations between the par-

[77] *Id.* ¶¶ 79-80.

[78] *Id.* ¶ 83 (emphasis in original).

[79] 33 I.L.M. 839 (1994).

[80] *Id.* at ¶¶ 3.14, 3.21 – 3.34.

[81] *Id.* at ¶ 5.18.

[82] *Id.* at ¶ 5.19.

ties" shall be taken into account in resolving disputes between them. An interpretation of this language to mean only any subsequent agreement among all of the parties to the GATT — and not simply to an agreement among the parties to the dispute — does not seem supportable by the text of Article 31(3)(c). The word "parties," as used in Article 31(3)(c), would seem to refer to the parties to the particular dispute, not to the parties to the multilateral agreement. In any event, the panel's textual emphasis on the word "parties" would itself seem to diminish the relevance of the reasoning of the *Tuna* report in the WTO, inasmuch as the signatories to the WTO are "Members," not "parties" as they were in GATT.

The *Tuna* panel also rejected the argument that practice under the other agreements could be considered "subsequent practice in the application of the treaty which establishes the agreement of the parties regarding its interpretation" as provided for in Article 31(3)(b) of the *Vienna Convention*. According to the panel, any such practice would constitute practice under those other agreements, not under GATT.[83] This interpretation, too, seems excessively narrow, and not justified by the text of the *Convention*.

In a report involving restrictions imposed by the United States on imports of shrimp from countries not meeting U.S. standards for protecting sea turtles in the shrimping process, all of the parties to the dispute were also parties to CITES.[84] As in *Tuna*, the panel found CITES not relevant to the dispute, but on more limited grounds that seem more persuasive than the verbal distinctions concerning "parties" drawn in *Tuna*. The United States restricted imports of shrimp, the panel noted, and shrimp are not an endangered species covered by CITES. Turtles were the endangered species, but the United States took no challenged trade action with regard to turtles. Moreover, the United States itself had informed the panel that CITES neither authorized nor prohibited the measures at issue.[85]

The issue of the impact of other international agreements between parties is likely to arise, as it did in *Tuna*, when one WTO Member imposes trade sanctions on the exports of another pursuant to an international agreement, such as an environmental agreement, to which both are parties. If the action would otherwise be inconsistent with its WTO obligations, the

---

[83] *Id.*

[84] *United States – Import Prohibition of Certain Shrimp and Shrimp Products,* WT/DS58/R (6 April 1998) ¶ 7.57.

[85] *Id.*

party taking the action might refer to its obligations under the other agreement in support of an argument that the inconsistency is excused by one or more of the exceptions set forth in GATT Article XX on the theory that the other agreement constitutes a modification of the WTO legal situation of the participating parties to the dispute.[86]

The *Tuna* panel did raise an issue that is highly germane to the issue of the relevance of other agreements between the parties, although it did so in a limited way. The panel considered whether the cited treaties could be considered to be subsequent agreements between the parties concerning the interpretation of GATT within the meaning of Article 31 of the *Vienna Convention*; it concluded, not surprisingly, that they could not be so considered.[87] However, the panel did not look to the question of whether GATT and the cited treaties could be considered successive treaties relating to the same subject matter within the meaning of Article 30 of the *Vienna Convention*. This result is consistent with the principle *pacta tertiis nec nocent nec prasunt*: a treaty binds only the contracting parties and neither rights nor duties arise under a treaty for a state not a party.

Article 30 is likely to be the more relevant provision of the *Vienna Convention*, particularly with regard to international environmental agreements. Article 30.3 specifies that when the parties to a dispute are signatories to both agreements, the latter in time prevails. Article 30.4(b) also specifies that as between a State party to both treaties, and a State party to only one of the treaties, the treaty to which both are parties governs. This would mean that in the event that a WTO Member is a party to an environmental agreement, and another Member is not a party to that agreement, the environmental agreement would not affect WTO rights and obligations. This result is consistent with the principle *pacta tertiis nec nocent nec prosunt:* a treaty binds only the contracting parties and neither rights nor duties arise under a treaty for a state not a party.

To the extent that other agreements are relevant to the rights and obligations of WTO Members under the covered agreements, the question arises as to who interprets the relevant provisions of those agreements. As

---

[86]On this issue see Aaditya Mattoo & Petros C. Mavroidis, *Trade, Environment and the WTO: How Real is the Conflict?*, in Ernst-Ulrich Petersmann (ed.), International Trade Law and the GATT/WTO Dispute Settlement System (Kluwer, 1997).

[87]*Id.* ¶ 5.19.

to agreements specifically brought into the WTO, it now seems settled that WTO panels and the Appellate Body interpret their terms for WTO purposes.

In *Bananas* both the panel and the Appellate Body considered the scope of a waiver of specified obligations granted by the GATT Council and extended by the WTO General Council to the European Communities (EC) with respect to the Lomé Convention, which required the EC to extend preferential treatment to goods originating in certain African, Caribbean, and Pacific (ACP) countries.[88] The substantive question was: What was required by the Lomé Convention? The EC and the ACP argued that the panel was not competent to answer that question. Rather, they contended, the panel should defer to the interpretation advanced by the EC and the ACP who, as parties, were competent to answer it.[89]

The panel disagreed. It noted that the EC and ACP countries initially had been granted a waiver by the GATT CONTRACTING PARTIES to permit the preferential treatment. That waiver subsequently was adopted by the WTO. Clearly, therefore, the waiver itself was a WTO agreement, within the competence of a WTO panel. "Since the waiver applies to action 'necessary . . . to provide preferential treatment . . . as required by the relevant provisions of the Fourth Lomé Convention,' the panel said, "we must also determine what preferential treatment is required by the Lomé Convention."[90] The Appellate Body affirmed, observing, "To determine what is 'required' by the Lomé Convention, we must look first to the text of that Convention and identify provisions of it that are relevant to trade in bananas.[91]

Because the waiver effectively incorporated the Lomé Convention into a WTO agreement, the panel's authority to interpret the waiver and, therefore, the Lomé Convention itself, parallels the authority that is likely to be claimed for the agreements explicitly referred to in the covered agreements, such as the intellectual property conventions. The report does not deal with

---

[88] *European Communities – Regime for the Importation, Sale and Distribution of Bananas*, WT/DS27/R (22 May 1997)(Adopted as Modified by the Appellate Body 25 September 1997).

[89] *Id.* at ¶¶ 7.95, 7.97.

[90] *Id.* at ¶ 7.97.

[91] *European Communities – Regime for the Importation, Sale and Distribution of Bananas*, *supra* note 6 ¶¶ 167, 169.

the situation in which the international agreement at issue is not, at least implicitly, a WTO Agreement.

[3] Agreements to which the WTO is a party

The WTO itself is a party to agreements with other organizations. Two of these involve the Bretton Woods organizations – the *Agreement between the International Monetary Fund and the World Trade Organization* and the *Agreement between the International Bank for Reconstruction and Development, the International Development Association and the World Trade Organization.*[92] The agreements are intended to strengthen the relationship between the WTO and the IMF and the World Bank. The Appellate Body has held that the agreement between the WTO and the IMF does not modify, add to, or diminish the rights and obligations of Members under the *WTO Agreement.*[93]

[92] *See, WTO Agreements with the Fund and the Bank, Approved by the General Council at its meeting on 7, 8 and 13 November 1996*, WT/L/195 (18 November 1996). The WTO has also entered into an *Agreement between the World Intellectual Property Organization and the World Trade Organization*, 35 ILM 754 and an *Agreement between the World Trade Organization and the Office International des Épizooties*, WT/L/272 (8 July 1998); *See also* § 5.05.

[93] *Argentina – Measures Affecting Imports of Footwear, Textiles, Apparel and Other Items*, AB-1998-1 (27 March 1998) (Adopted 22 April 1998) ¶ 72.

CHAPTER 4
The Panel Process

§ 4.01 OVERVIEW

With the establishment of the WTO and adoption of the Dispute Settlement Understanding, resolution of international trade disputes has entered a new and, in the context of international trade law, a highly legalistic era. Under GATT, dispute settlement often was called "conciliation," a term reflecting GATT's diplomatic heritage and its indifference, if not hostility, to legalism. The early GATT process was very much a diplomatic process, seeking to reconcile the conflicting views of the parties, sometimes ending in stalemate if this could not be accomplished. Gradually, GATT dispute settlement became more legalistic in form, but it remained largely diplomatic and, in the view of many, of limited effectiveness, particularly because the losing party could prevent consensus and, therefore, could prevent adoption of an adverse report of a GATT dispute settlement panel. While this did not happen in most instances, it happened often enough to cause dissatisfaction and was an always present threat that, by itself, might have discouraged resort to dispute settlement.[1]

Under the WTO, the GATT consensus requirement is reversed: consensus in the WTO is required to reject, rather than to adopt, the report. This has resulted in a far more juridical system. Although the DSB offers "good offices, conciliation and mediation" if the parties so desire, and although the WTO Members, acting collectively as the DSB, continue to have

[1]*See* § 1.01[5].

the last word as a formal matter, in a practical sense the last legal word really now lies with the panels and the Appellate Body. Thus, while panels and the Appellate Body are not courts, increasingly they bear a striking resemblance to courts, as can be seen from their reports themselves, particularly those of the Appellate Body.[2]

§ 4.02 CONSULTATIONS

[1] Form and content of the request

Dispute settlement begins with a formal request for consultations. In many instances, informal consultations may already have occurred between the Members concerned and the formal request is made only after the complaining Member concludes that the informal process has not been productive. Requests for consultations should be in writing and should be copied to the DSB and to the relevant Councils and Committees. The Councils are the Council for Trade in Goods, for Trade in Services, and for TRIPS. The Committees are those concerned with different substantive areas of the WTO agreements, such as the Committee on Anti-Dumping Practices, the Committee on Technical Barriers to Trade, and the Committee on Subsidies and Countervailing Measures. Once the substantive area of a consultation request has been determined, the relevant Committee should be identified for formal notification.

The request for consultations should specify the articles of the relevant WTO agreements under which consultations are sought. These normally would include Article 4 of the DSU, the corresponding provisions of other covered agreements, which are listed in footnote 4 to the DSU, and Article XXII or XXIII of GATT.

Article 4.5 requires that the complaining party "give the reasons for the request including identification of the measures at issue and an indication of the legal basis for the complaint."

It is important that the request for consultations be as broad in scope as possible, both in identifying the measures at issue and in indicating the

[2] *See*, David Palmeter, *The WTO Appellate Body's First Decision*, 9 LEIDEN JOURNAL OF INTERNATIONAL LAW 337, 356-358 (1996).

legal basis for the complaint, as these will limit the scope of any eventual panel request and that, in turn, will limit the scope of the terms of reference of the panel.[3] A measure that is not the subject of consultations cannot be referred to a panel.[4] Panels, in turn, may evaluate a measure only under the provisions of the covered agreements specified in the terms of reference, which incorporates the request for a panel.[5]

[2] Time elements

Members may request consultations with other Members at any time. The DSU admonishes, however, that, before bringing a case, a Member should consider whether action would be "fruitful."[6]

A Member receiving a request for consultations is required to meet two deadlines: (1) it must respond to the request within 10 days of receipt; and (2), in that response, it must agree to consult within 30 days after receipt, or within a time frame mutually agreed. If the receiving Member does not respond within 10 days, or if it fails to consult within 30 days or within a period otherwise agreed, the Member requesting consultations may proceed immediately to request the DSB to establish a panel.

[3] Confidentiality

Consultations are considered confidential and are without prejudice to the rights of a Member in any further proceedings.[7] Thus, a Member's

---

[3] *United States - Denial of Most-favoured-nation Treatment as to Non-rubber Footwear from Brazil*, BISD 39S/128 (Adopted 19 June 1992) at 147-148, ¶¶ 6.1 and 6.2.

[4] *United States - Anti-dumping Duties on Imports of Fresh and Chilled Atlantic Salmon*, BISD 41S/229 (30 November 1992) (Adopted 27 April 1994) ¶¶332-338.

[5] *Japan - Taxes on Alcoholic Beverages*, WT/DS8/R, WT/DS10/R, WT/DS11/R (11 July 1996) (Adopted as Modified by the Appellate Body 1 November 1996) ¶6.5.

[6] DSU Art. 13.7.

[7] DSU Art. 4.6.

offer of compromise or adjustment of a particular measure does not constitute an admission that the measure is inconsistent with its WTO obligations.

[4] Adequacy of consultations

Consultations under Article 6.7 of the DSU are a confidential bilateral process, without the involvement of the DSB, the panel, or the Secretariat, and with no official records kept. A panel, therefore, is not in a position to know what in fact was discussed during consultations, and, therefore, is not in a position to resolve disputes between the parties on this point. The function of the panel, therefore, is simply to ascertain that consultations were in fact held. "[T]here is nothing in the DSU that provides that a complainant cannot request a panel unless its case is adequately explained in consultations."[8] The panel request itself will set out the scope of the requested consultations, and the panel effectively must assume that all of the points contained in the request were the subject of consultations.

The Appellate Body has stated in *dicta* that all parties engaged in dispute settlement must be "fully forthcoming," and that, particularly in the consultation process, facts must be freely disclosed. Indeed, the Appellate Body said, the demands of due process implicit in the DSU make full disclosure of facts during consultations especially important, "For the claims that are made and the facts that are established during consultations do much to shape the substance and the scope of subsequent panel proceedings. If, in the aftermath of consultations, any party believes that all the pertinent facts relating to a claim are, for any reason, not before the panel, then that party should ask the panel in that case to engage in additional fact-finding."[9]

---

[8]*European Communities - Regime for the Importation, Sale and Distribution of Bananas*, WT/DS27/R (22 May 1997) (Adopted as Modified by the Appellate Body 25 September 1997) ¶7.20; *United States - Restrictions on Imports of Cotton and Man-Made Fibre Underwear*, WT/DS24/R (8 November 1996) (Adopted as Modified by the Appellate Body 25 February 1997) ¶7.61.

[9]*India – Patent Protection for Pharmaceutical and Agricultural Chemical Products*, AB-1997-5, WT/DS50/AB/R (19 December 1997) (Adopted 16 January 1998) ¶ 94.

While there do not appear to have been any instances in which a responding Member has opposed a request for the establishment of a panel based on the fact that a claim covered in the request was not the subject of consultations, it could happen. For this reason, complaining parties should consider maintaining a record of the topics discussed in the consultations. Parties sometimes use written questions, which serve the purpose.

[5] Third parties

Consultations are intended to resolve the dispute between the parties and, accordingly, the DSU provides only a limited role for third parties in the process. If the request is based on Article XXII of GATT, third parties with "a substantial trade interest," may notify the consulting Members and the DSB, within 10 days of the circulation of the initial request for consultations, of their desire to be joined in the consultations. They shall be joined unless the party to whom the original request for consultations was addressed objects. However, if the request for consultations is based on Article XXIII, third parties may not request to be joined. This distinction allows the requesting party to make the tactical decision as to whether it wants the presence, and presumably the support, of third parties or not. In many cases, requesting parties have used Article XXIII, presumably to keep "outsiders" out of the consultations.[10]

§ 4.03 GOOD OFFICES, CONCILIATION AND MEDIATION

Good offices, conciliation or mediation ("good offices") may be requested by any party to a dispute at any time.[11] These proceedings, and the positions the parties take during them, are confidential and without prejudice to their rights in further proceedings.[12] If the parties agree, good offices

[10] DSU Art. 4.11.

[11] DSU Art. 5.3.

[12] DSU Art. 5.2.

efforts may continue while the panel process proceeds.[13] The Director-General may offer good offices at any time during a dispute.[14]

When good offices are entered into within 60 days of the request for consultations, the complaining party must allow a period of 60 days from the date of the consultation request before requesting a panel, unless the party complained against agrees that the good offices effort failed to settle the dispute.[15]

Formal good offices efforts are rare, since the parties normally have exhausted all diplomatic efforts to resolve the matter prior to moving to the dispute settlement process. The DSU also provides more specific procedures for good offices in disputes involving developing countries. These are discussed in § 5.03[2].

§ 4.04 REQUEST FOR A PANEL

[1] Time elements

If the Member to which a request for consultations is made agrees within 10 days to consult within 30 days, and does so, the complaining Member may not ask for a panel until 60 days have elapsed from the date of the original request, unless the parties agree that further consultations would not be productive.[16] At the request of the complaining party, a meeting of the DSB shall be convened within 15 days, provided that at least 10 days advance notice of the meeting is given.

An exception is provided in cases of urgency, including those which concern perishable goods. In these instances, Members shall enter into consultations within 10 days of the receipt of the request for consultations, and the complaining Member may request a panel 20 days after the request, if consultations have not resolved the matter. The determination that a case is urgent would be made by the DSB. The DSU provides no standard for determining whether a case qualifies as urgent. More significant, since the

[13]DSU Art. 5.5.
[14]DSU Art. 5.6.
[15]DSU Art. 5.4.
[16]DSU Art. 4.7.

DSB acts by consensus, a determination that a case is urgent would require the agreement of the Member complained against, which suggests that "cases of urgency" are not likely to be frequent.

[2] Form and content

A request for a panel is made in writing to the DSB. If consultations were held the request should so specify. It is customary to give the date and place of the consultations. If consultations were not held because the Member complained against did not, within 10 days of the request, agree to consult within 30 days, the panel request should so state. This would be a rather unusual occurrence; accordingly, the Member making the request would be wise to include as much detail as possible in its request, including copies of any relevant correspondence.

The request should identify the specific measures at issue, and provide a brief summary of the legal basis of the complaint sufficient to present the problem clearly, although a complete elaboration of the complainant's legal argument is not required,[17] and it is not necessary to provide evidence. Nevertheless, a request that does no more than identify a measure and specify the provision with which it is alleged to be inconsistent is "at the outer limits of what is acceptable" and "references to a WTO agreement without mentioning any provisions or to unidentified 'other' provisions are too vague to meet the standards of Article 6.2 of the DSU."[18] "[T]he convenient phrase, 'including but not limited to', is simply not adequate to 'identify the specific measures at issue and provide a brief summary of the legal basis of the complaint sufficient to present the problem clearly' as required by Article 6.2 of the DSU."[19] Measures not included in the panel request are not within the terms of reference and may not be considered by the panel.[20]

Although Article 4.4 requires notification of consultation requests to the relevant WTO Councils and Committees, Article 6 requires that panel

---

[17]*European Communities - Regime for the Importation, Sale and Distribution of Bananas*, *supra* note 8, ¶ 7.28.

[18]*Id.* ¶¶7.29-7.30.

[19]*India - Patent Protection for Pharmaceutical and Agricultural Chemical Products*, *supra* note 9, ¶90.

[20]*Japan - Taxes on Alcoholic Beverages*, *supra* note 5, ¶ 6.5.

requests be made only to the DSB without further notification. If the request seeks other than the standard terms of reference the proposed terms of reference should be included.[21]

§ 4.05 ESTABLISHMENT OF PANEL

A panel will be established no later than the second meeting after the request for a panel first appears on the DSB's agenda, unless the DSB decides by consensus not to establish the panel.[22] The party requesting establishment of a panel normally would not join a consensus against its establishment. Rather, if it changed its position, the requesting party more likely would simply withdraw its request. A requesting party might agree not to establish a panel at a particular meeting of the DSB if it believes further consultations are desirable. It later could place the matter on the agenda of a subsequent meeting if further consultations were not successful.

Entitlement to a panel at the DSB meeting following that at which it first appears on the agenda means, in practice, that the party complained against can "block" establishment of a panel for one DSB meeting. Of course, the party complained against could agree to the establishment of a panel at the first meeting, in which case presumably there would be consensus to do so. This is not a frequent occurrence.

§ 4.06 COMPOSITION OF PANELS

[1] In general

Panels normally are composed of three individuals, with one serving as chair. The parties may agree, however, to a five member panel, provided they do so within 10 days of the establishment of the panel by the DSB.[23] Panelists generally are present or former members of non-party delegations to the WTO, or academics. They serve in their individual capacities, not as

[21] *See* § 4.07.

[22] DSU Art. 6.

[23] DSU Art. 8.5.

government representatives or representatives of other organizations. Members generally are required to permit their officials to serve as panelists (a time-consuming task that can take away from their other responsibilities), and are prohibited from giving them instructions or seeking to influence them with regard to matters before the panel.[24] If a dispute involves a developing country, at least one panelist shall be from a developing country if the developing country Member so requests.[25]

[2] Nominating panelists

Panelists are nominated by the Secretariat from Member delegations and from a roster of governmental and non-governmental individuals who are deemed qualified by virtue of their training or experience. Normally this is done by the Director of the Legal Affairs Division in collaboration with the Director of the division of the Secretariat having substantive responsibility for the matter in dispute. In antidumping and subsidy and countervailing duty disputes, the Director of the Rules Division usually suggests the names of proposed panelists to the parties. Members are directed not to oppose nominees of the Secretariat "except for compelling reasons."[26]

If the parties do not agree on panelists within 20 days of the establishment of the panel, either party may request the Director-General of the WTO, in consultation with the Chairman of the DSB and Chairman of the relevant Council or Committee, to name the panelists.[27] This has happened on occasion. In *Argentina - Measures Affecting Textiles and Clothing*, for example, the panel was established and the terms of reference were agreed upon on 16 October 1997, but the parties were unable to agree on the panelists. On 9 December, the European Communities requested the Director-General to determine the composition of the panel, which he did on 18 December.[28]

[24]DSU Art. 8.9.

[25]DSU Art. 8.10.

[26]DSU Art. 8.6.

[27]DSU Art. 8.7.

[28]*Constitution of the Panel Established at the Request of the European Communities, Note by the Secretariat*, WT/DS77/4 (7 January 1998). There have been a number of oth-

Panels established pursuant to the *General Agreement on Trade in Services* regarding specific service sectors shall have the necessary expertise relevant to the sector involved.[29] Somewhat redundantly, the *Annex on Financial Services* to GATS provides that, "Panels for disputes on prudential issues and other financial matters shall have the necessary expertise relevant to the specific financial service under dispute."[30]

§ 4.07 TERMS OF REFERENCE

The terms of reference determine the subject matter jurisdiction of the panel, and fulfil the due process objective of notifying the responding party – and potential third parties – of the claims at issue.[31] Accordingly, " the convenient phrase, 'including but not limited to', is simply not adequate to 'identify the specific measures at issue and provide a brief summary of the legal basis of the complaint sufficient to present the problem clearly' as required by Article 6.2 of the DSU."[32] However, "the requirements of Article 6.2 would be met in the case of a 'measure' that is subsidiary or so closely related to a 'measure' specifically identified, that the responding party can reasonably be found to have received adequate notice of the scope of the claims asserted by the complaining party." [33] Regardless of the panel's view of the legal implications of the facts, it may not go beyond its terms of reference.[34] The fact that a respondent first raises conformity with another provision of a covered agreement as a defense in its first written submission

---

ers, *e.g., European Communities - Regime for the Importation, Sale and Distribution of Bananas, supra* note 8, ¶¶ 1.3 - 1.5.

[29]*Decision on Certain Dispute Settlement Procedures for the General Agreement on Trade in Services* ¶4.

[30]*Annex* ¶4.

[31] *Brazil – Measures Affecting Desiccated Coconut*, AB-1996-4, WT/DS22/AB/R (21 February 1997)(Adopted 20 March 1997) §VI, at 22-23.

[32] *India – Patent Protection for Pharmaceutical and Agricultural Chemical Products, supra* note 9 ¶ 90.

[33] *Japan – Measures Affecting Consumer Photographic Film and Paper*, WT/DS44/R (31 March 1998) (Adopted 22 April 1998) ¶ 10.8.

[34] *United States – Anti-dumping Duties on Imports of Fresh and Chilled Atlantic Salmon, supra* note 4, ¶ 336.

does not bring the question of conformity within the panel's terms of reference for purposes of finding a violation of that other provision. [35]

[1] Standard terms of reference

Unless the parties within 20 days agree to the contrary, panels will proceed under standard terms of reference, as set out in Article 7.1, which instruct them:

> To examine, in light of the relevant provisions in (name of covered agreement(s) cited by the parties to the dispute), the matter referred to the DSB by (name of party) in document . . . and to make such findings as will assist the DSB in making the recommendations or in giving the rulings provided for in that/those agreement(s).

The "document" referred to with ellipses is the complainant's request for the establishment of a panel. That document will specify the measures claimed to be inconsistent with WTO obligations and the specific WTO provisions of the WTO obligations that are said to be violated.[36]

Some ambiguity surrounds the reference to the relevant provisions "cited by the parties" since it is only one party, the complainant, that provides a document to the DSB requesting the establishment of a panel. Provisions of WTO agreements cited by the other party in defense are not likely to be included in the complainant's request for a panel. For example, a complainant may argue that a measure is inconsistent with the national treatment provisions of Article III of GATT 1994. A respondent may agree, but argue that the inconsistency is excused by Article XX, which contains a series of exceptions to GATT obligations, including those of Article III. The complainant's request for a panel alleging that the measure is inconsistent with Article III need not refer to the respondent's affirmative defense based on Article XX.

In these circumstances, the respondent should not be prohibited from raising the Article XX defense since it is a specific answer provided by GATT

---

[35] *India – Patent Protection for Pharmaceutical and Agricultural Chemical Products*, *supra* note 9 ¶ 96.

[36] *See* § 3.02.

1994 to a claim of inconsistency with Article III, and since the DSU provides no avenue for the respondent to put the defense in the complainant's request and thus into the terms of reference. A respondent would be prudent, however, to make specific reference to the anticipated defense for the record at the DSB meeting at which the panel request is considered, and to note that it was the subject of consultations.

[2] Special terms of reference

If the parties agree, the DSB may authorize its chairman to draw special terms of reference. However, since GATT's adoption of the "Decision of 12 April 1989 on Improvements to the GATT Dispute Settlement Rules and Procedures" there have been no special terms of reference issued. The 1989 document contained standard terms of reference that essentially parallel those contained in the DSU.

§ 4.08 FUNCTION, AUTHORITY AND RESPONSIBILITIES OF PANELS

The formal function of panels is to assist the DSB in discharging its responsibilities under the DSU and the WTO agreements.[37] Given the near-automaticity of the WTO process for adopting reports, however, it is more realistic to say that panels, together with the Appellate Body, effectively discharge the responsibilities of the DSB.

Panels control the dispute settlement process within the confines of the rules set out in the DSB, establishing deadlines for written submissions and otherwise establishing the schedule.[38] While normally all of the relevant information is submitted by the parties, panels are not confined to the parties as sources of the information they need. They have the right to seek information and technical advice from any source they deem appropriate.[39] However, *ex parte* communications with the panel concerning matters

[37] DSU Art. 11.

[38] DSU Arts. 12.3, 12.4, 12.5.

[39] DSU Art. 13.1. *See* § 4.13 regarding burden of proof.

under consideration are not permitted.[40] Panels may consult experts to obtain their opinions and, with respect to scientific and technical matters, may request an advisory report from an expert review group.[41] Procedures governing the establishment and conduct of expert review groups are set out in Appendix 4 to the DSU.

As described more fully in §§ 4.17 – 4.21, few formal procedural rules govern the operations of panels. Consequently, some panels increasingly have begun to issue fairly detailed and specific Working Procedures soon after they have been composed, i.e., the panelists have been named. These procedures supplement the Working Procedures set out in Annex 3 to the DSU, and may cover topics ranging from the order of presentation at panel meetings, to the time limitations on the submission of evidence, to the form of submissions, including electronic copies.

§ 4.09 THIRD PARTIES AND MULTIPLE COMPLAINANTS

Because a measure taken by any WTO Member may affect the present interests of more than one other Member, and may potentially affect the interests of all Members, the DSU provides for multiple complaints as well as for third party participation in panel proceedings. As noted above, third parties may request to participate in consultations requested by another party and, if permission is denied, may request consultations on their own.[42]

[1] Third parties

Any Member having a substantial interest in a dispute, and having notified the DSB of that interest, may be heard by a panel and may make written submissions to the panel.[43] Third parties receive the first written

[40] DSU Art. 18.1.
[41] DSU Art. 13.2. *See* § 4.12[2] regarding experts.
[42] *See* §4.02 [5].
[43] DSU Art. 10.2.

submissions of the parties to the first meeting of the panel, but no provision is made for them to receive the second or any subsequent submissions.[44] They may present their views at a session of the first substantive meeting of the panel set aside for that purpose.[45] Third parties may not appeal a panel report; however, if a party appeals, third parties may participate.[46]

The DSU does not specify a time limit within which third parties must notify the DSB of their interest in a dispute between other parties. However, since Article 8.3 provides that citizens of Members who are parties or third parties may not serve as panelists without the approval of the parties, difficulties could arise if a Member notified the DSB of its interest after one of its citizens had been named to a panel. To minimize the likelihood of this occurring, the Secretariat has adopted the informal practice of not suggesting the names of possible panelists to the parties until 10 days after the DSB has voted to establish the panel.

Under GATT, third parties, with the agreement of the parties, sometimes participated more extensively than the DSU rules require.[47] Under the WTO, even in the absence of agreement among the parties, third parties have been permitted to observe the second substantive meeting of the panel, but were not permitted to make a second written submission.[48]

[2] Multiple complaints

When more than one Member requests the establishment of a panel related to the same subject matter, a single panel will be established whenever feasible.[49] The written submissions of each complainant will be made available to the other complainants, and each complainant shall have the right to be present when the other complainants present their cases to the panel.[50] The panel may issue a single report, unless one of the parties to

---

[44]DSU Art. 10.3.

[45]DSU Appendix 3.6.

[46]DSU Art. 17.4. *See* Chapter 6.

[47]*See, e.g., Japan - Trade in Semiconductors*, BISD 35S/116 (Adopted 4 May 1988) at 116-117, ¶ 5.

[48]*European Communities - Regime for the Importation, Sale and Distribution of Bananas, supra* note 8 ¶ 7.8.

[49]DSU Art. 9.1.

[50]DSU Art. 9.2.

the dispute requests separate reports, in which case separate reports shall be issued.[51]

§ 4.10 COUNTER-COMPLAINTS

Since WTO dispute settlement is not considered to be a contentious act, counter-complaints ("counter-claims") are not provided for in DSU procedure. Consequently, if a Member responding to a complaint files its own complaint against the original complainant, with regard to a distinct matter, the DSU provides that it should not be linked to the original complaint.[52] The two cases would proceed independently of each other.

§ 4.11 ROLE OF THE SECRETARIAT

The Secretariat has the responsibility of providing legal, historical and procedural assistance to panels.[53] It also provides secretarial and technical support. Generally panels are assisted by a representative of the Legal Affairs Division and by a representative of the Division of the Secretariat with substantive responsibility for the subject matter of the dispute. It is the role of the Legal Affairs Division to advise panelists on points of WTO law, and to assist the panel in maintaining coherent and consistent case law jurisprudence, unless the panel decides, for informed reasons, to depart from prior case law.[54]

---

[51] *Id.* In the first case involving multiple complainants, a single report was issued. *United States - Standards for Reformulated and Conventional Gasoline*, WT/DS2/R (29 January 1996) (Adopted as Modified by the Appellate Body 20 May 1966). In *European Communities - Regime for the Importation, Sale and Distribution of Bananas, supra* note 8, four separate reports were issued. The factual sections of the reports were identical, while the "findings" sections differed to take into account the fact that the complainants did not make the same arguments, but a consistent paragraph numbering system was used for all common findings. *See* ¶ 7.58.

[52] DSU Art. 3.10.

[53] DSU Art. 27.1.

[54] *See* § 3.03.

§ 4.12 EVIDENCE AND EXPERTS

[1] General

WTO panels, like international tribunals generally, are given considerable flexibility in evaluating evidence.[55] The DSU contains no technical rules concerning the production, admissibility, or sufficiency of evidence. Article 12, dealing with panel procedures, does not mention the subject. Appendix 3 to the DSU specifies only that, before the first meeting of the panel, the parties shall file written submissions in which they present the "facts of the case" as well as their arguments. Since most WTO disputes have dealt with the "measures" of Member governments, the text of the measure at issue generally has been the factual basis for the proceeding. Accordingly, panel proceedings have tended to emphasize legal argument — the WTO consequences of the measure at issue — rather than disputes over points of fact. As disputes have become increasingly complex, however, the factual component has increased, most notably in matters involving antidumping and sanitary and phytosanitary standards.

There clearly is now significant room for factual disputes in the WTO. In this regard, Article 13.1 makes clear the right of panels to "seek information and technical advice from any individual or body it deems appropriate." It goes on to state that, "A Member should respond promptly and fully to any request by a panel for such information." Indeed, also following normal international practice, responding parties in WTO proceedings have an affirmative obligation to cooperate in providing evidence to panels. [56] Article 13.2 also authorizes panels to seek information from "any relevant source."

The DSU does not establish time limits for the submission of evidence to a panel.[57] Moreover, the Working Procedures of Appendix 3 to the DSU do not constrain panels with hard and fast rules on deadlines for submitting evidence. Therefore, a panel could have refused to admit evidence offered two days before the second substantive meeting of the panel, but was not required to do so.[58]

---

[55] *Argentina - Measures Affecting Imports of Footwear, Textiles, Apparel and Other Items*, WT/DS56/R (25 November 1997) (Adopted as Modified by the Appellate Body 22 April 1998) ¶ 6.39.

[56] *See* § 4.13.

[57] *Argentina – Measures Affecting Imports of Footwear, Textiles, Apparel and Other Items*, AB-1998-1, WT/DS56/AB/R (27 March 1998) (Adopted 22 April 1998) ¶ 79.

[58] *Id.* ¶ 80.

In *Australia – Measures Affecting Importation of Salmon*, which involved restrictions placed on imports because of alleged health risks, a risk assessment conducted by a third country was submitted to the panel by the complainant after a deadline set by the panel. This document was accepted because it was part of the complainant's reply to statements by experts advising the panel who had referred to it.[59] However, another exhibit submitted after the second substantive meeting of the panel and after its meeting with the experts was rejected.[60]

[2] Experts

In addition to authorizing panels to seek information from "any relevant source," Article 13.2 also authorizes them "to consult experts to obtain their opinion on certain aspects of the matter." Appendix 4 to the DSU sets forth rules for establishing an expert review group, and the procedures that such groups should follow.

Article 13.2 contemplates a written report from an expert review group, and the rules of Appendix 4 reflect this. However, in the first instance of the use of experts in a WTO proceeding, the panel elected to proceed in a different fashion. In *EC Measures Concerning Meat and Meat Products (Hormones)*, the panel chose not to receive a consensus report of the experts as a group, but rather, to obtain the opinions of the experts individually.[61] This practice was affirmed by the Appellate Body.[62]

None of the parties requested the appointment of experts in *United States – Import Prohibition of Certain Shrimp and Shrimp Products*, but all of them submitted studies by experts and quoted from the same scientific

[59] WT/DS18/R (12 June 1998) ¶ 8.5; *See* § 4.12[2].

[60] *Id.* ¶ 8.4.

[61] *EC Measures Concerning Meat and Meat Products (Hormones), Complaint by the United States*, WT/DS26/R/USA (18 August 1997), and *EC Measures Concerning Meat and Meat Products (Hormones), Complaint by Canada*, WT/DS48/R/Can (18 August 1997) (Adopted as Modified by the Appellate Body 13 February 1998) ¶¶ 8.7, 8.8 and 8.9. The panel also proceeded under Article 11 of the *Agreement on the Application of Sanitary and Phytosanitary Measures* which also provides for the use of experts. *See* § 5.05.

[62] *EC Measures Concerning Meat and Meat Products (Hormones)*, AB-1997-4, WT/DS26/AB/R and WT/DS48/AB/R, (16 January 1998) (Adopted 13 February 1998) ¶¶ 146-149.

documents to support opposite views. Accordingly, the panel, on its own initiative, sought expert advice pursuant to Articles 13.1 and 13.2 of the DSU.[63] The panel asked the parties to suggest experts, and also obtained curricula vitae from the Secretariat. Five were selected, and were asked to serve in their individual capacities.[64] The parties were given time by the panel to comment in writing on the replies of the experts to the questions of the panel.[65]

Similarly, in *Australia – Measures Affecting Importation of Salmon*, neither party requested the panel to seek expert advice, but neither objected.[66] Four experts were chosen from names of individuals submitted by the parties and from the Office international des épizooties.[67] The parties were given the opportunity to comment on the list of potential experts on the basis of their curricula vitae, and to state "any compelling objections" they might have to particular individuals.[68] In consultation with the parties, the panel prepared specific questions, which were submitted to each expert individually. The experts were requested to provide written responses to the questions they felt qualified to address. The written submissions of the parties, including the written versions of their oral presentations, were provided to each expert. The written responses of the experts were given to the parties, who in turn were given the opportunity to comment on these responses.[69] The experts met with the panel and the parties to discuss their responses to the questions.[70]

In *Japan – Measures Affecting Consumer Photographic Film and Paper*, the panel, faced with difficult translation issues, named a two-member panel of experts to advise it.[71]

The Appellate Body has stated that a panel is not duty bound to consult with particular experts; and, just as panels have discretion to determine

[63] WT/DS58/R (15 May 1998) ¶ 5.1.
[64] *Id.* ¶¶ 5.5 – 5.7.
[65] *Id.* ¶ 7.10.
[66] *Supra*, note 59 ¶ 6.1.
[67] *Id.* ¶ 6.2.
[68] *Id.* ¶ 6.3.
[69] *Id.* ¶ 6.4.
[70] *Id.* ¶ 6.5.
[71] WT/DS44/R (31 March 1998) (Adopted 22 April 1998) ¶¶ 1.9-1.10.

how to seek expert advice, so also do they have discretion to determine whether to seek expert advice at all.[72]

[3] Subsequent evidence

Information and evidence developed after the challenged action has occurred normally is not considered by the panel. Rather, panels review the evidence used by the Member in making its determination.[73] In *Hormones*, the panel rejected evidence that was not used in making the challenged determination. The EC provided no evidence that the studies it referred to before the panel or the scientific conclusions reached in those studies were actually taken into account by the EC.[74]

> According to the terms of reference given to us as a dispute settlement panel, we have no mandate to reexamine the risk assessment referred to by the European Communities in light of this 'new evidence', nor to make our own risk assessment.[75]

However, evidence in the form of invoices relating to transactions that took place after consultations were initiated was accepted by a panel since, the panel said, its purpose was to try to understand the way the tariff system at issue functioned, and evidence of these later transactions further confirmed the evidence for transactions that took place in preceding years.[76]

---

[72] *Argentina – Measures Affecting Imports of Footwear, Textiles, Apparel and Other Items, supra* note 57 ¶ 84.

[73] *United States - Measure Affecting Imports of Woven Wool Shirts and Blouses from India*, WT/DS33/R (6 January 1997) (Adopted as Affirmed by the Appellate Body 23 May 1997), ¶ 7.20-21. The panel contrasted this limitation on panels with what it described as the ability of the Textiles Monitoring Body to consider subsequent developments. The Appellate Body, however, described the panel's statements with regard to the Textile Monitoring Body's ability to consider subsequent evidence *dicta*. *United States - Measure Affecting Imports of Woven Wool Shirts and Blouses from India*, AB-1997-1, WT/DS33/AB/R (25 April 1997) (Adopted 23 May 1997), §V at 19.

[74] *EC Measures Concerning Meat and Meat Products (Hormones), supra* note 61, *Complaint by the United States*, ¶ 8.114, *Complaint by Canada*, ¶ 8.117.

[75] *Id.* ¶ 8.115 (US) and ¶ 8.118 (Canada).

[76] *Argentina - Measures Affecting Imports of Footwear, Textiles, Apparel and Other Items, supra* note 55, ¶ 6.63.

In the same case, invoices representing imports from countries other than the complainant also were accepted because, "The issue before the Panel is whether Argentina's measures lead to the imposition of duties above its bound rate of 35 percent *ad valorem*, irrespective of the source."[77]

[4] Municipal law

Municipal law may serve as evidence of facts and may provide evidence of state practice; it may also constitute evidence of compliance or non-compliance with international obligations.[78] A panel, therefore, is not confined to treating municipal law as a fact to be proved, but also may examine it to determine compliance with WTO obligations. "[T]he Panel was simply performing its task in determining whether India's 'administrative instructions' for receiving mailbox applications were in conformity with India's obligations under Article 70.8(a) of the *TRIPS Agreement*." [79]

[5] Quantum of evidence

The question of the quantum of evidence that will satisfy a party's burden of proof (*See* § 4.13) will depend upon the specific circumstances of a particular case. This may well depend upon the evidence that is, in the panel's view, available to the parties.

In *Indonesia – Certain Measures Affecting the Automobile Industry*, the panel noted that evidence with regard to the planned introduction of certain models "is very general, and supporting documentation, with the exception of newspaper reports and letters prepared by GM, Ford and Chrysler for the purposes of this dispute, is non-existent."[80] The panel went on to explain that it did "not mean to suggest that in WTO dispute settlement there are any rigid evidentiary rules regarding the admissibility of newspaper reports or the need to demonstrate factual assertions through

---

[77] *Id.* ¶ 6.60.

[78] *India - Patent Protection for Pharmaceutical and Agricultural Chemical Products*, *supra* note 9, ¶ 65.

[79] *Id.* ¶ 66.

[80] WT/DS54/R, WT/DS55/R, WT/DS59/R, WT/DS64/R (2 July 1998) (Adopted 23 July 1998) ¶ 14.233.

contemporaneous source information."[81] However, the panel went on, "the affected companies certainly had at their disposal copious evidence in support of the claims of the complainants."[82] This would have included, the panel observed, actual business plans, corporate minutes, and internal decision memoranda relating to the approval and subsequent abandonment of the plans in question. The fact that contemporaneous company documents were not submitted, and that complainant relied instead upon news reports of its own industry's activities, led the panel to conclude that the complainant had not demonstrated the effects of the subsidies in question "by positive evidence."[83]

It may be important to note that the panel in *Indonesia – Automobiles* was confronted with a situation in which the complaining party used news articles to document the alleged adverse effects upon its own industry. The situation could well be different when a party relies on press reports to document the activities of the other party or its industry, since press reports may be the only evidence available to the party.

§ 4.13 BURDEN OF PROOF[84]

[1] General

The burden of proof has been called "the law's response to ignorance."[85] It "compensates for the many uncertainties of litigation, allowing the judicial system to reach determinate outcomes in the absence of relevant information."[86] As dispute proceedings, first in GATT and now in the WTO, grew more complex and more juridical, the question of burden of proof became an increasingly important part of panel reports. This trend is likely to continue.

[81] *Id.* ¶ 14.234.

[82] *Id.*

[83] *Id.* ¶ 14.236.

[84] *See, generally,* Rutsel Silvestre J. Martha, *Presumptions and Burden of Proof in World Trade Law*, 14 Journal of International Arbitration No. 1, at 67 (March 1997); Mojtaba Kazazi, Burden of Proof and Related Issues: A Study on Evidence Before International Tribunals (Kluwer 1996).

[85] Richard H. Gaskin, Burdens of Proof in Modern Discourse 4 (Yale 1992).

[86] *Id.*

In the WTO, as in any mature legal system, the party asserting a fact, whether claimant or respondent, is responsible for providing the proof of that fact.[87] Once the asserting party has presumptively established a fact, it is the responsibility of the other party to provide evidence and argument sufficient to rebut the presumption.[88] The burden of establishing an affirmative defense rests with the party asserting it.[89]

Some confusion may arise concerning burden of proof in WTO proceedings, particularly among lawyers trained in the common law, because, contrary to what prevails in most common law proceedings, WTO panels are not confined to the factual record made by the parties. A panel may seek information "from any individual or body which it deems appropriate."[90] In this, they follow the practice of courts in the civil law system, as do most international tribunals. For example, in *Indonesia – Certain Measures Affecting the Automobile Industry*, the panel was faced with the question of whether the subsidies at issue were "specific" subsidies within the meaning of the Articles 1 and 2 of the Agreement on Subsidies and Countervailing Measures. The complaining parties, of course, claimed that they were and the responding party agreed. By itself, however, this was not necessarily enough for the panel: "In light of the views of the parties, *and given that nothing in the record would compel a different conclusion*, we find that the measures in question are specific subsidies within the meaning of Articles 1 and 2 of the SCM Agreement."[91] In this regard, it should be noted that Article 6.8 of the SCM Agreement provides that, except in certain limited circumstances, "the existence of serious prejudice should be determined on the basis of the information submitted to or obtained by the panel."

In common law jurisdictions, in contrast, after the complainant has presented its case, the responding party normally may move for judgment on the ground that all of the evidence presented by the complainant does not constitute a violation of the law. There is no counterpart to such a motion in WTO practice. While a complainant whose initial submission does not adequately document a violation by a respondent obviously runs an enormous risk, the respondent does not have a legal right to judgment at

---

[87] *United States - Measure Affecting Imports of Woven Wool Shirts and Blouses from India*, AB-1997-1, *supra* note 73, §IV, at 16.

[88] *Id.*, at 15.

[89] *Id.*, at 18.

[90] DSU Art. 13.1.

[91] *Supra* note 80 (emphasis added).

that point, since the possibility remains that additional evidence, supporting the complainant, has otherwise been made available to the panel.[92]

In fact, in WTO proceedings, as in international legal proceedings generally, there is a "rule of collaboration" which requires the parties, including the respondent, to cooperate in the presentation of evidence to the panel.[93] "[T]he most important result of the rule of collaboration appears to be that the adversary is obligated to provide the tribunal with relevant documents which are in its sole possession. This obligation does not arise until the claimant has done its best to secure evidence and has actually produced some *prima facie* evidence in support of its case."[94]

[2] "General rule-exception" analysis

A significant development in WTO jurisprudence regarding burden of proof concerns the Appellate Body's apparent rejection of the so-called "general rule - exception" analysis that was used in a number of GATT panel reports.[95] Under this analysis, the party invoking an exception to a

[92]This system is not totally unfamiliar to trade lawyers in the United States, despite their common law training. Antidumping and countervailing duty investigations before both the Department of Commerce and the United States International Trade Commission proceed in a fashion that greatly resembles the civil law procedure followed in the WTO. Proceedings before both agencies are "investigative," not adversarial, and thus, while parties have the burden of proving their claims, at the risk of having them not be accepted, the agency record is not necessarily confined to information supplied by the parties.

[93]*Argentina - Measures Affecting Imports of Footwear, Textiles, Apparel and Other Items, supra* note 55, ¶ 6.40. For the provisions of the *Agreement on Subsidies and Countervailing Measures* requiring Members to cooperate in the development of evidence concerning actionable subsidies, *see* § 5.09[4].

[94]*Id.* "We do not consider that the fact that the United States submitted copies of customs documents affects their probative value. The United States did try to obtain the original copies in Argentina's possession. Before an international tribunal, parties do have a duty to collaborate in doing their best to submit to the adjudicatory body all the evidence in their possession. In the absence of the originals and after careful examination of the evidence, we consider that the copies submitted by the United States constitute sufficient evidence to allow us to make the conclusions we have reached." *Id.* at ¶ 6.58. *See also, supra* note 9 and accompanying text.

[95]*See, e.g., Norway - Procurement of Toll Collection Equipment for the City of Trondhiem*, BISD 40S/319 (Adopted 13 May 1992) at ¶ 4.5: "Since Article V:16(e) was an ex-

general principle of GATT — such as most-favored-nation or national treatment — effectively had a heavier burden of proof than the party invoking the provision embodying the general principle. The exception was interpreted more narrowly or more strictly than other provisions.

The Appellate Body, however, from the start has demonstrated an emphasis on text.[96] It later observed that Articles XX and XI:(2)(c)(i) of GATT are limited exceptions from other obligations, in the nature of affirmative defenses, and that the party invoking them has the burden of proving their applicability.[97] In this observation, the Appellate Body was relying on the language of the provisions themselves, and not on broader principles. In *EC Measures Concerning Meat and Meat Products (Hormones)* it was particularly explicit. After stating that the burden of proof of showing an inconsistency with a provision is not avoided by describing that provision as an exception, the Appellate Body said:

> [M]erely characterizing a treaty provision as an "exception" does not by itself justify a "stricter" or "narrower" interpretation of that provision than would be warranted by examination of the ordinary meaning of the actual treaty words, viewed in context and in the light of the treaty's object and purpose, or, in other words, by applying the normal rules of treaty interpretation.[98]

The Appellate Body's conclusion seems to be supported by the customary rules of interpretation of public international law as set out in Articles 31 and 32 of the *Vienna Convention on the Law of Treaties.* These articles do not give grounds for preferring one portion of the text over an-

---

ceptions provision, its scope had to be interpreted narrowly and it would be up to Norway, as the Party invoking the provision, to demonstrate the conformity of its actions with the provision;" *United States - Measures Affecting Alcoholic and Malt Beverages,* BISD 39S/206 (Adopted 19 June 1992) at ¶ 5.41: "The Panel also noted the practice of the CONTRACTING PARTIES of interpreting these Article XX exceptions narrowly, placing the burden on the party invoking the exception to justify its use."

[96] *United States - Standards for Reformulated and Conventional Gasoline,* AB-1996-1, WT/DS2/AB/R (29 April 1996) (Adopted 20 May 1996), III.B at 18, observing that the so-called "primarily aimed at" test developed in GATT jurisprudence to interpret the phrase "relating to" in Article XX(g) is "not itself treaty language."

[97] *United States - Measure Affecting Imports of Woven Wool Shirts and Blouses from India, supra* note 73 at 14.

[98] *EC Measures Concerning Meat and Meat Products (Hormones), supra* note 62 ¶ 104.

other, construing the former broadly and the latter narrowly. The better justification for the narrow construction of some provisions of GATT lies in the fact that their wording is narrow, rather than in assumed policy of favoring one article over another.

§ 4.14 CONFIDENTIAL INFORMATION[99]

Confidential information provided to a panel "shall not be revealed without formal authorization from the individual, body, or authorities of the Member submitting it."[100]

Invoices submitted as evidence with the name of the importer and all relevant data that could help identify the importer or the exporter deleted were accepted by a panel because "it is often the practice in disputes, such as this one, for a party to protect commercial in-confidence information such as the names and other information of the private entities involved."[101]

While complainants cannot be required to submit confidential information to panels, neither may they invoke confidentiality as a basis for their failure to submit positive evidence.[102]

§ 4.15 STANDARD OF REVIEW[103]

The Dispute Settlement Understanding contains no explicit standard of review. Article 11 simply instructs panels to make "an objective assessment of the case and the applicability of and conformity with the relevant

[99]The *Agreement on Implementation of Article VI of GATT 1994* (the Antidumping Agreement), the *Agreement on Implementation of Article VII of GATT 1994* (Customs Valuation), and the *Agreement on Technical Barriers to Trade* contain special provisions regarding confidential information. *See* §§ 5.07, 5.08.

[100]DSU Art. 13.1.

[101]*Argentina - Measures Affecting Imports of Footwear, Textiles, Apparel and Other Items, supra* note 55, ¶¶ 6.53 and 6.59. Panel proceedings also are confidential, and submissions to panels may be confidential. *See*, § 4.18.

[102] *Indonesia – Certain Measures Affecting the Automobile Industry, supra* note 80 ¶ 14.235.

[103]Article 17.6 of the Antidumping Agreement contains a separate standard of review. *See* § 5.07.

covered agreements."[104] A policy of total deference to the findings of the national authorities could not ensure an "objective assessment" as envisioned by Article 11.[105] A panel review is not a substitute for the proceedings conducted by national investigating authorities. Thus, "the task of the Panel is to examine the consistency of the US action with the international obligations of the United States, and not the consistency of the US action with the US domestic statute implementing the international obligations of the United States."[106]

The Appellate Body has stated that issue of alleged failure to apply an appropriate standard of review as to factual issues ultimately resolves itself into the issue of whether a panel made an objective assessment of the matter before it, including an objective assessment of the facts.[107]

§ 4.16 CLAIMS AND DEFENSES NOT RAISED

[1] Claims

It is not always necessary for a complaining party to include a discussion of all of its claims in its first written submission to the panel, although such an omission might not be advisable as a tactical matter. In *European Community - Regime for the Importation, Sale and Distribution of Bananas*, Mexico, Guatemala, and Honduras in their first written submissions to the panel, omitted any reference to some claims that had been made in their request for the establishment of the panel, which had been made jointly with other parties.[108] The panel declined to consider these claims on the ground that to do so would be unfair to the respondent, as it would have little or no time to respond.

The Appellate Body, however, disagreed, apparently concluding that what the panel considered to be a claim was actually an argument in support of a claim: "There is no requirement in the DSU or in GATT practice for arguments on all claims relating to the matter referred to the DSB to be

[104] *United States - Restrictions on Imports of Cotton and Man-Made Fibre Underwear, supra* note 8, ¶¶ 7.8, 7.9.

[105] *Id.* ¶7.10.

[106] *Id.* ¶7.12.

[107] *EC - Measures Concerning Meat and Meat Products (Hormones), supra* note 62 ¶ 119.

[108] *See supra* note 8, at ¶ 7.57.

set out in the complaining party's first written submission to the panel."[109] The Appellate Body added that, "Any omissions in the arguments contained in the first written submissions were rectified in joint presentations with other Complaining Parties made at the first meeting of the parties with the panel, as well as in their joint written rebuttal submission and in their joint representations made at the second meeting of the panel."[110]

GATT panels declined to consider claims raised by third parties that were not raised by the complaining party. Such claims normally would not be within the panel's terms of reference.[111]

[2] Defenses

It was the practice of GATT panels not to consider potential defenses not raised by the responding party.[112] In this respect, panels have respected the international law maxim, *non ultra petita*, that is, adjudicatory bodies should not move beyond that which has been requested.

§ 4.17 FIRST WRITTEN SUBMISSIONS

Soon after it is established, if possible within one week, the panel will consult with the parties and establish a time-table for the proceedings.[113]

[109]AB - 1997 - 3, WT/DS27/R (9 September 1997) (Adopted 25 September 1997), ¶145. Article 4 of Appendix 3 to the DSU provides that prior to the first meeting of the panel, the parties shall transmit written submissions "in which they present the facts of the case and their arguments."

[110]*Id.* ¶146.

[111]"GATT practice has been for panels to make findings only on the issues raised by the parties to the dispute," *United States -Denial of Most-favoured-nation Treatment as to Non-rubber Footwear from Brazil, supra* note 3, ¶ 6.19.

[112]*EEC - Quantitative Restrictions against Import of Certain Products from Hong Kong*, BISD 30S/129 (Adopted 12 July 1983) at 138, ¶ 26; *US - Imports of Sugar from Nicaragua*, BISD 31S/67 (Adopted 13 March 1984) at 74, ¶ 4.4; *Japanese Imports of Leather*, BISD 31S/94 (Adopted 16 May 1984) at 111, ¶ 44; *EEC - Restrictions in Imports of Dessert Apples - Complaint by Chile*, BISD 36S/93 (Adopted 22 June 1989) at 133, ¶ 12.30; *EEC - Regulation on Imports of Parts and Components*, BISD 37S/131 (Adopted 16 May 1990) at 194, ¶ 5.11.

[113]DSU Art. 12.3.

This will include a time-table for written submissions.[114] Normally, the complaining party will present its first submission two-to-three weeks prior to the responding party, unless the panel decides, after consultation with the parties, that they should make their initial submissions simultaneously.[115] This normally would occur three-to-six weeks after the panel is established.

The first submissions of all parties should set forth their view of the facts of the case and their arguments flowing from those facts.[116] The complainant's submission normally would include such things as the texts or other information concerning the "measure" complained of, together with any relevant translations. The *Bananas* case to the contrary notwithstanding, it usually would not be advisable for a complaining party — or any party — to omit any arguments in its first submission.[117]

The responding party's later-filed first submission inherently will be in the nature of a rebuttal, but it also should set out any affirmative defenses that may be claimed, keeping in mind that a party asserting an affirmative defense has the burden of establishing it.[118] Parties are entitled to claim confidential treatment for their submissions; however, those doing so must furnish non-confidential summaries to the other parties, which may be disclosed to the public.[119] In addition, parties may disclose their own submissions.[120]

§ 4.18 FIRST MEETING OF THE PANEL

The few formal rules that govern the proceedings of panels may be stated briefly. Panels meet in closed sessions, and the parties, including interested third parties, attend only by invitation of the panel.[121] A panel's deliberations as well as the documents submitted to it are confidential, although, as noted in the previous section, parties may make their own submissions public, and non-confidential summaries that may be made public

---

[114] DSU Art. 12.5.

[115] DSU Art. 12.4; App. 3, Art. 12(a)(2).

[116] DSU Appendix 3.4.

[117] *See* § 4.16.

[118] *See* § 4.13.

[119] DSU Appendix 3.2

[120] DSU Appendix 3.3.

[121] *Id.*

are required of confidential submissions.[122] Parties are required to provide to the panel written versions of their oral statements.[123] All submissions are made available to all parties.[124]

The complaining party presents its case first, followed by the party against which the complaint was brought.[125] The panel may, at any time, put questions to the parties.[126] Parties often request permission to submit answers in writing at a later session of a panel meeting. Panels often permit parties to present written or verbal questions to each other. To avoid prolonged argument on legal issues, this permission may be confined to factual matters. Panels sometimes require parties to serve copies of their answers to any questions, including questions from the panel, upon the other parties.

Third parties meet with the panel, and with the parties to the proceeding, at a separate session of the first substantive meeting.[127] They are, however, entitled to be present at all sessions of the first meeting. They also receive copies of the first written submissions of the parties to the dispute.[128]

Panels sometimes require parties to include requests for preliminary rulings in their first written submissions. They may also require responses from other parties prior to the first meeting of the panel.

Parties are not prohibited from submitting additional evidence after the first meeting of the panel. According to one panel, "Until the WTO Members agree on different and more specific rules on this regard, our main concern is to ensure that 'due process' is respected and that all parties to a dispute are given all the opportunities to defend their position to the fullest extent possible."[129] An additional two weeks were given to the party complained against to respond to the evidence submitted after the first meeting.[130]

However, some panels have required parties to submit all factual evidence no later than the panel's first meeting with the parties, except with respect to rebuttal evidence or answers to questions from the panel or other parties. When this has been done, panels have provided for exceptions upon

---

[122]*Id.*

[123]DSU Appendix 3.9.

[124]DSU Appendix 3.10.

[125]DSU Appendix 3.5.

[126]DSU Appendix 3.8.

[127]DSU Appendix 3.6.

[128]*Id. But see* § 4.09.

[129]*Argentina - Measures Affecting Imports of Footwear, Textiles, Apparel and Other Items*, *supra* note 55, ¶ 6.55.

[130]*Id.*

a showing of good cause, while granting the other parties appropriate time for reply.

§ 4.19 SECOND WRITTEN SUBMISSIONS

The parties submit their second written submissions to the panel simultaneously.[131] These are the formal rebuttal submissions, which would include rebuttal not only to the first submission of the other party, but also rebuttal to oral statements made at the first panel meeting. The second submission for the respondent is, in essence, a second rebuttal, inasmuch as its first submission, filed after the complaining party's first submission, itself was primarily in the nature of a rebuttal.

The second submission, particularly for the complaining party, generally is a crucial document. Other than the statement presented at the second meeting of the panel, it is the only opportunity the complaining party has to rebut the arguments of the responding party, since the latter's first submission will have been made after the complainant's first submission.

§ 4.20 SECOND MEETING OF THE PANEL

The second meeting of the panel considers the rebuttal arguments of the parties, and any other issues the panel may wish to review. Third parties normally do not participate in, or attend, the second panel meeting, nor receive the second written submissions of the parties. However, in one dispute, the third parties requested that they be allowed to be present at all meetings between the panel and the parties to the dispute.[132] The panel agreed to permit the third parties to observe the second substantive meeting of the panel with the parties, but declined to offer further participation.[133]

Just as the second submissions are extremely important, so is the second meeting of the panel. By this time the panel will have had the opportunity of hearing the parties during the first meeting, possibly receiving their

---

[131]DSU Art. 12.6.

[132]*European Communities - Regime for the Importation, Sale and Distribution of Bananas, supra* note 8, ¶¶ 7.4 to 7.9.

[133]*Id.*

responses to questions posed, and simply to reflect on the issues. The second meeting normally will be the panel's last opportunity to request information from the parties and to hear their responses to issues that may be troubling the panel. It also normally will be the last opportunity of the parties to make their case to the panel.

§ 4.21 INTERIM REVIEWS

[1] Descriptive portions of the report

Interim panel reports are reviewed by the parties at two stages during the proceeding. The first interim review occurs after the panel's consideration of the rebuttal submissions of the parties; at this point the interim report sets forth only its "descriptive" portions — a statement of the facts and a summary of the arguments of the parties.[134] The parties may comment on this portion of the report within a time set by the panel, usually two weeks.[135] The same procedure was followed under GATT practice. In practice, remarks by the parties to the descriptive part of the report are almost always agreed to by the panels.

[2] Full interim report

After consideration of the comments of the parties on the descriptive portion of the report, the panel then issues an interim report that includes not only its descriptive portion, but also its findings and recommendations. This usually occurs two-to-four weeks after submission of comments on the descriptive portion.[136]

Again within a time set by the panel, usually one week, parties may submit a written request for a review of precise aspects of the interim report, including a further meeting with the panel to review the issues identified in the written request.[137] The review, including the possible meeting

[134]DSU Art. 15.1.
[135]DSU Appendix 3.12(f).
[136]DSU Art. 15.2; Appendix 3.12(g).
[137]DSU Art. 15.2; App. 3.12(h).

with the parties, normally will occur within two weeks.[138] If no review is requested, the interim report is considered to be the final report.[139] The DSU requires that the findings of the final panel report include a discussion of the arguments made at the interim review stage.[140] However, it does not limit the panel to modifying only those paragraphs of the interim report commented upon by the parties.[141]

[3] Request for further review

The main purpose of requiring identification of the precise issues to be reviewed is to provide the other party with adequate notice of the issues so that it may prepare a rebuttal.[142] Therefore, merely enumerating the numbers of the paragraphs of the findings section of the interim report for which review is requested, and not stating the precise aspects of those paragraphs for which review is requested, normally would not meet the requirements of Article 15.2 of the DSU.[143] However, where the written request for review of the findings section related only to such factual aspects as the correct reflection of the requestor's arguments and the names and references of scientific experts, the responding party normally would not be prejudiced.[144]

§ 4.22 COMPUTATION OF TIME

Prompt resolution of disputes was an important goal of the negotiators of the Uruguay Round and, consequently, the DSU imposes a number

[138]DSU Appendix 3.12(j).

[139]DSU Art. 15.2.

[140]DSU Art. 15.3.

[141]*EC Measures Concerning Meat and Meat Products (Hormones)*, *supra* note 61, ¶7.6.

[142]*Id.* ¶7.4.

[143]*Id.*

[144]*Id.*

of time limits on the various stages of the process. However, the DSU does not provide flexibility for many of these limits, particularly if they expire on weekends or holidays. Accordingly, the DSB subsequently agreed on the following practice:

> When, under the DSU (and its special or additional rules and procedures), a time-period within which a communication must be made or action taken by a Member to exercise or preserve its rights expires on a non-working day of the WTO Secretariat, any such communication or action will be deemed to have been made or taken on the WTO non-working day if lodged on the first working day of the WTO Secretariat following the day on which such time-period would normally expire.[145]

The fact that this practice would extend some time-periods by a day or more would not serve to extend subsequent time-periods;[146] consequently, these subsequent time-periods could in fact be shortened.

The DSU calls for panels normally to issue their final reports to the parties within six months from the date of the composition of the panel.[147] "In no case should the period from the establishment of the panel to the circulation of the report to the Members exceed nine months."[148] Despite this relatively clear injunction, some reports, in complex cases, have exceeded the nine month deadline.[149] In truth, in some of these cases it is not possible to meet the nine month deadline set out in the DSU. It appears that the Secretariat, therefore, construes the word "should" to be hortatory, not mandatory, and that the Dispute Settlement Body and the parties thus far have agreed.

---

[145]*Expiration of Time-Periods in the DSU, Proposal by the Chairman*, WT/DSB/W/10 and WT/DSB/W/10/Add .1 (20 July 1995). The proposal was agreed to by the DSB at its meeting of 27 September 1995, WT/DSB/M/7 (27 October 1995) agenda item 10.

[146]*Id.*

[147]DSU Art. 12.8.

[148]DSU Art. 12.9.

[149]For example, the panel in *Bananas* was composed on 7 June 1996, but its final report was not circulated until 22 May 1997, more than 11 months later. *European Communities - Regime for the Importation, Sale and Distribution of Bananas*, *supra* note 8. Similarly, the panel in *Hormones* was constituted on 2 July 1996, but its report was not circulated until 18 August 1997, more than 13 months later. *EC Measures Concerning Meat and Meat Products (Hormones), Complaint by the United States*, *supra* note 61.

§ 4.23 "NON-VIOLATION" COMPLAINTS AND COMPLAINTS INVOLVING "OTHER" SITUATIONS

Most disputes involve claims under Article XXIII(1)(a) that a Member has failed to carry out its obligations under an agreement. The Dispute Settlement Understanding elaborates and applies Article XXIII(1)(a) to the covered WTO agreements. In addition, Article XXIII of GATT, however, also provides two other bases for complaints:

> (b) the application by another contracting party of any measure, whether or not it conflicts with the provisions of this Agreement; or
> (c) the existence of any other situation.

These are the so-called "non-violation nullification and impairment complaints" and the "other situation" complaints.[150] The somewhat unusual notion that one Member can nullify or impair its commitments to another Member without violating an agreement is grounded in the fact that the benefits governments expect to obtain from trade agreements may be negated by actions of another government that could not reasonably have been anticipated at the time of the negotiation. The "other factors" provision is an even broader basis for proceeding. Article 26 of the DSU provides special procedures for dealing with these two types of complaints.

When a Member brings a "non-violation" complaint of the type described in Article XXIII(1)(b), it must comply with all of the requirements that apply to other complaints. In addition, the complaining Member must present a detailed justification in support of its position.[151] However, Article 26 does not state where or when the complaining party must do this: in its request for consultations, in its request for the establishment of a panel, or in its submissions to the panel. Presumably, a detailed justification would not be necessary in the request for consultations, so long as the request

---

[150]GATT panels found "non-violation" nullification and impairment in four of 14 instances in which it was alleged: *Australia - Subsidy on Ammonium Sulphate*, BISD II/188 (Adopted 3 April 1950); *Germany - Imports of Sardines*, BISD 1S/53 (Adopted 31 October 1952); *Germany - Import Duties on Starch and Potato Flour*, BISD 3S/77 (Noted 16 February 1955); *European Communities - Payments and Subsidies Paid to Processors and Producers of Oilseeds and Related Animal Feed Proteins*, BISD 37S/86 (Adopted 25 January 1990).

[151]DSU Art. 26.1(a).

gives "the reasons for the request including identification of the measures at issue and an indication of the legal basis for the complaint."[152] Prudence would dictate, however, that the complaining Member should present as detailed a justification as possible in its request for consultations, as well as in its panel request, at least until a panel or the Appellate Body makes clear that it is not necessary to do so. A simple reference to Article XXIII as the legal basis for a request for the establishment of a panel will not suffice to include a claim for an Article XXIII:1(b) violation within a panel's terms of reference. Explicit reference to Article XXIII:1(b) is necessary.[153]

If the panel agrees with the complaining Member, there is, nevertheless, no obligation on the responding Member to withdraw the measure.[154] However, in such cases, the panel or the Appellate Body shall recommend that the responding Member concerned make a mutually satisfactory adjustment.[155]

A party alleging nullification and impairment of benefits based on "any other situation" also shall present a detailed justification in support of its argument.[156] As with allegations of non-violation nullification and impairment, prudence would dictate that this justification be included both in the request for consultations and in the request for the establishment of a panel.

In cases encompassing findings concerning both "other situation" claims and violation or non-violation claims, the panel shall prepare and circulate separate reports for the other disputes and the "other situation" dispute.[157]

The DSU applies to "other situation" disputes only to the point when the report has been circulated to the Members. Consideration for adoption, and surveillance and implementation of recommendations and rulings of "other situation" reports are governed by the Decision of 12 April 1989, the so-called "Montreal Rules."[158] The most significant consequence of this is

[152]DSU Art. 4.5.

[153] *Australia – Measures Affecting Importation of Salmon, supra* note 59 ¶ 8.28.

[154]DSU Art. 26.1(b).

[155]*Id. See* Chapter 8 with regard to implementation.

[156]DSU Art. 26.2(a).

[157]DSU Art. 26.2(b).

[158]DSU Art. 26.2. The "Montreal Rules" are published at BISD 36S/61. *See also*, §§ 7.08 and 8.08.

that the Montreal Rules contain GATT's requirement of a positive consensus to adopt and act upon an adopted report.[159] This is the only remaining relic of the former system's consensus practice in dispute settlement, and is likely to mean few "other situation" disputes, since the losing party can always prevent consensus.

Article XXIII:3 of the *General Agreement on Trade in Services* ("GATS") contains special provisions concerning non-violation complaints involving services. These are discussed in § 5.11[3].

§ 4.24 REPRESENTATION BY PRIVATE ATTORNEYS

The legal complexity of the WTO Agreements – 558 pages of text in the English version – increased the demand for the services of lawyers, a phenomenon that had begun under GATT in the late 1980s and early 1990s. Many Members, particularly developing country Members, did not have the resources to support a permanent staff of legal experts, and found themselves in need of legal help, particularly in disputes involving developed countries that were well-staffed with legal expertise. Traditionally, however, private attorneys did not present cases directly to the panels; this task was performed by government officials. Private attorneys advised, counseled, drafted submissions, and waited in the coffee lounge during panel meetings, available to answer questions.

In *Bananas*, some third parties included private attorneys in their delegations. Upon objection from the complaining party, the panel excluded the private attorneys from attendance in the panel meetings.[160] When the case reached the Appellate Body, the issue arose again, but with a different result: the Appellate Body held that it is for the Member concerned to determine who shall represent it, and that this may include private attorneys.[161] The Appellate Body's action, however, did not reverse the panel's decision since the issue had not been appealed; the question simply re-

[159]Montreal Rules ¶ G.3.

[160] *European Communities – Regime for the Importation, Sale and Distribution of Bananas, supra* note 8 ¶¶ 7.10-7.12.

[161] See *§ 6.03[16].*

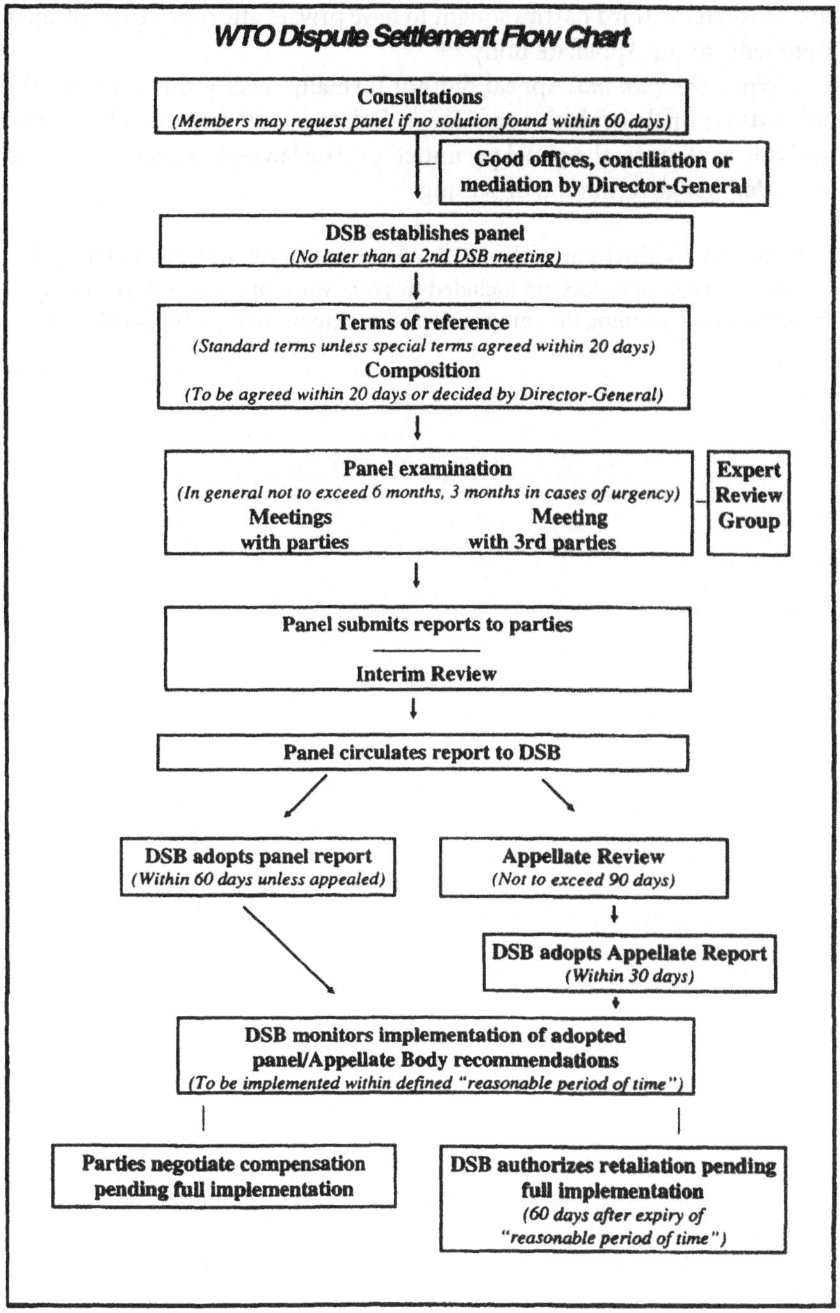
WTO Dispute Settlement Flow Chart
Consultations
(Members may request panel if no solution found within 60 days)
Good offices, conciliation or mediation by Director-General
DSB establishes panel
(No later than at 2nd DSB meeting)
Terms of reference
(Standard terms unless special terms agreed within 20 days)
Composition
(To be agreed within 20 days or decided by Director-General)
Panel examination
(In general not to exceed 6 months, 3 months in cases of urgency)
Meetings with parties
Meeting with 3rd parties
Expert Review Group
Panel submits reports to parties
Interim Review
Panel circulates report to DSB
DSB adopts panel report
(Within 60 days unless appealed)
Appellate Review
(Not to exceed 90 days)
DSB adopts Appellate Report
(Within 30 days)
DSB monitors implementation of adopted panel/Appellate Body recommendations
(To be implemented within defined "reasonable period of time")
Parties negotiate compensation pending full implementation
DSB authorizes retaliation pending full implementation
(60 days after expiry of "reasonable period of time")

curred when the third parties sought to have private attorney's present their arguments to the Appellate Body.[162]

While the *Bananas* appeal did not formally reverse the panel on the point, its rationale left little room for excluding private lawyers. Thus, when the issue next arose, the panel permitted private lawyers to present the case for a Member government, observing:

> [W]e find no provision in the WTO Agreement or the DSU, including the standard rules of procedure included therein, which prevents a WTO Member from determining the composition of its delegation to WTO panel meetings.[163]

[162] The third parties could not appeal issues of their own, but were confined to addressing the issues appealed by the parties themselves. *See* § 6.02.

[163] *Indonesia – Certain Measures Affecting the Automobile Industry*, *supra* note 80 ¶ 14.1.

CHAPTER 5

Special Rules and Procedures

§ 5.01 OVERVIEW

Appendix 2 to the Dispute Settlement Understanding lists a number of special rules and procedures contained in specific covered agreements that apply when the provisions of those agreements are in issue. To the extent that there is a difference between the provisions of the DSU and any of these special rules, the special rules prevail.[1] In addition, the DSU contains several provisions applicable to disputes involving developing countries. These too prevail over the standard rules of the DSU when applicable. Finally, the DSU contains special rules that apply to "non-violation" and "other situation" complaints of the type described in Article XXIII (1)(b) and (c) of GATT, as well as arbitration.

§ 5.02 DEVELOPING COUNTRIES

Developing countries have long been a concern of the GATT and now of the WTO.[2] Article XVIII of the original GATT deals with Governmental Assistance to Economic Development, a topic of primary interest to developing countries. The entirety of Part IV of GATT, dealing with Trade and Development, was added in the 1960s at the behest of the developing countries. In 1966 GATT adopted an Understanding regarding the application of

[1]DSU Art. 1.2.

[2]*See, generally*, Robert E. Hudec, GATT and the Developing Countries (Trade Policy Research Centre 1988).

dispute settlement procedures to developing countries.[3] Article 3.12 of the DSU makes certain of the provisions of this 1966 Understanding applicable to developing countries as optional alternatives to the corresponding DSU provisions. In addition, several articles of the DSU contain provisions that apply specifically to developing countries. Finally, Article 27 of the Agreement on Subsidies and Countervailing Measures provides for special and differential treatment for developing countries.[4]

§ 5.03 THE 1966 UNDERSTANDING

The 1966 Understanding provides alternative provisions to four DSU articles to developing countries which bring complaints under any WTO agreement against a developed country Member. These are Article 4 (Consultations); Article 5 (Good Offices, Conciliation and Mediation); Article 6 (Establishment of Panels); and Article 12 (Panel Procedures).[5]

[1] Consultations

Despite the fact that the DSU offers the 1966 Understanding as an alternative to the consultation provisions of Article 4 of the DSU, there do not appear to be any important differences between the Understanding and Article 4. The Understanding simply refers to steps to be taken "[i]f consultations between a less-developed contracting party and a developed contracting party in regard to any matter falling under paragraph 1 of Article XXIII do not lead to a satisfactory settlement."[6] The Understanding has no provisions governing the course and conduct of consultations, apart from paragraph 4's reference to a "two months" time frame which would closely coincide with the 60 days provided for in Article 4. Accordingly, it does not seem likely that developing countries will often invoke the Understanding in lieu of Article 4.

---

[3]*Procedures Under Article XXIII*, BISD 14/S 18.

[4]*See*, § 5.09[8].

[5]DSU Art. 3.12.

[6]Understanding ¶ 1.

[2] Good offices, conciliation or mediation

The provisions for good offices, conciliation or mediation ("good offices") contained in the Understanding are more elaborate than those contained in the DSU and, in an appropriate case, could offer an attractive alternative to a developing country complainant.

Perhaps the most important difference is that, under the DSU, good offices are undertaken only if both parties agree.[7] The Understanding, in contrast, permits a developing country complainant, if consultations are unsuccessful, to refer the matter to the Director-General who may use his good offices with a view to facilitating a solution.[8] This provision permits the Director-General to become involved in the matter even over the opposition of the developed country respondent.

The Understanding also requires the parties, at the request of the Director-General, to furnish all relevant information.[9] This requirement could be a useful vehicle for developing country complainants that, during consultations, experience difficulty in obtaining relevant information concerning developed country programs.

[3] Establishment of panels

The 1966 Understanding provides that after two months of consultations, the Director General shall — at the request of either of the parties — bring the matter to the attention of the DSB, to whom he shall submit a report.[10] A panel shall be appointed "forthwith,"[11] rather than at the meeting of the DSB following the meeting at which the request first appears on the agenda, as is normally the case.[12]

---

[7]DSU Art. 5.1.

[8]Understanding ¶ 1.

[9]Understanding ¶ 2.

[10]Understanding ¶ 4. The text of this paragraph actually refers to the CONTRACTING PARTIES or the GATT Council. Their dispute settlement responsibilities are now handled by the DSB.

[11]Understanding ¶ 5.

[12]DSU Art. 6.1.

[4] Panel procedures

A panel established pursuant to the Understanding is to submit its findings and recommendations within 60 days from the date on which the matter was referred to it.[13] This short deadline contrasts sharply with the six-to-nine months normally provided to panels.[14] The DSU therefore relaxes the requirement of the Understanding by permitting a panel to extend the 60 day limit if it considers the time insufficient.[15]

§ 5.04 OTHER DEVELOPING COUNTRY PROVISIONS OF THE DSU

[1] Consultations

Members are required by Article 4.10 of the DSU to "give special attention to the particular problems and interests of developing country Members" in the consultation process. Article 12.10 gives this general requirement some degree of specificity when a measure of a developing country is the subject of the consultations. The parties may agree to extend the time for consultations and, if they cannot agree to do so, the Chairman of the Dispute Settlement Body, after consulting with the parties, may extend the consultation period.

[2] Panel process

The difficulties developing countries may have in dealing with the complex WTO process are recognized by a further requirement of Article 12.10. When examining a complaint against a developing country Member, the panel shall accord sufficient time for the developing country to prepare and present its argumentation in defense of its measure. However, any extra time provided may not extend the normal time limits for the panel to issue the report, or for its recommendations and rulings to be implemented.

[13]Understanding ¶ 7.

[14]DSU Art. 12.9.

[15]DSU Art. 3.12.

When a developing country is involved as either complainant or respondent, panels are required to state in their reports explicitly how they have taken into account, when raised by a developing country, any relevant provisions on differential and more-favourable treatment for developing countries in the particular agreement at issue.[16]

In any dispute in which a developing country is involved, the panel shall include at least one panelist from a developing country, if the developing country Member involved in the dispute so requests.[17] Finally, the Secretariat provides legal advice and assistance to developing country Members upon request.[18]

§ 5.05 AGREEMENT ON THE APPLICATION OF SANITARY AND PHYTOSANITARY MEASURES

The *Agreement on the Application of Sanitary and Phytosanitary Measures* ("SPS Agreement"), applies to measures designed to protect human, plant, and animal life or health from pests and disease.[19] Such measures are, for the most part, highly technical, and Article 11 of the SPS Agreement, therefore, specifies that panels should seek the advice of experts.[20] A panel may establish an advisory technical experts group or consult with relevant international organizations, either on their own initiative or upon the request of a party.[21]

Experts have assisted panels in *EC – Measures Concerning Meat and Meat Products (Hormones)*[22], *Australia – Measures Affecting Importation of Salmon*[23] and *Japan – Measures Affecting Agricultural Products*[24]

---

[16]DSU Art. 12.11.

[17]DSU Art. 8.10.

[18]DSU Art. 27.2.

[19]*See* definition in SPS Agreement, Annex A.

[20]SPS Agreement Art. 11.2.

[21]*Id., See,* 4.12[2]

[22] WT/DS26/R/USA and WT/DS48/R/ Can (18 August 1997) (Adopted as Modified by the Appellate Body 13 February 1998).

[23] WT/DS18/R (12 June 1998).

[24] WT/DS76. *See* § 4.12[2] for a discussion of panel procedures with regard to experts.

An agreement between the WTO and the Office International des Épizooties provides that the organizations may agree "on administrative arrangements for designating scientific and technical experts with a view to the appliaiton of the provisions of the SPS Agreement, notably as provided for in Article 11, paragraph 2, in respect of dispute settlement."[25]

§ 5.06 AGREEMENT ON TECHNICAL BARRIERS TO TRADE

The *Agreement on Technical Barriers to Trade* ("TBT Agreement") applies to standards and technical regulations applicable to all products, including agricultural and industrial products, other than those covered by *Agreement on the Application of Sanitary and Phytosanitary Measures.*[26] A technical regulation is a "[d]ocument which lays down product characteristics or their related processes and production methods, including the applicable administrative provisions, with which compliance is mandatory."[27] A standard is a "[d]ocument approved by a recognized body, that provides, for common and repeated use, rules, guidelines or characteristics for products or related processes and production methods, with which compliance is not mandatory."[28]

The TBT Agreement specifies that consultations and the settlement of disputes shall be governed by the Dispute Settlement Understanding.[29] In addition, it authorizes a panel, at the request of a party or on its own initiative, to establish a technical expert group to assist in questions of a technical nature, requiring detailed consideration by experts.[30] Annex 2 to the TBT Agreement sets out simple procedures for technical expert groups: their terms of reference are set by the panels, to whom they report; partici-

[25] *Agreement between the World Trade Organization and the Office International des Épizooties*, WT/L/272 (8 July 1998) ¶ 10. (The Organization International des Épizooties, headquartered in Paris, comprises 151 member countries. Its mission is to inform governments of the occurrence and course of animal diseases; coordinate studies devoted to the surveillance and control of animal diseases; and harmonize regulations for trade in animals and animal products among its members).

[26] TBT Agreement Art. 1.3 and 1.5.

[27] TBT Annex 1.1.

[28] TBT Annex 1.2.

[29] TBT Agreement Art. 14.1.

[30] TBT Agreement Art. 14.2.

pation is restricted to persons of recognized experience and standing in the field; citizens of parties to the dispute shall not serve without the joint agreement of the parties, other than in exceptional circumstances when the need for specialized expertise cannot be satisfied otherwise; officials of governments of parties to the dispute may not serve, and governments or organizations shall not give instructions to experts, who serve in their individual capacities.[31]

Technical expert groups, in turn, may consult and seek information and technical advice from any source they deem appropriate.[32] Parties shall have access to all relevant information provided to an expert group, other than confidential information, which shall not be released without formal authorization from the government, organization or person providing the information.[33] If confidential information is not released, a non-confidential summary will be provided by the government, organization or person supplying the information.[34]

A draft report of the expert group shall be submitted for comment to the Members. Comments shall be taken into account in the final report which is circulated both to the Members and to the panel.[35] There is no comparable provision in the SPS Agreement, raising the issue as to whether a panel established under the TBT Agreement could use experts in their individual capacity, rather than as a group, as was done by a panel under the SPS Agreement.[36] Arguably, a TBT panel could seek expert advice pursuant to Article 13.1 of the DSU, which permits panels to seek advice from any individual or body it deems appropriate. However, this could raise a question as to whether the provisions for experts in the TBT Agreement supplant those in the DSU for TBT panels, pursuant to Article 1.2 of the DSU, or whether they are in addition to those rules.

Several provisions of the TBT Agreement require that Members take reasonable measures available to them in achieving compliance with the Agreement by local governmental bodies and non-governmental organizations.[37] The TBT Agreement's provisions regarding experts may be invoked

[31] TBT Annex 2.1-2.3.

[32] TBT Annex 2.4.

[33] TBT Annex 2.5.

[34] *Id.*

[35] TBT Annex 2.6.

[36] *See*, § 5.05.

[37] TBT Agreement Arts. 3, 4, 7, 8 and 9.

when a Member considers that another Member has not achieved satisfactory results under these provisions and its trade interests are significantly affected. In these circumstances the results of the dispute settlement process shall be the equivalent to those as if the body in question were a Member.[38]

§ 5.07 AGREEMENT ON IMPLEMENTATION OF ARTICLE VI OF GATT 1994 (ANTIDUMPING AGREEMENT)

[1] General

Article 17 of the *Agreement on Implementation of Article VI of GATT 1994* (the "Antidumping Agreement") covers consultations and dispute settlement concerning antidumping matters.[39] The distinction between the word "matter" as used in Article 17 and the word "measure" as used in the DSU was subject of the first WTO panel report to consider an antidumping dispute.

In *Guatemala – Anti-Dumping Investigation Regarding Portland Cement from Mexico*, Guatemala argued that only "measures" identified in Article 17.4 may be referred to panels.[40] Three such measures are identified in Article 17.4: a final antidumping measure; a price undertaking; or a provisional measure having a significant impact. The panel rejected this argument, noting that Article 17.5 requires the panel "to examine the matter" referred to it. The panel noted that this language is different from the language of Article 6 the DSU, which requires that a request for the establishment of a panel "identify the specific measures at issue."[41] The panel therefore read Article 17.4 as a timing provision, one that established when a "matter" might properly be the subject of dispute settlement: only after a Member took one of the three "measures" itemized in Article 17.4. Accordingly, the panel proceeded to consider the propriety of the matter of the initiation of the investigation, an event not specified in Article 17.4.

---

[38] TBT Agreement Art. 14.4.

[39] For a general discussion of the Antidumping Agreement, *see*, David Palmeter, *A Commentary on the WTO Anti-Dumping Code*, 30 JOURNAL OF WORLD TRADE, No. 4, at 43 (August 1996).

[40] WT/DS60/R (19 June 1998) ¶ 7.4.

[41] *Id.* ¶ 7.15.

The term "measure" in the DSU, the panel concluded, "should be understood as a shorthand reference to the many and varied situations in which obligations under the WTO Agreements might not be fulfilled by a Member, giving rise to a dispute, for which a resolution is provided in the DSU."[42]

[2] Standard of review

Perhaps the most significant part of Article 17 is paragraph 6 which provides a standard of review for panels considering antidumping measures. No other agreement contains an explicit standard of review.[43]

Article 17.6(i) requires panels to defer to the factual conclusions reached by the authorities of the Member imposing antidumping duties "if the establishment of the facts was proper and the evaluation was unbiased and objective, even though the panel might have reached a different conclusion."

In *Guatemala – Cement from Mexico*, in considering whether the evidence available to the authorities was sufficient to justify the initiation of the investigation, the panel quoted extensively, with approval, from the GATT panel report in *United States – Measures Affecting Imports of Softwood Lumber from Canada*.[44] The panel stated that its task was not to evaluate anew the evidence and information available to the authorities, but to examine "whether an unbiased and objective investigating authority evaluating that evidence could properly have determined that sufficient evidence of dumping, injury, and causal link existed to justify initiating the investigation."[45]

Article 17.6(ii) provides a standard of review to be applied to questions of law. It first instructs panels to interpret the relevant provisions of

---

[42] *Id.* ¶ 7.26.

[43] During the Uruguay Round, negotiators reached a *Decision on Review of Article 17.6 of the Agreement on Implementation of Article VI of the General Agreement on Tariffs and Trade 1994* in which they agreed to review the antidumping standard of review within three years "with a view to considering the question of whether it is capable of general application." The three-year deadline was not met.

[44] BISD 40S/358 (Adopted 17 October 1993).

[45] *Guatemala – Anti-Dumping Investigation Regarding Portland Cement from Mexico* ¶ 7.57.

the Anti-Dumping Agreement in accordance with the customary rules of interpretation of public international law. It next instructs panels, when they find that a provision of the Agreement admits of more than one permissible interpretation, to uphold the decision of the authorities if they reach one of those permissible interpretations. The panel in *Guatemala – Cement from Mexico* referred to the second instruction of Article 17.6(ii), but concluded that the relevant articles did not permit the interpretation adopted by Guatemala.[46]

The panel did not deal with the customary rules of interpretation of public international law at this point in its report, nor did it deal with an argument put forth by Professors Steven P. Croley and John H. Jackson concerning the interaction between the two instructions of Article 17.6(ii).[47] Prof. Croley and Prof. Jackson note that the customary rules of interpretation of public international law, as codified in Articles 31 and 32 of the *Vienna Convention on the Law of Treaties*, themselves resolve textual ambiguities. Thus, "Once a panel has invoked Articles 31 and 32 of the *Vienna Convention*, it presumably will have already settled on a nonambiguous, nonabsurd interpretation."[48]

Article 17.6(ii) thus seems to create a dilemma for panels wishing to avoid "a reading that would result in reducing whole clauses or paragraphs of a treaty to redundancy or inutility."[49] The reading adopted by the panel completely ignores the first sentence of Article 17.6(ii) and thus risks reducing it to redundancy or inutility. But, conversely, if the first sentence is read as requiring resolution by the customary rules of public international law in all cases, the second sentence becomes superfluous. Perhaps the best way of proceeding is sequentially, beginning with the first sentence. If the customary rules of interpretation of public international law, for some unusual reason, fail to provide an interpretation, then the second sentence may come into play. This procedure reduces neither sentence to redundancy or inutility. It simply provides that the second sentence is not reached unless it is needed.

---

[46] *Id.* footnote 232.

[47] *WTO Dispute Procedures, Standard of Review, and Deference to National Governments*, 90 AMERICAN JOURNAL OF INTERNATIONAL LAW 193 (April 1996).

[48] *Id.* 201.

[49] *United States – Standards for Reformulated and Conventional Gasoline*, AB-1996-1, WT/DS2/AB/R (29 April 1996) (Adopted 20 May 1996) at 23.

[3] Confidential information

Many of the relevant facts in antidumping investigations are confidential. In this regard, Article 17.7, in conformity with the DSU, specifies that confidential information disclosed to the panel shall not be disclosed without formal authorization of the submitter, but that if confidential information is withheld, a non-confidential summary will be released.[50]

An additional provision in Article 17 deals, indirectly, with the issue of confidentiality. Article 17.5(ii) provides that panels shall examine matters based upon "the facts made available in conformity with appropriate domestic procedures to the authorities of the importing Member." This raises the possibility that panels will decide disputes without the benefit of all of the information provided to the authorities, since the "domestic procedures" of a Member might preclude the disclosure of information made available to the Member on a confidential basis by firms involved in an investigation.

This issue apparently arose under GATT in *United States - Imposition of Anti-Dumping Duties on Imports of Fresh and Chilled Atlantic Salmon from Norway*, where the panel was permitted to review "data derived from" responses submitted by companies to a questionnaire issued by the United States International Trade Commission.[51] It is not clear whether these were the actual questionnaire responses or some compilation made from them. There also is no indication that the complainant and its counsel were permitted to review the information. One commentator reports that the panel was given "extremely limited access" to the confidential information, and "a matter of hours to review the material."[52]

[4] Overlap with countervailing duties

There is considerable substantive overlap between antidumping and countervailing duty proceedings, particularly with regard to questions of injury. To further consistency in these areas, the Ministers at the Uruguay

---

[50]*See* § 4.14.

[51]BISD 41S/229, (30 November 1992) (Adopted 27 April 1994)at ¶ 516.

[52]J.C. Thomas, *The Need for Due Process in WTO Proceedings*, 31 Journal of World Trade Law, No. 1, 45, at 48 (February 1997).

Round issued a Declaration "recognizing the need for the consistent resolution of disputes arising from anti-dumping and countervailing duty measures."[53] This is likely to mean, in practice, that parties, panels, and the Appellate Body will treat prior reports dealing with injury under the Antidumping Agreement as the equivalent of a report under the *Agreement on Subsidies and Countervailing Measures* and *vice versa*.[54]

§ 5.08 AGREEMENT ON IMPLEMENTATION OF ARTICLE VII OF GATT 1994 (CUSTOMS VALUATION AGREEMENT)

A Technical Committee on Customs Valuation, established by Article 18.2 of the *Agreement on Implementation of Article VII of GATT 1994* (the "Customs Valuation Agreement") serves, *inter alia*, as an institutionalized expert group available to assist panels and parties to disputes.

An important difference between the Technical Committee on Customs Valuation and other expert groups is that the Technical Committee is directed to provide, upon request, advice and assistance to Members engaged in consultations.[55] This responsibility is in addition to the normal expert group responsibility, which the Technical Committee also has, of carrying out an examination of any question requiring technical consideration upon the request of a panel.[56]

The terms of reference for the Technical Committee are set by the panel, and the panel, in turn, is required to take the Committee's report into consideration in its own deliberations.[57] If the Committee is unable to reach consensus on the matter referred to it, the panel will afford the parties an opportunity to present their views on the matter.[58]

---

[53]*Declaration on Dispute Settlement Pursuant to the Agreement on Implementation of Article VI of the General Agreement on Tariffs and Trade 1994 or Part V of the Agreement on Subsidies and Countervailing Measures.*

[54]*See* § 3.03.

[55]Customs Valuation Agreement Art. 19.3.

[56]*Id.* Art. 19.4.

[57]*Id.*

[58]*Id.*

Article 19 to the Customs Valuation Agreement makes clear that the DSU is generally applicable to disputes arising under the Agreement.[59] It also provides that confidential information provided to the panel shall not be disclosed without formal authorization of the submitter, but that when such information is not disclosed, a non-confidential summary shall be provided.[60]

§ 5.09 AGREEMENT ON SUBSIDIES AND COUNTERVAILING MEASURES

The entire subject of subsidies and countervailing measures — usually termed "countervailing duties" — is contentious, and the *Agreement on Subsidies and Countervailing Measures* (the "SCM Agreement"), in its complexity, reflects this policy contentiousness. The SCM Agreement deals with three types of subsidy: (1) prohibited; (2) actionable; and (3) permitted, as well as with domestic measures taken to offset, or "countervail," prohibited and actionable subsidies. It also establishes a Permanent Group of Experts with the responsibility, *inter alia*, of assisting panels in disputes concerning prohibited subsidies.[61]

[1] Prohibited subsidy procedures

Subsidies that are contingent upon export performance or upon the use of domestic rather than imported goods are prohibited by the SCM Agreement.[62] Reflecting the concern of the Members of the WTO with such subsidies, the SCM Agreement provides expedited procedures for dealing with disputes concerning them.

---

[59] *Id.* Art. 19.1.

[60] *Id.* Art. 19.5. *See also* §§ 4.14 and 4.17.

[61] SCM Agreement Art. 24.3. As noted above at § 5.07[4], there is considerable substantive overlap between countervailing duty and antidumping proceedings, particularly with regard to questions of injury, and, to further consistency in these areas, the Ministers at the Uruguay Round issued a Declaration "recognizing the need for the consistent resolution of disputes arising from anti-dumping and countervailing duty measures."

[62] SCM Agreement Art. 3.1.

Whenever a Member has reason to believe that a prohibited subsidy is being granted or maintained by another Member, it may request consultations with that other Member. The request for consultations must include a statement of available evidence with regard to the existence and nature of the subsidy.[63] The Member requested to consult must do so "as quickly as possible."[64] If no mutually agreed solution is reached within 30 days of the request for consultations, the matter may be referred to the Dispute Settlement Body for the immediate establishment of a panel.[65] This contrasts sharply with regular DSU proceedings which provide for 60 days consultations before a request for the establishment of a panel can be made, and for the establishment of a panel at the second meeting after a request first was placed on the agenda of the DSB.[66] Apart from the time limits specified in the SCM Agreement, the time periods specified in the DSU for the conduct of dispute settlement panels are reduced by half.[67]

No provision is made for interim reports of panels concerned with prohibited subsidy disputes. Instead, panels are directed simply to submit their final reports to the parties to the dispute and to circulate the final report to the Members within 90 days of the date of the composition of the panel and the establishment of its terms of reference.[68] If the measure in question is found to be a prohibited subsidy, the panel shall recommend that it be withdrawn without delay; in this regard, the panel will specify the time within which the measure must be withdrawn "without delay."[69]

Expedited provisions also govern the appeal of prohibited subsidy panel reports, and the adoption and implementation of those reports.[70]

[2] Procedures before the Permanent Group of Experts

Panels established to consider prohibited subsidies may request the assistance of the Permanent Group of Experts ("PGE") with regard to the

[63]SCM Agreement Art. 4.2.

[64]*Id.* Art. 4.3.

[65]*Id.* Art. 4.4.

[66]DSU Arts. 4.7 and 6.1.

[67]SCM Agreement Art. 4.12.

[68]*Id.* Art. 4.6.

[69]*Id.* Art. 4.8.

[70]*See* § 8.07.

issue of whether the measure in question is or is not a prohibited subsidy.[71] The PGE's conclusions on that question "shall be accepted by the panel without modification."[72]

The SCM Agreement also provides that the PGE "shall provide an opportunity for the Member applying or maintaining the measure to demonstrate that the measure in question is not a prohibited subsidy."[73] It is not clear from this language whether the accused Member has the burden of establishing that the measure is not prohibited, or that the accuser has the burden of establishing that it is.[74]

The PGE has issued Draft Rules of Procedure, Part III of which deals with Assistance to Panels.[75] These rules reflect the accelerated pace of prohibited subsidy proceedings. Parties, and any interested third parties may make written submissions within seven days of the request of a panel to the PGE for assistance.[76] The submission should address the issue of whether the measure identified by the panel is a prohibited subsidy, and should contain any relevant information concerning the measure, including legislation, regulations, or other documentation relating to the establishment and operation of the measure.[77] Parties to the dispute, but not third parties, may submit written rebuttal within fourteen days of the request for assistance.[78]

At the request of a party, or on its own initiative, the PGE may hold one hearing which, normally, will take place 21 days after the request for assistance.[79] Party requests for a hearing should be included in their initial written submissions.[80] Third parties, as well as parties, may be present at the hearing, but only for the duration of their oral presentations.[81]

In exceptional circumstances, where strict adherence to these time periods would result in "manifest unfairness," the PGE may, at the request of

[71] *Id.* Art. 4.5.

[72] *Id.*

[73] *Id.*

[74] *See* § 4.13 concerning burden of proof.

[75] *Draft Rules of Procedure for the Permanent Group of Experts*, G/SCM/W/365/Rev.1, 26 June 1996 (hereafter PGE Rules).

[76] PGE Rule 9(1).

[77] PGE Rule 9(2).

[78] PGE Rule 9(3).

[79] PGE Rule 10 (1).

[80] PGE Rule 10 (2).

[81] PGE Rule 10(3) and 10(4).

a party, modify the time period for filing documents or scheduling a hearing.[82] Documents filed by a party or a third party must be served, by the most expeditious means possible, on each of the other parties to the dispute and to third parties.[83] This service requirement is unusual in WTO practice; the PGE Rules do not specify how a service list is to be compiled so that parties may comply with this requirement.

The PGE may be consulted by any Member, and may give confidential advisory opinions, which may not be invoked in any dispute settlement proceeding involving actionable subsidies.[84]

[3] Actionable subsidy procedures

Actionable subsidies are those which, though not prohibited, cause "adverse effects to the interests of other Members."[85] Adverse effects are those which cause injury to the domestic industry of another Member, nullify or impair benefits accruing to another Member, or cause serious prejudice to the interests of another Member.[86]

A request for consultations regarding an actionable subsidy must include a statement of available evidence with regard to both the existence and nature of the subsidy, and the adverse effects, i.e., the injury, nullification and impairment, or serious prejudice.[87] In the event that serious prejudice is alleged, the available evidence may be limited to specific factors: the level of the subsidization; whether the subsidy covers operating losses sustained by an industry or, in some instances, a single enterprise; or whether it constitutes forgiveness of debt.[88] Annex V to the SCM Agreement sets out procedures for developing information concerning serious prejudice.[89]

---

[82] PGE Rule 13 (2).
[83] PGE Rule 15 (2) and (3).
[84] SCM Agreement Art. 24.4.
[85] SCM Agreement Art. 5.
[86] *Id.*
[87] SCM Agreement Art. 7.2.
[88] SCM Agreement Art. 7, n. 19. The factors are set out in detail in Art. 6.1.
[89] *See*, § 5.09[4].

As is the case with prohibited subsidies, a Member receiving a consultation request shall enter into consultations "as quickly as possible."[90] If consultations do not result in an agreed solution within 60 days, establishment of a panel may be requested, and the panel will be established absent consensus to the contrary.[91] The composition of the panel and its terms of reference shall be established within 15 days from the date when it is established.[92] The final report of the panel shall be circulated to all Members within 120 days.[93] Expedited provisions also govern the appeal of actionable subsidy panel reports, and the adoption and implementation of those reports.[94]

[4] Procedures for developing information concerning serious prejudice

To establish that a program is inconsistent with the actionable subsidy provisions of the SCM Agreement, the complaining Member must demonstrate adverse effects — injury to its domestic industry, nullification or impairment, or serious prejudice. Information regarding injury to a domestic industry as well as that relating to nullification and impairment to the complaining Member is information uniquely available to that Member. However, information regarding serious prejudice may be uniquely in the possession of the Member complained against or of third parties.[95] Annex V to the SCM Agreement contains procedures for developing information concerning serious prejudice.

Members are required to cooperate in the development of evidence to be provided to a panel examining an allegation of an actionable subsidy.[96]

[90]SCM Agreement Art. 7.3.

[91]SCM Agreement Art. 7.4.

[92]*Id.*

[93]SCM Agreement Art. 7.5.

[94]*See* §§ 5.09[4] and 8.07.

[95]Serious prejudice is defined in Art. 6 of the SCM Agreement and includes, *inter alia*, the ad valorem level of the subsidy, whether it is used to cover operating losses or debt forgiveness, or whether the effect is to displace or impede imports of a Member in third country markets, or to undercut prices.

[96]SCM Agreement Annex V.1.

In this regard, the parties to the dispute, as well as any interested third parties, are required to notify the DSB, as soon as a panel has been requested, of the organization within its territory responsible for administering the information requirement, and the procedures to be followed in requesting information.[97] The DSB, upon request, shall initiate the procedure necessary to obtain relevant information from the government of the subsidizing Member.[98] This process may include the presentation of questions to both the complaining Member and the subsidizing Member.[99]

When third-country effects are at issue, a party to the dispute may collect third-country information through the use of questions to the government of the third-country Member.[100] The information to be supplied by third-country Members is that which already is available or readily can be made available; third-country Members are not required to make a market or price analysis specially for the purpose of responding to questions.[101] However, if a party undertakes a detailed market analysis at its own expense, the authorities of the third-country should cooperate by making available all non-confidential information which is normally maintained by the government.[102]

A representative shall be appointed by the DSB to serve the function of facilitating the timely completion of the information-gathering process,[103] which shall be completed within 60 days of the date on which the matter was referred to the DSB.[104] One of the responsibilities of the representative is to advise the panel of the reasonableness of any requests for information and the efforts made by parties to comply with these requests in a cooperative and timely manner.[105]

If the subsidizing Member, or third-country Members, fail to cooperate in the information-gathering process, the complaining Member shall present its case based on the evidence available to it.[106] The panel shall make

[97]*Id.*

[98]SCM Agreement Annex V.2.

[99]*Id.*

[100]SCM Agreement Annex V.3.

[101]*Id.*

[102]*Id.*

[103]SCM Agreement Annex V.4.

[104]SCM Agreement Annex V.5.

[105]SCM Agreement Annex V.8.

[106]SCM Agreement Annex V.6.

its determination based on the best information available.[107] In making that determination, "the panel should draw adverse inferences from instances of non-cooperation by any party involved in the information-gathering process."[108] The panel retains its basic power to seek additional information on its own initiative.[109]

[5] Multiple subsidy procedures

A Member may wish to argue that a subsidy is both prohibited and actionable, or that it is otherwise inconsistent with Article XVI of GATT. However, the time-tables prescribed for these procedures differ greatly. Allegations of prohibited subsidies and actionable subsidies are subject to different time-tables under the terms of Articles 4 and 7 of the SCM Agreement, while Article XVI proceedings would be subject to the even different times provided for in the DSU.

This issue arose when Canada requested the establishment of a panel to determine whether export financing for civil aircraft provided by Brazil was a prohibited subsidy as well as a violation of Articles XVI and XXIII of GATT.[110] Canada withdrew the request after the procedural problem was raised by Brazil in the DSB, and subsequently refiled the request with the Article XVI and XXIII counts dropped.[111] Several months later, Brazil in turn sought consultations with Canada concerning the latter's programs affecting exports of civil aircraft. In this instance, Brazil filed two separate requests for consultations, the first alleging that the programs were prohibited subsidies, the second that they were actionable.[112]

---

[107] *Id.*

[108] SCM Agreement Annex V.7.

[109] SCM Agreement Annex V.9.

[110] *Brazil - Export Financing Programme for Aircraft, Request for Establishment of a Panel by Canada*, WT/DS46/2 (17 September 1996).

[111] *Brazil - Export Financing Programme for Aircraft, Request for the Establishment of a Panel by Canada*, WT/DS46/4 (4 October 1996). This request also was withdrawn prior to the meeting at which it was to be considered. World Trade Organization, *WTO Focus*, No. 21, at 2 (August 1997).

[112] *Canada - Measures Affecting the Export of Civilian Aircraft*, WT/DS/70 and WT/DS/71 (10 March 1997).

[6] Non-actionable subsidies

Subsidies which are not "specific," or those which provide assistance for certain research activities or to disadvantaged regions, as well as those that promote adaption of existing facilities to new environmental requirements, are not actionable provided they meet the criteria of the SCM Agreement.[113] Members who claim that their subsidy programs are non-actionable are required to notify the details of those programs to the Committee on Subsidies and Countervailing Measures in advance of their implementation.[114] Upon request of a Member, the Committee shall review a notification to determine whether the program meets the criteria for a non-actionable subsidy.[115]

The determination of the Committee will be submitted to binding arbitration at the request of any Member.[116] In addition, an allegation that the conditions set out in a notified program have been violated may also be submitted to binding arbitration.[117] The arbitration body shall present its conclusions to the Members within 120 days from the date when the matter first was referred to the arbitrator. While the arbitration provisions of the DSU generally apply to the arbitration proceeding, the Committee has adopted additional procedures for the initiation of the arbitration.[118] If a program has not been notified as a non-actionable subsidy, it nevertheless shall be treated as non-actionable if it is found to be so during the dispute settlement process.[119]

Notwithstanding the fact that a program is non-actionable, it may be subject to a dispute settlement procedure that could lead to countermeasures. If a Member believes that the program has resulted in serious adverse effects to its industry, it may request consultations with the Member implementing the non-actionable program.[120] The implementing Member shall

[113]SCM Agreement Arts. 8.1 and 8.2.

[114]SCM Agreement Art. 8.3.

[115]SCM Agreement Art. 8.4.

[116]SCM Agreement Art. 8.5. *See* § 5.15 concerning arbitration.

[117]*Id.*

[118]*Id. See*, §5.15.

[119]SCM Agreement Art. 10, n. 35.

[120]SCM Agreement Art. 9.1.

consult "as quickly as possible" "to clarify the facts of the situation and to arrive at a mutually acceptable solution.[121]

If no mutually acceptable solution is reached in 60 days, the requesting Member may refer the matter to the Committee on Subsidies and Countervailing Measures which, if it determines, within 120 days, that the adverse effects exist, may recommend to the subsidizing Member that it modify the program.[122] If the Committee's recommendation is not followed within six months, the Committee shall authorize the requesting Member to take appropriate countermeasures commensurate with the nature and degree of the effects determined to exist.[123]

[7] Countervailing Measures

Countervailing measures, in the form of duties, may be taken to offset subsidies that injure a domestic industry. Disputes concerning the imposition of countervailing measures are governed generally by the Dispute Settlement Understanding.

Footnote 35 to Article X of the SCM Agreement specifies that countervailing measures may be imposed to offset both prohibited and actionable subsidies. However, they may not be imposed if countermeasures under dispute settlement procedures have been imposed. Countervailing measures may not be imposed against non-actionable subsides. Even if a program has not been properly notified as non-actionable, it nevertheless may not be countervailed if it is found to conform to the substantive requirements for a non-actionable subsidy.

[8] Developing countries

Article 27 of the SCM Agreement provides for special and differential treatment of developing countries. With regard to dispute settlement, it provides that the prohibited subsidy provisions shall not apply for a period

[121]SCM Agreement Art. 9.2.

[122]SCM Agreement Arts. 9.3 and 9.4.

[123]SCM Agreement Art. 9.4.

of eight years from the date of entry into force of the WTO Agreement, provided certain substantive standards are met.[124] During this period, the actionable subsidy provisions of Article 7, with their requirement of a showing of adverse effects, applies to what otherwise would be prohibited subsidies.[125]

§ 5.10 AGREEMENT ON TEXTILES AND CLOTHING (ATC)

[1] Overview

International trade in textiles and clothing ("textiles") traditionally has been, and, at least temporarily, effectively remains subject to a strict regulatory regime, the Arrangement Regarding International Trade in Textiles, commonly known as the "MFA." The *Agreement on Textiles and Clothing* ("ATC") brings textile trade into the GATT/WTO system by phasing out the import quotas established by the MFA over a period of 10 years.[126] During this transition period, restrictions continue to apply, subject to the rules of the ATC. This system of restrictions is supervised by the Textiles Monitoring Body ("TMB").[127] Its responsibilities include resolving disagreements over such matters as changes in import restrictions, and, if necessary, making findings and recommendations to the parties. In addition, pursuant to the ATC, the TMB has established its own rules of procedure.[128] Ultimately, if a matter remains unresolved despite TMB recommendations, it may be referred to the Dispute Settlement Body for consideration by a panel pursuant to the Dispute Settlement Understanding.[129] Prior consultations pursuant to the DSU are not required.[130]

As described more fully below, the role and function of DSU panels differ substantially from those of the TMB. Unlike panels, for example, the

---

[124]The substantive standards are set out in paragraphs 2 through 5 of Article 27.

[125]SCM Agreement Art. 27.7.

[126]ATC Art. 8.

[127]ATC Art. 8.1.

[128]ATC Art. 8.2. *See* §5.10[3].

[129]ATC Art. 8.10.

[130]*Id.*

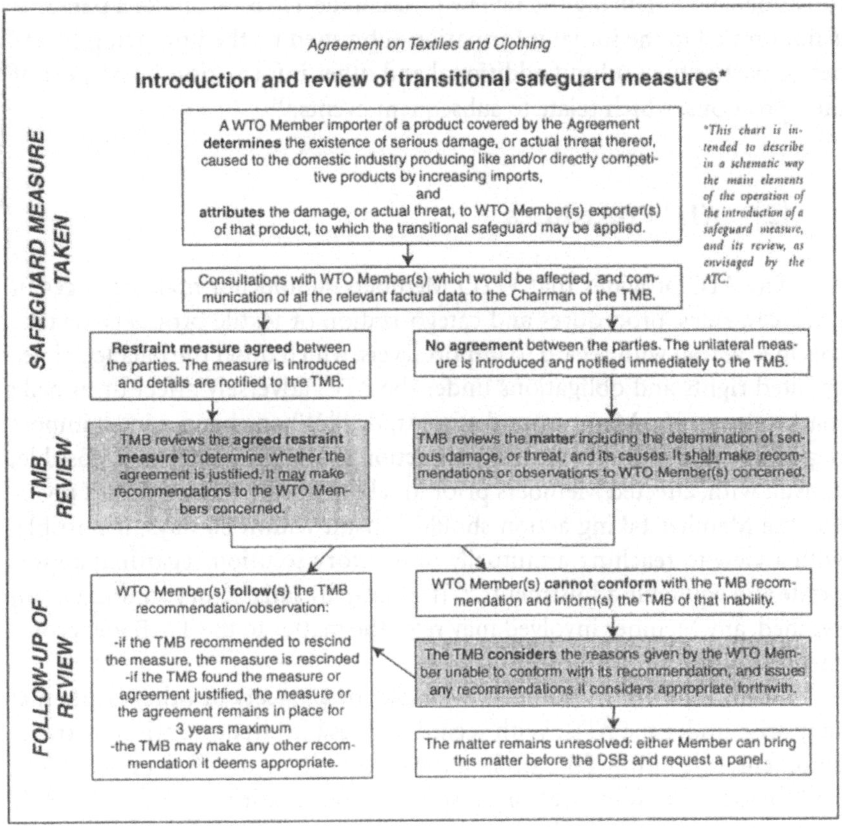

TMB is not limited to any specific terms of reference.[131] The function of the TMB is to supervise the implementation of the ATC generally; panels have no such general responsibility.[132] The TMB's membership is composed of constituencies; DSU panelists, by contrast, are not selected on the basis of

[131] *United States - Measure Affecting Imports of Woven Wool Shirts and Blouses from India*, WT/DS33/R (6 January 1997) (Adopted as Affirmed by the Appellate Body 23 May 1997), ¶7.19.

[132] *Id.*

constituencies.[133] During the review process, the TMB — unlike a panel — is not limited to the initial information submitted by the importing Member, as parties may submit additional and other information in support of their positions, which relate to subsequent events.[134]

[2] ATC Procedures

The ATC provides that WTO Members should not make changes in practices, rules, procedures and categorization of textile products, or take specified action with regard to import levels, which upset the balance of negotiated rights and obligations under the ATC, adversely affect or impede market access of a Member, or disrupt trade.[135] When changes in an import regime are made, the Member taking action should inform, and if possible, consult with, affected Members prior to taking action.[136] If this is not possible, the Member taking action should consult within 60 days, if possible, with a view to reaching a mutually satisfactory solution regarding appropriate and equitable adjustments.[137] If a mutually satisfactory solution is not reached, any Member involved may refer the matter to the TMB for recommendations.[138]

Referral to the TMB is also available for a variety of other issues that may arise under the ATC. With regard to possible circumvention by transshipment, re-routing, false declarations of origin or of official documents, and inadequate measures in response, consultations should be held promptly, within 30 days if possible.[139] Any measures taken to counter these activities must be notified to the TMB. If a mutually agreed solution is not reached, any Member concerned may refer the matter to the TMB for review and recommendations.[140] Should any Member believe that no action,

---

[133] *Id.*

[134] Id. ¶7.20. The Appellate Body, however, termed this statement *dicta*. *United States - Measure Affecting Imports of Woven Wool Shirts and Blouses from India*, WT/DS33/AB/R (25 April 1997) (Adopted 23 May 1997), §V, at 19.

[135] ATC Art. 4.2, 4.3.

[136] ATC Art. 4.4.

[137] *Id.*

[138] *Id.*

[139] ATC Art. 5.2.

[140] ATC Art. 5.4.

or inadequate action is being taken in response to false declarations concerning fibre content, quantities, description or classification, frustrating the objectives of the ACT, it should consult promptly with the Member concerned. If a solution is not reached, any Member involved may refer the matter to the TMB for recommendations.[141]

In certain circumstances Members may impose import restraints pursuant to a "transitional safeguard mechanism."[142] The WTO panel on *Cotton and Man-Made Fibre Underwear* concluded that, consistent with prior GATT practice, this provision should be interpreted narrowly.[143] This point was not reviewed on appeal; however, subsequent decisions of the Appellate Body cast serious doubt on this "narrow interpretation" conclusion.[144]

Transitional safeguard restraints are applied on a Member-by-Member basis, not on a most-favored-nation basis.[145] The Member proposing to take safeguard action must consult with the Members which would be affected by the measure.[146] The request for consultations must be accompanied by specific and relevant information with regard to the impact of the imports on the domestic industry concerned and the source of the imports.[147] The Member should also state the level of the proposed restraint, and communicate the request for consultations, together with the relevant data, to the Chairman of the TMB.[148] Consultations should be held "without delay," and normally would be completed within 60 days of the date on which the request was received.[149]

If the Members concerned agree on a restraint measure, the details must be communicated to the TMB within 60 days from the date of the conclusion of the agreement.[150] The TMB shall determine whether the agreement is consistent with the safeguard requirements of the ATC, and

---

[141]ATC Art. 5.6.

[142]ATC Art. 6.

[143]*United States - Restrictions on Imports of Cotton and Man-Made Fibre Underwear*, WT/DS24/R (8 November 1996) (Adopted as Modified by the Appellate Body 25 February 1997), ¶ 7.21.

[144]*See* § 4.13.

[145]ATC Art. 6.4.

[146]ATC Art. 6.7.

[147]*Id.*

[148]*Id.*

[149]*Id.*

[150]ATC Art. 6.9.

shall make such recommendations as it deems appropriate to the Members.[151] If the Members concerned do not agree on a restraint measure within 60 days from the date on which the request for consultations was requested, the Member which proposed to take safeguard action may apply the restraint, in accordance with the requirements of the ATC, within 30 days following the 60-day period for consultations.[152] At the same time, the Member applying the restraint must refer the matter to the TMB.[153] Either Member may refer the matter to the TMB prior to the expiration of the 60-day period for consultations.[154] The TMB shall make its recommendations to the Members concerned within 30 days.[155]

In "highly unusual and critical circumstances, where delay would cause damage which would be difficult to repair," safeguard restraints may be imposed provisionally.[156] In such a case, the request for consultations and the notification to the TMB shall be made by the Member taking action no more than five working days after the action is taken.[157] The TMB shall be notified at the conclusion of the consultations if they do not produce agreement; in no case shall it be notified later than 60 days from the date of implementation of the action.[158] The TMB shall examine the matter and make its recommendations to the Members concerned within 30 days.[159] If consultations are successful, the Members shall notify the TMB upon their conclusion, but in any case, no later than 90 days from the date of the implementation of the action.[160] The TMB may make such recommendations as it deems appropriate to the Members concerned.[161]

Members shall endeavor to accept in full the recommendations of the TMB.[162] If a Member is unable to do so, it shall inform the TMB as to why it is unable to do so not later than one month after receipt of the recommen-

[151] *Id.*

[152] ATC Art. 6.10.

[153] *Id.*

[154] *Id.*

[155] *Id.*

[156] ATC Art. 6.11.

[157] *Id.*

[158] *Id.*

[159] *Id.*

[160] *Id.*

[161] *Id.*

[162] ATC Art. 8.9.

dations.[163] The TMB may then issue any further recommendations it deems appropriate and, if the matter remains unresolved, either Member may bring it before the Dispute Settlement Body, invoking Article XXIII:2 of GATT 1994, and the relevant provisions of the Dispute Settlement Understanding.[164]

[3] Textiles Monitoring Body Working Procedures

The TMB consists of a chairman and 10 members.[165] The ATC provides that its membership is to be balanced and broadly representative of the Members, and shall be rotated at "appropriate intervals."[166] The members of the TMB are appointed by WTO Members designated by the WTO Council for Trade in Goods; they serve in their personal capacities.[167]

The TMB's Working Procedures with regard to dispute settlement are brief. Representatives of parties to a dispute shall be invited to present their views fully to the TMB, and to answer questions put by TMB Members.[168] If a member of the TMB is a representative of a party to a dispute, that member should not present the party's case.[169] Parties to a dispute may designate a representative who may be present during the discussion phase of the TMB's consideration of the dispute. If a national of a party to a dispute is a member of the TMB, the designated representative may not be present during the drafting of recommendations, findings or observations. However, the representative of party to a dispute of which no member of the TMB is a national may be present, but may not take part during the drafting of the recommendations, findings or observations.[170] Parties to the dispute are required to notify the Chairman of the TMB, in writing, prior to the TMB's examination of the dispute of the composition of their delegations.[171]

---

[163] ATC Art. 8.10.

[164] *Id.*

[165] ATC Art. 8.1.

[166] *Id.*

[167] *Id.*

[168] *Working Procedures for the Textiles Monitoring Body, Annex to Textiles Monitoring Body, Report of the First Meeting*, G/TMB/R/1, ¶ 6.1.

[169] *Id.*

[170] *Id.* ¶6.2.

[171] *Id.* ¶6.3.

Unless otherwise decided by the TMB, support material, working documents or information prepared by the Secretariat shall be confidential to the TMB and shall have no official standing.[172] Information supplied to the TMB by WTO Members shall remain confidential to the TMB, if supplied on a confidential basis.[173] The TMB Working Procedures do not require a non-confidential summary.[174]

§ 5.11 GENERAL AGREEMENT ON TRADE IN SERVICES (GATS)

[1] General

The consultation and dispute settlement provisions of the Dispute Settlement Understanding apply to consultations concerning disputes under the *General Agreement on Trade in Services* ("GATS").[175] Additionally, at the request of a Member, the Council for Trade in Services or the Dispute Settlement Body may consult with any Member or Members with regard to any matter for which regular consultations have not produced a satisfactory solution.[176]

[2] Double taxation treaties

A Member may not request consultations (or dispute settlement) under the national treatment provisions of Article XVII of GATS with regard to measures that fall within the scope of international agreements between them concerning the avoidance of double taxation.[177] In the case of

---

[172]*Id.* ¶4.3.

[173]*Id.* ¶ 4.4. At its first meeting, the TMB decided to continue discussion on the adoption of the following sentence: "In cases where the TMB has based its recommendations, findings or observations *inter alia* on confidential information provided to it by a party to a dispute, the TMB should ensure that the other party directly concerned [can] have access to such information." TMB, *Report of the First Meeting*, G/TMB/R/1, ¶ 5 at 2 (26 July 1995).

[174]*See* § 4.17.

[175]GATS Art. XXII:1 and Art. XXIII:1.

[176]GATS Art. XXII:2.

[177]GATS Art. XXII:3.

disagreement between the Members as to whether a measure falls within the scope of such an agreement, and if the agreement in question was entered into after the date of entry into force of the WTO Agreement, either Member may bring the matter before the Council on Trade in Services, which shall refer the question to binding arbitration.[178] If the agreement existed on the date on which the WTO Agreement entered into force, the question may be brought before the Council only with the consent of both parties to the agreement.[179]

[3] Non-violation nullification and impairment[180]

If a Member considers that any benefit it could reasonably have expected to accrue to it under a specific commitment of another Member under Part III of GATS is being nullified or impaired as a result of the application of a measure which does not conflict with GATS, it may have recourse to the DSU.[181] If nullification and impairment is found, the Member affected would be entitled to a mutually satisfactory adjustment on the basis of Article XXI:2 ("Modification of Schedules"). If an agreement cannot be reached on the basis of Article XXI:2, the compensation and suspension of concessions provisions of Article 22 of the DSU apply.[182]

[4] Modification of schedules

A Member may modify or withdraw any service commitment made in its Schedule of specific commitments at any time after three years have elapsed from the date on which the commitment entered into force, in accordance with the provisions of Article XXI of GATS. However, compensatory adjustments in its Schedule must be made at the request of an affected Member.[183]

At the request of an affected Member, the Member proposing to modify or withdraw a commitment, shall enter into negotiations with regard to

[178] *Id.*

[179] *Id.*, n. 1.

[180] *See* § 4.23.

[181] GATS Art. XXIII:3.

[182] GATS Art. XXIII:3. *See* Chapter 8.

[183] GATS Art. XXI:2.

compensatory adjustments, and "shall endeavor to maintain a general level of mutually advantageous commitments not less favourable to trade than that provided for in Schedules of specific commitments prior to such negotiations."[184] If agreement is not reached before the end of the period provided for negotiations, the affected Member may refer the matter to arbitration. Any affected Member that wishes to enforce a right that it may have to compensation must participate in the arbitration.[185] The proposed modification or withdrawal may not occur until compensatory adjustments have been made in conformity with the findings of the arbitration.[186]

[5] Air transport services

GATS does not apply to air traffic rights, however granted, or to services directly related to the exercise of traffic rights, other than measures affecting aircraft repair and maintenance services, the selling and marketing of air transport services, and computer reservation systems.[187] The DSU may be invoked with regard to air transport services only where obligations or specific commitments have been assumed by a Member, and only where any dispute settlement procedures in bilateral or other multilateral agreements or arrangements have been exhausted.[188]

§ 5.12 AGREEMENT ON TRADE-RELATED ASPECTS OF INTELLECTUAL PROPERTY RIGHTS (TRIPS)

The non-violation nullification and impairment provisions and the "other situation" provisions of GATT Article XXIII: (b) and (c) do not apply to disputes under the *Agreement on Trade-Related Aspects of Intellectual Property Rights* ("TRIPS") for a period of five years from the date of entry into force of the WTO Agreement.[189] During this five-year period,

[184]*Id.*

[185]GATS Art. XXI:3 (a).

[186]GATS Art. XXI:4(a).

[187]*Annex on Air Transport Services*, ¶¶ 2-3.

[188]*Id.* ¶ 4.

[189]*Agreement on Trade-Related Aspects of Intellectual Property Rights* ("TRIPS") Art. 64.2.

the Council for TRIPS shall examine the scope and modalities for non-violation and "other situation" complaints.[190]

§ 5.13 AGREEMENT ON GOVERNMENT PROCUREMENT

[1] Background

The *Agreement on Government Procurement* ("GPA") is a plurilateral agreement applicable only to the minority of WTO Members that have signed it. The GPA is not listed in Appendix 2 of the DSU with the agreements whose special dispute settlement provisions take precedence over the DSU in case of conflict, although it contains special dispute settlement provisions. It is, however, listed in Appendix 1 as one of the agreements covered by the DSU, but with the *proviso* that the applicability of the DSU shall be subject to a decision of the parties to the GPA setting out the terms for the applicability of the DSU and the GPA's special terms.

On 8 July 1996, the Committee on Government Procurement officially notified the Dispute Settlement Body that the special or additional rules and procedures contained in the GPA, Article XXII:2-7, would be applicable to disputes involving the GPA.[191] Article XXII:1 specifies that the DSU is applicable to disputes under the GPA, subject to the remaining paragraphs of the Article.

[2] Proposals and DSU notification

A party that believes that benefits accruing to it under the GPA are being nullified or impaired by the actions of another party, whether or not those actions violate the GPA, may begin dispute settlement by making written representations or proposals to the other party.[192] The written representations or proposals should be notified to the DSB at the same time.[193]

---

[190]TRIPS Art. 64.3.

[191]Committee on Government Procurement, *Special or Additional Rules and Procedures on Dispute Settlement in the Agreement on Government Procurement (1994)*, GPA/5, 19 July 1996.

[192]GPA Art. XXII:2. For non-violation nullification and impairment, *see* § 4.23.

[193]*Id.*

The GPA does not specify that consultations should be requested. Presumably, however, inasmuch as the DSU applies, the panel process would begin with a request for consultations in accordance with Article 4 of the DSU. The consultation request presumably would include, or accompany, the written representations and proposals required by Article XXII:2. Pursuant to Article 4.4, this consultation request should simultaneously be notified to the Committee on Government Procurement.

[3] DSB authority

Although Article XXII gives overall dispute settlement authority to the DSB, only WTO Members party to the GPA may participate in decisions or actions taken by the DSB with respect to GPA disputes.[194] In the event of disputes involving the GPA and another covered agreement, however, all DSB Members shall participate in the non-GPA aspects of the DSB's activities.[195]

[4] Terms of reference

Unless the parties to the dispute within 20 days of the establishment of a panel agree otherwise, the following standard terms of reference shall apply to GPA disputes:

> To examine, in the light of the relevant provisions of this Agreement and of (name of any other covered Agreement cited by the parties to the dispute), the matter referred to the DSB by (name of party) in document . . . and to make such findings as will assist the DSB in making the recommendations or in giving the rulings provided for in this Agreement.[196]

[5] Time limits

Article XXII imposes tighter time limits on GPA dispute settlement than apply generally under the DSU. This could create difficulties of the

---

[194]GPA Art. XXII:3.

[195]GPA Art. XXII:4.

[196]GPA Art. XXII:4.

kind experienced under the *Agreement on Subsidies and Countervailing Measures* when other agreements, with different time-tables, are included in the dispute.[197]

Panels shall "attempt" to provide their final reports to the parties not later than four months, or, in case of delay, seven months from the date on which the composition and terms of reference of the panel were agreed.[198] This contrasts with the six and nine months specified in the DSU.[199] Further, "every effort shall be made" to reduce by two months the DSU's nine to 12 month limit between the date of the establishment of the panel until the report is considered for adoption, and the DSU's 15 to 18 month period from the date of the establishment of the panel until the date of determination of the reasonable period of time for compliance with an adopted report.[200] In addition, in the case of a disagreement as to the existence or consistency with a covered agreement of measures taken to comply with the recommendations and rulings of an adopted report, the time for the panel to resolve the dispute is set at 60 days, rather than the 90 days provided for by the DSU.[201]

[6] No cross-retaliation

Notwithstanding DSU Article 22.2, concessions granted under the GPA shall not be suspended as a result of a dispute involving another covered agreement, nor shall concessions granted under any other covered agreement be suspended as a result of a dispute involving the GPA.[202]

§ 5.14 AGREEMENT ON TRADE IN CIVIL AIRCRAFT

The *Agreement on Trade in Civil Aircraft* ("TCA"), like the *Agreement on Government Procurement*, is a plurilateral agreement, listed in Appendix 1 to the DSU as a covered agreement, but not in Appendix 2 as one whose dispute settlement terms automatically prevail over the DSU. Unlike the

[197] *See* § 5.09[5].
[198] GPA Art.XXII:6.
[199] DSU Art. 12.8, 9.
[200] GPA Art. XXII:6, referring to DSU Art. 20.1 and 21.4.
[201] *Id.*, referring to DSU Art. 21.5.
[202] GPA Art. XXII:7. *See* § 8.06[2].

GPA, however, the Committee on Trade in Civil Aircraft has not notified the DSB of the adoption of a decision setting out the terms for the application of the DSU to the TCA. This creates considerable legal uncertainty, as the Committee on Trade in Civil Aircraft itself has recognized.[203]

The uncertainty is compounded by the fact that the specific dispute settlement procedures of the TCA incorporate the somewhat dated rules of the GATT's 1979 *Understanding Regarding Notification, Consultation, Dispute Settlement and Surveillance.*[204]

§ 5.15 ARBITRATION[205]

[1] Generally

Parties who wish may by-pass WTO dispute settlement altogether and arbitrate their differences.[206] Apart from instances in which the DSU permits a single Member to seek arbitration of a particular issue, mutual agreement to arbitrate is required.[207] Agreement to arbitrate must be notified to all WTO Members "sufficiently in advance of the actual commencement of the arbitration process."[208]

However, other Members may become party to an arbitration proceeding only upon agreement of the parties that have agreed to arbitration.[209] Thus, unlike regular dispute settlement before panels established by the DSB, third parties have no rights as such in arbitration. However, they may seek dispute settlement on their own if they are affected by the measure in question.

---

[203]Committee on Trade in Civil Aircraft, *Report (1997) of the Committee on Trade in Civil Aircraft*, WT/L/247 (26 November 1997): "At the meeting of 16 June 1997 (TCA/M/5), the Chairman recalled that significant legal uncertainty surrounded the relationship between the Agreement and other WTO Agreements as a result of the continuing failure to adapt the Agreement to the WTO Structure."

[204]TCA Art. 8.8. The *Understanding* is set out at BISD 26S/210.

[205]For arbitration of issues surrounding implementation of panel reports, *see* Chapter 8.

[206]DSU Art. 25.1.

[207]DSU Art. 25.2. These instances are noted in the subsequent subsections.

[208]DSU Art. 25.2.

[209]DSU Art. 25.3.

The parties to arbitration are required (1) to notify awards to the DSB and to any relevant Council or Committee of the WTO and (2) abide by the arbitration award.[210] Arbitration awards must be consistent with the WTO agreements, and should not nullify or impair benefits under those agreements, or impede the attainment of any objective of those agreements.[211]

[2] Non-actionable subsidies

An individual Member may request arbitration of a determination by the Committee on Subsidies and Countervailing Measures as to whether a program qualifies as a non-actionable subsidy, or the failure of the Committee to make such a determination.[212] An individual Member also may request arbitration of alleged violation, in individual cases, of the conditions for non-actionability set out in a notified program.[213]

The arbitrator is required to present its conclusions within 120 days from the date of referral. In all other aspects, the DSU applies to non-actionable subsidy arbitrations.[214]

The *SCM Agreement* also provides for arbitration of whether counter-measures taken in response to actionable and prohibited subsidies are appropriate.[215]

The arbitration rules adopted by the Committee on Subsidies and Countervailing Measures for Article 8.5 issues require that requests for arbitration be addressed to the chair of the Committee and that they include the basis for the request, the specific questions to be addressed by the arbitration body, and a brief summary of the information on which the request is based.

Rule 8 of the Committee's procedures provides that the only parties to an arbitration proceedings shall be the Member which has notified the subsidy in question, the Member which requested the arbitration, and any other Member that has become a party. Third parties may participate, but

---

[210] DSU Art. 25.3.

[211] DSU Art. 3.5.

[212] SCM Agreement Art. 8.5.

[213] *Id.*

[214] *Id.*

[215] SCM Agreement Arts. 4.11 and 7.10. *See* § 8.06[1].

they are not considered "parties" to the proceeding. Members wishing to become parties may do so by notifying the Committee chair, within 15 days of the date of circulation of the initial request, and including in the notification the information required for a request for arbitration. Members wishing simply to become third parties may do so by notifying the Committee chair, in writing, within 20 days of the circulation of the request for arbitration. Third parties may intervene only with respect to specific questions raised by the parties.

[3] Services

In specified circumstances, Members may modify or withdraw commitments in their Schedule of Commitments made pursuant to the *General Agreement on Trade in Services*. However, such a step requires compensatory adjustments.[216] If an agreement is not reached concerning compensatory adjustments, an affected Member may refer the matter to arbitration.[217] Any affected Member wishing to enforce a right to compensation must participate in the arbitration.[218]

[216] GATS Art. XXI.
[217] GATS Art. XXI:3(a).
[218] *Id.*

CHAPTER 6

The Appellate Process

§ 6.01 OVERVIEW

The WTO Appellate Body consists of seven Members, three of whom serve on any particular case.[1] Its jurisdiction is limited to issues of law covered in a panel report and to legal interpretations developed by a panel.[2] The Appellate Body may uphold, modify or reverse the legal findings and conclusions of a panel.[3] However, if it modifies or reverses the findings, it may not remand the matter to the panel for further proceedings.[4] The Appellate Body's proceedings are confidential.[5] As is the case with panels, *ex parte* communications with the Appellate Body concerning matters under its consideration are not permitted.[6]

§ 6.02 RIGHT OF APPEAL

Only parties to the dispute, not third parties, may appeal a panel report. In the event of an appeal, third parties which have notified the DSB of a substantial interest in a manner, pursuant to DSU Article 10.2, may make

[1]DSU Art. 17.1.
[2]DSU Art. 17.6.
[3]DSU Art. 17.13.
[4]*See* § 6.05.
[5]DSU Art. 17.10.
[6]DSU Art. 18.1.

written submissions to, and be given an opportunity to be heard by, the Appellate Body.[7]

§ 6.03 APPELLATE BODY RULES

[1] Overview

The DSU requires the Appellate Body to prepare working procedures, in consultation with the Chairman of the DSB and the Director-General.[8] These were issued in early 1996, shortly after the Members of the Appellate Body were appointed, and constitute the rules by which the appellate process is conducted.[9] Part I of the Rules deals with internal organizational matters, while Part II deals with the process.

Most of the terms used by the Appellate Body are self-explanatory. A few terms, however, are specialized: the Appellate Body uses the term "participant" for those who participate as appellants, appellees, or third parties in an appeal. Appellants and appellees are simply "participants," while third parties in the appeal are "third participants." The terms "party to the dispute" and "third party" refer to those who participated in the panel process. A list of definitions is set out at the beginning of the Working Procedures.

[2] Divisions of the Appellate Body

The DSU specifies that three of the seven Members of the Appellate Body shall hear a case.[10] In its rules, the Appellate Body has used the term "division" for this group of three members.[11] The Members constituting a division are selected on the basis of rotation on a non-disclosed basis intended to insure random selection, unpredictability and opportunity for all Members to serve regardless of their national origin.[12] The Members of a division select a Presiding Member whose responsibilities include coordinat-

---

[7]DSU Art. 17.4.

[8]DSU Art. 17.9.

[9]WT/AB/WP/3 (28 February 1997) *replacing* WT/AB/WP/1 (15 February 1996).

[10]DSU Art. 17.1.

[11]Appellate Body Rule (hereafter "AB Rule") VI(1).

[12]AB Rule VI(2).

ing the overall conduct of the proceeding, chairing oral hearings and meetings, and coordinating the drafting of the appellate report.[13]

[3] Decision making and collegiality

Decisions relating to an appeal are taken only by Members of the division hearing the appeal.[14] If a division cannot reach consensus, the decision will be made by majority vote.[15] The DSU specifies that opinions of the Appellate Body shall be anonymous.[16] It does not discuss the possibility of a dissenting opinion.

To further collegiality, all Members of the Appellate Body receive all documents filed in all appeals, including those Members not serving on the division deciding the case. All Members also exchange views on each appeal before the division finalizes the appellate report for circulation to WTO Members.[17] The division, however, retains "full authority and freedom" to decide the appeal.[18]

[4] Documents

No document is considered filed with the Appellate Body unless it is received by the Appellate Body Secretariat within the time period set out for filing in the appellate rules.[19] Unless specifically provided for in the rules to the contrary, every document filed must be served on all other parties, including third parties, to the dispute before the panel, and participants, including third participants, in the appeal.[20] Documents must be

[13] AB Rule VII.
[14] AB Rule III(1).
[15] AB Rule III(2).
[16] DSU Art. 17.11.
[17] AB Rule IV(2) and (3).
[18] AB Rule IV(4).
[19] AB Rule XVIII (1).
[20] AB Rule XVIII (2).

served by the most expeditious means available, including delivery to the service address of the participants, transmission by facsimile, expedited courier or expedited mail service.[21] Each filed document shall include proof of service.[22]

The division may authorize participants, including third parties, to correct clerical errors in their submissions, provided the corrections are made within three days of the filing. A copy of the revised version must be filed with the Appellate Body Secretariat and served upon the other participants.[23]

[5] Commencement of an appeal

An appeal is commenced by notification in writing to the DSB in accordance with Article 16.4 of the DSU, and with simultaneous filing of a Notice of Appeal with the Appellate Body Secretariat.[24] The notice of appeal should contain:

(a) the title of the panel report under appeal;
(b) the name of the party filing the Notice of Appeal;
(c) the service address, telephone and facsimile numbers of the party to the dispute; and
(d) a brief statement of the nature of the appeal, including the allegations of errors in the issues of law covered in the panel report and in the legal interpretations developed by the panel.[25]

Appellees are not required to notify the Secretariat, the appellant, or other parties of their intent to participate prior to filing a written Appellee's Submission pursuant to Rule 22.[26]

---

[21] AB Rule XVIII(4).
[22] AB Rule XVIII(3).
[23] AB Rule XVIII(5).
[24] AB Rule XX(1).
[25] AB Rule XX(2).
[26] *See* § 6.03[8].

Failure to note a particular finding of a panel in the claims of error set out in the Notice of Appeal will result in exclusion of the finding from the scope of the appeal.[27]

[6] Working schedule

Immediately after the commencement of an appeal, the division will prepare a working schedule for the appeal. It will contain the dates for the filing of documents and a timetable for the division's work and, if possible, the date for an oral hearing. The Appellate Body Secretariat shall serve the working schedule on the appellant, the parties to the dispute, and any third parties.[28] This is likely to include finalization of the service list, since it is only the appellant, in its Notice of Appeal, that is required to furnish a service address, but all participants are required to serve all documents on all other participants.

Because the DSU calls for a decision by the Appellate Body within 60 days as a "general rule," and in no case in less than 90 days from the initiation of the appeal, the working schedule will reflect these tight time constraints.[29] Time limits and their impact, which give the Appellate Body little room for maneuver, are noted *passim* in the sections below which discuss the appellate process, and are treated in greater detail in § 6.04.

[7] Appellant's submission

The Appellant's written submission must be filed within 10 days of the Notice of Appeal, and served on the other parties to the dispute and third parties. The submission must be dated and signed by the appellant, and contain:

---

[27] *European Communities – Regime for the Importation, Sale and Distribution of Bananas*, AB-1997-3, WT/DS27/AB/R (9 September 1997) (Adopted 25 September 1997), ¶ 152.

[28] AB Rule XXVI.

[29] DSU Article 17.5.

(a) the legal arguments in support of the appellant's position, including a precise statement of the grounds for appeal, including the specific allegations of errors in the issues of law covered in the panel report, and in the legal interpretations developed by the panel;
(b) a precise statement of the provisions of the covered agreements and other legal sources relied on; and
(c) the nature of the decision or ruling sought.[30]

Apart from the oral hearing and possible written responses to inquiries from Members of the Appellate Body, the appellant's submission is the only opportunity the appellant has to make its case on appeal. Since the document must be filed and served within 10 days of the Notice of Appeal, and since that Notice might have to be filed in as little as 20 days after the circulation of the panel report,[31] appellants frequently will wish to begin their preparation for appeal as early as the circulation to the parties of the full interim report containing the panel's proposed findings and recommendations.[32]

It should be noted that parties that have prevailed before the panel may, nevertheless, appeal that result. This is unlikely to be a common occurrence, since prevailing parties normally would not be expected to question the result. However, in *Woven Shirts and Blouses*, India, the prevailing party, appealed from certain issues of law and legal interpretations in the panel report. India argued, in essence, that the panel reached the correct conclusion by an erroneous route. The Appellate Body disagreed, and upheld the panel's legal findings, as well as its conclusions.[33]

[8] Appellee's submission

Any party to the dispute before the panel wishing to respond to allegations raised in an appellant's submission may file a written submission with the Secretariat, serving a copy on the appellant, other parties to the

[30] AB Rule XXI.

[31] *See* § 6.04[1].

[32] *See* § 4.21[2].

[33] *United States – Measure Affecting Imports of Woven Wool Shirts and Blouses from India*, AB-1977-1, WT/DS33/AB/R (25 April 1997) (Adopted 23 May 1997).

dispute and third parties.[34] The submission must be made no later than 25 days after the filing of the Notice of Appeal, which means that, normally, potential appellees will have access to appellant's arguments for only 15 days, since those normally would be filed 10 days after notice of appeal.[35]

The appellee's submission, which must be dated and signed, should set out:

(a) a precise statement of the grounds for opposing the specific allegations of errors in the issues of law covered in the panel report and in the legal interpretations developed by the panel that have been raised in the appellant's submission, and in the legal arguments raised by the appellant in support of its points;
(b) an acceptance of, or opposition to, each ground set out in the appellant's submission;
(c) a precise statement of the provisions of the covered agreements and other legal sources relied on; and
(d) the nature of the decision or ruling sought.[36]

[9] Multiple appeals

Within 15 days after the date of the filing of the Notice of Appeal, a party to the dispute before the panel, other than the original appellant, may join in that appeal or may itself appeal on the basis of other alleged errors in the issues of law covered in the panel report and legal interpretations developed by the panel.[37] This would be accomplished by filing and serving a written submission in conformity with the requirements set out in Article 21(2) for appellants' submissions.[38] These are, typically, "cross-appeals" by the prevailing party seeking to protect the result, particularly in light of the fact that the Appellate Body lacks remand authority.[39]

[34] AB Rule XXII(1).
[35] *Id. See also* § 6.03[7].
[36] AB Rule XXII(2).
[37] AB Rule XXIII(1).
[38] AB Rule XXIII(2).
[39] *See* § 6.05.

The original appellant, any appellee, and any other party to the dispute that wishes to respond to a later appeal may do so by filing a written submission within 25 days after the date of the filing of the Notice of Appeal. Such submission should conform to the requirements set out in Article 22(2) for appellees' submissions.[40]

[10] Third participants

Any third party before the panel may file a written submission stating its intention to participate as a third participant in the appeal, and stating the grounds and legal arguments in support of its position. This submission must be made within 25 days of the date of filing of the Notice of Appeal.[41] A third participant who has filed a written submission may appear and make oral argument or presentations at the Appellate Body's hearing.[42]

[11] Record on appeal

The parties have no responsibility for preparing or filing the record on appeal. This is the direct responsibility of the Director-General and the indirect responsibility of the Secretariat.[43] The record includes, but is not limited to:

a) written submissions, rebuttal submissions, and supporting evidence attached to the submissions by the parties and third parties to the panel dispute;
b) written arguments submitted at the panel meetings with the parties to the dispute and third parties, the records of those meetings, and any written answers to questions posed at the meetings;
c) correspondence relating to the dispute between the panel or the WTO Secretariat and the parties to the dispute or third parties;
d) any other documentation submitted to the panel.

---

[40] AB Rule XXIII(3).

[41] AB Rule XXIV.

[42] AB Rule XXVII (3).

[43] AB Rule XXV (1).

[12] Oral hearing

The Appellate Body's rules require an oral hearing in each appeal. This normally will be held 30 days after the Notice of Appeal.[44] The Secretariat will notify all interested parties and participants of the date as soon as possible.[45] The Presiding Member of the Appellate Body, who chairs the hearing, may set time-limits for oral arguments and presentations.[46] Third participants who have filed submissions may appear at the hearing.[47]

[13] Written responses to questions

At any time during the appellate process, and particularly during the hearing, Members of the division may address questions to participants and third participants and specify the time periods in which responses should be made. They may also request memoranda, usually on a legal question, and again set the time for response.[48] Any questions, responses, or memoranda shall be made available to other participants and third participants, who shall be given an opportunity to reply.[49]

[14] Failure to appear and withdrawal of appeal

Where a participant fails to file a submission within the required time, or fails to appear at the hearing, the division shall, after hearing the views of the participants, issue such order as it deems appropriate. This could include dismissal of the appeal.[50]

An appellant may withdraw its appeal at any time by notifying the Appellate Body.[51] Where a mutually agreed solution to a dispute which is the

[44] AB Rule XXVII (1).
[45] AB Rule XXVII (2).
[46] AB Rule XXVII (4).
[47] AB Rule XXVII (3).
[48] AB Rule XXVIII (1).
[49] AB Rule XXVIII (2).
[50] AB Rule XXIX.
[51] AB Rule XXX (1).

subject of an appeal has been notified to the DSB pursuant to Article 3.6 of the DSU, it shall be notified as well to the Appellate Body.[52]

[15] Prohibited subsidy cases

Part II of the *Agreement on Subsidies and Countervailing Measures* provides a special, "fast-track" procedure for dealing with disputes concerning alleged prohibited subsidies.[53] This Agreement reduces the time provided for appeals of prohibited subsidy cases from the normal 60-90 days to 30-60 days.[54] Pursuant to Rule 31 of its Working Procedures, the Appellate Body, accordingly, has established a separate, shorter, time-table for appeals of prohibited subsidy cases. These basically cut the already truncated appellate time limits in half.

[16] Representation by private attorneys

The Appellate Body has held that it is for a WTO Member to decide who should represent it as members of its delegation in an oral hearing of the Appellate Body, and that this may include private lawyers.[55]

§ 6.04 TIME ELEMENTS

Because the DSU imposes tight time constraints on the appellate process, the Appellate Body's rules in turn impose tight time constraints on

---

[52] AB Rule XXX (2).

[53] *Agreement on Subsidies and Countervailing Measures* Art. 4. *See* § 5.09[1].

[54] *Id.* Art. 4.9.

[55] *European Communities – Regime for the Importation, Sale and Distribution of Bananas*, AB-1997-3, WT/DS27/AB/R (9 September 1997) (Adopted 25 September 1997), ¶¶ 10-12.

the participants. These constraints themselves can have tactical importance.

[1] Limits imposed by the DSU

A panel report shall be adopted, absent consensus to the contrary, at a meeting of the Dispute Settlement Body occurring within 60 days after its circulation to the Members — unless a party to the dispute formally notifies the DSB of its intention to appeal.[56] However, the report shall not be considered for adoption until 20 days after it has been circulated.[57] If a meeting of the DSB is not scheduled between the 20th and 60th days after circulation, a special meeting shall be held to consider the report.[58]

The practical impact of these provisions taken together is that a party wishing to appeal a panel report must so notify the DSB and file a Notice of Appeal prior to any meeting scheduled between the 20th and 60th days after circulation of the report, or prior to any special meeting convened to consider the report.

The Appellate Body, as noted previously, normally must issue its decision within 60 days from the date a party formally notifies its decision to appeal. When the Appellate Body considers that it cannot provide its report within 60 days, it is to inform the DSB of this fact, in writing. According to the DSU, "In no case the appellate proceedings take longer than 90 days."[59] However, on occasion the Appellate Body, like some panels, simply has found it impossible to complete the task even within 90 days. When this has occurred, the Appellate Body, "after consultation with the parties to the dispute," has informed the DSB that it would not be able to circulate its report by the 90th day, and has specified a date on which it intended to circulate its report.[60]

---

[56]DSU Art. 16.4.

[57]DSU Art. 16.1.

[58]DSU Art. 16.4, n. 7.

[59]DSU Art. 17.5.

[60]*See, EC Measures Concerning Meat and Products (Hormones) Complaint by the United States*, WT/DS/11 (10 December 1997) and *Complaint by Canada*, WT/DS/9 (10 December 1997).

[2] Limits imposed by the Appellate Body

The short time limits allowed the Appellate Body by the DSU in turn result in the imposition of short time limits on the participants in an appeal. However, the *Working Procedures for Appellate Review* provide that the time limits set out in any of the rules for filing documents or for an oral hearing may, in exceptional circumstances, "where strict adherence to a time period set out in these Rules would result in a manifest unfairness, a party to the dispute, a participant, a third party or a third party participant may request" that the Appellate Body modify the time limits set out in its working schedule.[61] Obviously, the Appellate Body's flexibility in granting extensions of time is very limited.

The Appellate Body has adopted the DSB's *Decision on Expiration of Time-Periods in the DSU* for the appeal process.[62] In computing any time period stipulated in the DSU, or in the special or additional provisions of the covered agreements, or its own rules, the day from which the time period begins to run shall be excluded, and the last day of the time-period shall be included, subject to the *Decision on Expiration of Time-Periods in the DSU*.[63]

[3] Timing – tactical considerations

The Working Procedures, which designate the date of the Notice of Appeal as Day Zero, require the appellant's submission on Day 10. Practical consequences flow both from the decision to date everything from Day Zero, instead of allowing a fixed number of days from the previous event, and from the decision to allow the appealing party 10 days from Day zero to file its submission.

The decision to measure each action from Day zero can crucially shorten the time allowed for some actions. For example, if an appeal is filed on a Wednesday, Day 10 falls on Saturday; the appellant's submission then

[61]AB Rule XVI(2).

[62]AB Rule XVII(2) referring to WT/DSB/M/7. *See* § 4.22.

[63]AB Rule XVII(1).

becomes due on the following Monday, Day 12.[64] Appellant thus gains two days, while appellee gains one, since, with Day Zero on Wednesday, Day 25 is Sunday, appellee's submission would be due on Monday, Day 26. More important for the cross-appeal process, an appellee's cross-appeal remains due on Day 15, a Thursday. Thus, an appellee's time to consider and prepare a cross-appeal after reviewing appellant's submission is cut from five days to three — from Monday to Thursday. Even the full 15 days for filing a cross-appeal submission is extremely short, particularly when five of those days overlap with the 15 days scheduled by the Working Procedures for the response on the merits of appellees to the appellant's submission.

In practice, this is likely to mean that prevailing parties must operate on the assumption that the Report will be appealed, and begin their review and preparation for cross-appeals when the Report is issued, rather than begin only if the losing party appeals. This is particularly the case because of the Appellate Body's lack of remand authority.

§ 6.05 LACK OF REMAND AUTHORITY

With the establishment of an Appellate Body, the legal system of the World Trade Organization has acquired an important characteristic of all mature legal systems: the separation of the judicial power from the other organs of governance (or, in this case, of the organization). Panels were not — and are not — formally independent of the organization.

The significance of an appellate tribunal to consider appeals only of questions of law should not be underestimated. It appears to have no international counterpart. Even the International Court of Justice is a court of original jurisdiction which decides both questions of fact and of law, and from which there is no appeal. Yet this important institution lacks one of the most important powers of an appellate body: the power to remand cases to the lower tribunal — the panel — whose decision has been appealed.

[64]*See*, Dispute Settlement Body, *Expiration of Time-Periods in the DSU, Proposal by the Chairman*, WT/DSB/W/10 (20 July 1995). If Monday is a holiday, timing could become even more skewed. *See* Ch. 4, note 145 and accompanying text.

The Appellate Body's lack of remand authority has important policy implications.[65] It also has important practical implications for parties and participants.

In the first case to be appealed, *United States – Standards for Reformulated and Conventional Gasoline*, the Appellate Body reversed the panel's conclusion that a rule prescribing quality standards for gasoline was not a measure "relating to" an exhaustible natural resource within the meaning of Article XX(g) of GATT.[66] This was the only issue appealed.

Because of its conclusion on the meaning of the phrase "relating to" in Article XX(g), the panel had found it unnecessary to decide whether the measure was "made effective in conjunction with restrictions on domestic production or consumption," as is also required by Article XX(g). The panel, additionally, found it unnecessary to consider whether the measure was inconsistent with the requirements of the chapeau of Article XX, as the complaining parties had argued.

When the Appellate Body reversed the Panel on "relating to," its choices were limited. It could not remand the case. It either could tell the appellees to start the panel process over, or, it could decide the necessary undecided issues itself, *de novo.* It chose to do the latter, and upheld the panel's conclusion that the Gasoline Rule was not justified by Article XX(g), albeit for reasons different from those given by the panel. It could hardly have done otherwise. To have sent the complainants back to the starting line a year after they had begun the process, simply because the panel — reasonably practicing judicial economy — chose not to decide all of the complainants' claims, would have been an unacceptable result to most WTO Members, particularly in the first matter to proceed through the new dispute settlement process.

In *Canada – Certain Measures Concerning Periodicals*, the issue arose again.[67] Canada successfully appealed the panel's conclusions regarding the first sentence of Article III:1 of GATT. The panel, however, also had concluded that, in light of its decision as to the first sentence, it need not consider Article III's second sentence, and this aspect of its decision was not appealed. Canada therefore argued that the Appellate Body lacked jurisdic-

[65] *See* David Palmeter, *The WTO Appellate Body Needs Remand Authority*, 32 Journal of World Trade No. 1 (February 1998).

[66] AB-1996-1, WT/DS2/AB/R (29 April 1996) (Adopted 20 May 1996).

[67] AB-1997-2, WT/DS31/AB/R (30 June 1997) (Adopted 30 July 1997).

tion to consider the unappealed second sentence. The Appellate Body disagreed:

> "As the legal obligations in the first and second sentences are two closely-linked steps in determining the consistency of an internal tax measure with the national treatment obligations of Article III:2, the Appellate Body would be remiss in not completing the analysis of Article III:2. In the case at hand, the Panel made legal findings and conclusions concerning the first sentence of Article III:2, and because we reverse one of those findings, we need to develop our analysis based on the Panel Report in order to issue legal conclusions with respect to Article III:2, second sentence, of the GATT 1994."[68]

Here again the Appellate Body decided an issue *de novo*. In doing so in *Gasoline*, the Appellate Body said that the Panel had "erred in law in failing to decide" the remaining Article XX issues.[69] In *Periodicals*, however, the Appellate Body abandoned this unusual terminology. Rather than find the panel in error for not reaching the second sentence of Article III:I, the Appellate Body simply said that it "would be remiss in not completing the analysis" begun by the panel.

The Appellate Body's apparent change from charging panels with error for not reaching issues to simply taking on the responsibility of "completing the analysis" no doubt stems from its intervening decision in *United States – Measure Affecting Imports of Woven Wool Shirts and Blouses from India.*[70] There it endorsed the practice of judicial economy by panels, holding that, "A panel need only address those claims which must be addressed in order to resolve the matter in issue in the dispute."[71]

But if panels may continue to exercise judicial economy — and there are good reasons why they should[72] — it is not clear that the Appellate Body

[68]*Id.* §VI.A, at 25.

[69]*United States – Standards for Reformulated and Conventional Gasoline, supra* note 66, at 29.

[70]AB-1997-1, WT/DS33/AB/R (25 April 1997) (Adopted 23 May 1997).

[71]*Id.* § VI, at 22.

[72]The principle of judicial economy not only economizes on judicial resources, it also avoids deciding issues that do not have to be decided in order to reach a conclusion on the dispute before the panel. It is, therefore, a less expansive approach which seems appropriate to bodies reviewing the programs and actions of sovereign governments. One panel, however, anticipated possible reversal and decided an issue it apparently

will continue "completing the analysis." The practice is problematic because it amounts to *de novo* review, and *de novo* decisions of the Appellate Body do not themselves benefit from appeal. They are effectively unreviewed and unreviewable, lacking the "second look" normal appellate review provides. The Appellate Body may become reluctant to make such determinations since, for all practical purposes, their decisions are final.[73]

Gasoline was the first case through this unusual system, and it no doubt presented the panel, the Appellate Body, and the participants with an unanticipated issue.[74] In *Periodicals* the issue arose for only the second time, suggesting that this nuance still was not appreciated.

For prevailing parties who are not prepared to appeal issues not reached by a panel practicing judicial economy, however, there is a risk that at some point the Appellate Body may simply decline to "complete the analysis." It is worth noting that in each case in which it did so, it confined itself to other portions of the particular article that was the subject of reversal: GATT Article XX(g) in *Gasoline* and GATT Article III:2 in *Periodicals*. Thus, it is not clear, even from these cases, that the Appellate Body would "complete the analysis" if that meant considering an entirely different article of a covered agreement.

However, an appeal of undecided issues may not necessarily guarantee their consideration by the Appellate Body. In *European Communities – Measures Affecting the Importation of Certain Poultry Products*, two of the "issues" raised by Brazil before the panel were not the subject of legal findings or conclusions by the panel.[75] These issues related to the participation

---

would not have decided otherwise: "[W]e believe it necessary to make our findings clear on the issue of transparency in order to avoid a legal vacuum in the event that, upon appeal, the Appellate Body were to reverse our findings on Article 70.8." *India – Patent Protection for Pharmaceutical and Agricultural Chemical Products*, WT/DS50/R (5 September 1997), ¶7.44.

[73]This is because Appellate Body reports are adopted by the Dispute Settlement Body and unconditionally accepted by the parties unless there is consensus not to adopt. DSU Art. 17.14. *See* § 1.04.

[74]The Appellate Body's 15 February 1996 *Working Procedures* were published only six days prior to the Notice of Appeal in the *Gasoline* case. WT/DS2/6 (21 February 1996).

[75] This portion of the discussion is based upon ¶ 107 of the Appellate Body report, WT/DS69/AB/R (13 July 1998).

of non-WTO Members in tariff-rate quotas. Brazil had included both issues in its notice of appeal and in its appellant's submission.

The Appellate Body, like the panel, did not decide these issues. Instead, it referred to Article 17.6 of the DSU, which limits appeals "to issues of law covered in the panel report and legal interpretations developed by the panel," and to Article 17.13 of the DSU, which specifies that the Appellate Body may only, "uphold, modify or reverse the legal findings and conclusions of the panel." Since the panel did not deal with these issues, the Appellate Body reasoned, there was "no finding nor any 'legal interpretation developed by the panel' that may be the subject of an appeal of which the Appellate Body may take cognizance."

In this portion of its opinion, the Appellate Body's does not refer to its opinions in *Gasoline* or *Periodicals*. It does not explain why the *Poultry* panel had not "erred in law," as the *Gasoline* panel had done, in failing to decide those issues. Nor does it explain why it would not "be remiss in not completing the analysis" as it did in *Periodicals*.

However, in a later portion of its opinion, dealing with different issues, the Appellate Body returned to its *Gasoline-Periodicals* approach.[76] The Appellate Body noted that Brazil did not include a claim relating to Article 5.5 of the *Agreement on Agriculture* in its notice of appeal, nor in its appellant's submission did it include a claim that the panel erred in failing to make a finding with regard to Article 5.5. However, the European Communities later filed an appellant's submission with regard to Article 5.1(b) of the *Agreement on Agriculture*. Brazil then argued, in reply, that if the panel's finding on Article 5.1(b) were reversed, it would be necessary for the Appellate Body to address "the issues arising under Articles 5.5 and 4.2 of the *Agreement on Agriculture*."

The Appellate Body did reverse the panel's finding relating to Article 5.1(b) and confronted Brazil's argument. It began its discussion with the statement, "We are aware of the provisions of Article 17 of the DSU that state our jurisdiction and our mandate."[77] It then quoted Articles 17.6 and 17.13, as it had in the portion of its opinion dealing with the participation of non-Members in tariff rate quotas. However, the opinion, citing *Gasoline* and *Periodicals*, states that in "certain appeals" "reversal of a panel's finding

[76] This portion of the discussion is based upon ¶ 155 of the Appellate Body report.

[77] This portion of the discussion is based upon ¶ 156 of the Appellate Body report.

on a legal issue may require us to make a finding on a legal issue which was not addressed by the panel." Thus, "we believe we should complete *our* analysis" by making a finding with respect to Article 5.5 "which was not addressed by the Panel for reasons of judicial economy."[78]

The fact that the Appellate Body's discussion of undecided issues in the portion of its opinion dealing with tariff-rate quotas does not refer to its discussion with regard to undecided issues under the *Agreement on Agriculture*, and *vice versa*, engenders some confusion. The Appellate Body does not explain why the provisions of Article 17 prevent it from deciding the issues in one instance, but not in the other. To be sure, the opinion describes a difference in how the undecided issues arose before it. With regard to the tariff-rate quota issues, the Appellate Body does not say why they were not addressed by the panel. In any event, the Appellate Body was not there confronted with a situation in which its action in reversing the panel made the issues relevant.

Reversal was the operative act that made the issues relevant under the *Agreement on Agriculture* as well as in *Gasoline* and *Periodicals*. If this is the distinction that was drawn by the Appellate Body in *Poultry*, however, it does not say so. Moreover, it would seem to be a distinction without a difference. Certainly the impact on the complaining party with regard to the tariff-rate quota issues is short of satisfactory. It properly raised the issues before both the panel and the Appellate Body. But, after completion of the entire panel and appellate processes, that party never received a ruling on those issues.

---

[78] *Id.* (Emphasis added; note that the Appellate Body refers to "our" analysis, whereas in *Periodicals* it referred to "the" analysis, which suggests the analysis begun by the panel. Whether this modification of terminology has any significance is not clear).

CHAPTER 7

Adoption and Implementation of Reports

§ 7.01 OVERVIEW

If the Dispute Settlement Understanding arguably is the most significant achievement of the Uruguay Round, its provisions concerning adoption and implementation of reports arguably are the most significant parts of the DSU. Under GATT, a consensus in favor of a report was required for its adoption. In practice, this meant that a dissatisfied party could block consensus and prevent adoption of a report. The DSU reverses this requirement. WTO reports are adopted unless there is a consensus *not* to adopt them.[1] This "negative consensus" requirement has made WTO dispute settlement into what is, in all probability, the most effective area of adjudicative dispute settlement in the entire area of public international law.

§ 7.02 CONSIDERATION AND ADOPTION OF REPORTS

The DSB has a minimum of 20 days from the date of circulation of a final report to consider its adoption.[2] In addition, Members having objections to a report must give their reasons in writing at least 10 days prior to

[1] DSU Art. 16.4.
[2] DSU Art. 16.1.

the DSB meeting at which the report will be considered.[3] Parties to a dispute have the right to participate fully in the DSB's consideration of a report.[4]

Panel reports shall be adopted within 60 days after the circulation of the panel report to the Members, unless a party formally notifies the DSB of its intention to appeal, or unless the DSB decides by consensus not to adopt the report. If a DSB meeting is not scheduled for the period between the 20th day after circulation of a report and the 60th day, a special meeting of the DSB shall be held to consider adoption.[5] An Appellate Body report shall be adopted by the DSB and unconditionally accepted by the parties to the dispute within 30 days of its circulation, unless the DSB decides by consensus not to adopt it.[6] If a DSB meeting is not scheduled during this period, a special meeting shall be held to consider and Appellate Body report.[7]

In cases involving prohibited subsidies, a panel report will be adopted within 30 days unless it is appealed or unless the DSB decides by consensus not to adopt it.[8]

§ 7.03 NOTIFICATION OF IMPLEMENTATION INTENTIONS

When a panel or the Appellate Body concludes that a measure is inconsistent with the requirements of a covered agreement, it recommends that the "Member concerned" bring its measure into conformity with that agreement.[9] When the report is adopted, its recommendations and rulings become those of the DSB itself. At a DSB meeting held within 30 days of the adoption of a report, the Member concerned must inform the DSB of its intentions concerning the DSB's recommendations and rulings.[10] If a DSB meeting is not scheduled within the next 30 days, a special meeting will be

---

[3]DSU Art. 16.2.

[4]DSU Art. 16.3.

[5]DSU footnote 7.

[6]DSU Art. 17.14.

[7]DSU footnote 8.

[8]SCM Agreement Art. 4.8. *See* § 5.09[1].

[9]DSU Art. 19.1. However, in situations involving "non-violation" complaints, the Member is not required to withdraw the measure. DSU Art. 26.1(a).

[10]DSU Art. 21.3.

called for the purpose of hearing from the Member concerned regarding its intentions.[11]

§ 7.04 "REASONABLE PERIOD OF TIME"

If it is not practicable to comply immediately with the DSB's recommendations and rulings, the Member concerned shall have a "reasonable period of time" to do so. The reasonable period of time shall be:

a) a period proposed by the Member concerned, provided it is approved by the DSB; in the absence of DSB approval,
b) a time mutually agreed by the parties to the dispute within 45 days of the adoption of the report; in the absence of such an agreement,
c) a period determined through binding arbitration within 90 days of adoption of the report.[12]

The prevailing Member has clear control over the first two alternatives, but there is some ambiguity regarding the interplay of the second and third.

As to the first alternative, if the period proposed by the Member concerned is acceptable to the Member that prevailed in the dispute, then it may be approved by the DSB; however, if it is not acceptable to the prevailing Member, that Member could prevent the consensus needed to approve it.[13] Similarly, as to the second alternative, the prevailing Member, by definition, must consent to an agreement of the parties reached within 45 days.

What is not clear is whether the parties have more than 45 days to reach an agreement, and, if so, how many more days. The scheme calls for a decision by an arbitrator within 90 days from the date of adoption of the report, so there clearly is some practical limit to how long beyond 45 days an attempt to reach agreement can go. If the parties negotiate, for example, for 100 days, the 90 day limit on an arbitral decision would be impossible. For this reason, it is possible to read Article 21.3(b) as affording a Member the

[11] DSU footnote 11.

[12] DSU Art. 21.3. With regard to Arbitration generally, *see* § 5.15.

[13] The consensus requirement is set out in the *Marrakesh Agreement Establishing the World Trade Organization* Article IX:1.

right to impose a legal objection to a referral to arbitration beyond the contemplated 45 days.

However, arbitration has been requested more than 45 days after adoption of the report. In *Japan – Taxes on Alcoholic Beverages*, the report was adopted on 1 November 1996, while arbitration was not requested until 24 December, some 54 days after adoption. The issue of the timeliness of the request for arbitration, however, does not appear to have been raised. Instead, by agreement of the parties and the arbitrator, the 90 day period for arbitration itself was extended for two weeks. The parties gave written assurances that, despite the departure from the 90 day limit, they would treat the arbitrator's award as binding. They also agreed that all of the original parties to the dispute could participate in the arbitration, although only the United States had requested arbitration.[14]

If the parties cannot agree on an arbitrator within 10 days of referring the matter to arbitration, the arbitrator shall be appointed by the Director-General within an additional 10 days.[15] The arbitrator may be either an individual or a group.[16] In *Japan – Taxes on Alcoholic Beverages*, after the parties were unable to agree on an arbitrator, the Director-General appointed as a single arbitrator the Presiding Member of the division of the Appellate Body which had heard the appeal from the decision of the panel.[17] In *Bananas*, the Director-General again appointed a single arbitrator, this time a Member of the division of the Appellate Body which heard the appeal.[18] In *Hormones* the Director-General appointed two arbitrators, a Member of the Appellate Body and the former chair of the Dispute Set-

[14]*Arbitration under Article 21(3)(c) of the Understanding on Rules and Procedures Governing the Settlement of Disputes, Award of the Arbitrator Julio Lacarte-Muro*, WT/DS8/15, WT/DS10/15, WT/DS11/13 (14 February 1997), at 1. In *European Communities – Regime for the Importation, Sale and Distribution of Bananas*, negotiations also exceeded 45 days. The report was adopted 25 September and the request for arbitration was made 17 November, some 53 days later. WT/DS27/13, G/L/209 (20 November 1997).

[15]DSU footnote 12.

[16]DSU footnote 13.

[17]*Op. cit.*

[18]*European Communities – Regime for the Importation, Sale and Distribution of Bananas, Arbitration under Article 21.3(c) of the Understanding on Rules and Procedures Governing the Settlement of Disputes, Award of the Arbitrator Said El-Naggar*, WT/DS27/15 (7 January 1998).

tlement Body and the General Council. However, the latter appointee was unable to accept the nomination, so the proceeding went forward with a single arbitrator.[19]

The DSU does not mandate a specific period as the reasonable period of time, but offers as "a guideline for the arbitrator" that the reasonable period normally should not exceed 15 months from the date of adoption of the report.[20] In *Japan – Taxes on Alcoholic Beverages*, the complaining party argued for a period of less than 15 months; Japan argued for a longer period. The arbitrator found that neither party had made a case for departing from the 15 month guideline, which, he concluded, was the reasonable period of time.[21]

In *Bananas*, the arbitrator agreed with the European Communities that 15 months plus one week was a reasonable period of time. The extra week moved the deadline to 1 January 1999. In making his award the arbitrator said:

> The Complaining Parties have not persuaded me that there are "particular circumstances" in this case to jusitify a shorter period of time than stipulated by the guideline in Article 21.3(c) of the DSU. At the same time, the complexity of the implementation process, demonstrated by the European Communities, would suggest adherence to the guideline, with a slight modification, so that the "reasonable period" of time for implementation would expire by 1 January 1999.[22]

In *Hormones*, the third "reasonable period of time" arbitration, the arbitrator said that, "the 15-month guideline is an outer limit or a maximum in the usual case. For example, when implementation can be effected by administrative means, the reasonable period of time should be considerably shorter than 15 months."[23] The time allowed "should be the shortest period possible within the legal system of the Member to implement the recommendations and rulings of the DSB."[24] In *Hormones*, the arbitrator explicitly

---

[19] *EC Measures Concerning Meat and Meat Products (Hormones), Arbitration under Article 21.3(c) of the Understanding on Rules and Procedures Governing the Settlement of Disputes, Award of the ArbitratorJulio Lacarte-Muro*, WT/DS26/15, WT/DS48/13 (29 May 1998).

[20] DSU Art. 21.3(c).

[21] *Op. cit.* at p.9 (14 February 1997).

[22] Op cit. at ¶ 19.

[23] Hormones, supra note 19, ¶25.

[24] *Id.* ¶ 26.

took into account the mechanics of implementation in the EC, denied the arguments of Canada and the United States for a shorter period, and settled on 15 months.[25]

§ 7.05 DISPUTES REGARDING IMPLEMENTATION

The initial decision as to whether steps taken to bring a measure into compliance with a covered agreement, in accordance with the rulings and recommendations of the DSB, belongs to the Member taking those steps. The complaining Member may disagree as to whether in fact compliance has taken place. When disagreement occurs as to the existence or consistency with a covered agreement of measures taken to comply, that further disagreement itself shall be decided through recourse to dispute settlement.[26]

Whenever possible, this shall be done through referral to the original panel, which should circulate its report within 90 days of referral of the matter. When the panel considers that it cannot provide its report within 90 days, it will inform the DSB in writing of the reasons for the delay, together with an estimate of the time within which it will submit its report. No maximum time is provided in the DSU.[27] In proceedings under the *Agreement on Government Procurement*, the 90 day period is reduced to 60 days.[28]

The question of compliance with the recommendations of an adopted report is closely linked to the question of remedies. These are considered in Chapter 8.

§ 7.06 SURVEILLANCE BY THE DSB

Implementation of all adopted recommendations and rulings is kept under surveillance by the DSB until the process is completed, and the issue of implementation may be raised in the DSB by any Member at any time.[29] Unless it is (by consensus) agreed to the contrary, six months after estab-

---

[25] *Id.* ¶ 48.

[26] DSU Art. 22.5.

[27] *Id.*

[28] GPA Art. XXII:6. *See* § 5.13[5].

[29] DSU Art. 21.6.

lishment of the reasonable period of time for implementation, the issue of implementation is placed on the agenda of the DSB and remains on the agenda until the issue is resolved.[30]

At least 10 days prior to each meeting of the DSB, the Member subject to the recommendations and rulings is required to provide the DSB with a written status report of its progress in the implementation of the DSB's recommendations and rulings.[31] When a Member does not implement within a reasonable period of time, surveillance by the DSB continues even if compensation has been provided or the DSB has authorized "sanctions" or "retaliation" in the form of suspension of concessions.[32] Compensation and retailiation are considered to be temporary measures, and are not preferred to full implementation.[33] This process usually creates an incentive for Members to implement adopted rulings and recommendations.[34]

§ 7.07 PROHIBITED AND ACTIONABLE SUBSIDIES

The provisions of the *Agreement on Subsidies and Countervailing Measures* ("SCM Agreement") dealing with the adoption and implementation of reports concerning prohibited and actionable subsidies reflect the accelerated procedures the SCM Agreement provides generally for these issues.

If the measure is found by the panel to be a prohibited subsidy, the report shall recommend that it be withdrawn without delay. The report also will include the panel's recommendation as to the time within which the measure must be withdrawn.[35] A report dealing with either prohibited or actionable subsidies shall be adopted by the DSB within 30 days of its issuance, unless it is appealed or unless the DSB decides by consensus not to adopt it.[36] If a report dealing with either prohibited or actionable subsidies

---

[30]*Id.*

[31]*Id.*

[32]*See* § 8.05.

[33]DSU Art. 22.1.

[34]As an example of an agreement concerning implementation, *see, Japan – Taxes on Alcoholic Beverages, Mutually Acceptable Solution on Modalities for Implementation*, WT/DS8/17, WT/DS10/17, WT/DS11/15 (30 July 1997).

[35]SCM Agreement Art. 4.7.

[36]SCM Agreement Art. 4.8, 7.6.

is appealed, the appellate report shall be adopted by the DSB and unconditionally accepted by the parties unless the DSB decides by consensus not to adopt it within 20 days of its issuance to the Members.[37]

If a meeting of the DSB is not scheduled during the 30 day period for consideration of a panel report dealing with prohibited or actionable subsidies, or the 20 day period for dealing with an appellate report on either prohibited or actionable subsidies, a special meeting shall be held for the purpose of adopting the report.[38]

§ 7.08 "OTHER SITUATION" COMPLAINTS

The DSU provides that when the provisions of Article XXIII:1(c), involving so-called "other situations," are applicable to a covered agreement, the DSU itself applies only up to and including the point in the proceedings where the panel report has been circulated to the Members. Adoption of the report, as well as surveillance and implementation of rulings, is governed by the Montreal Rules.[39] The Montreal Rules retain GATT's requirement of a positive consensus for the adoption of a report. Consequently, few disputes are likely to be brought under this provision.[40]

---

[37]SCM Agreement Art. 4.9, 7.7.

[38]SCM Agreement nn. 3, 8, and 9.

[39]DSU Art. 26.2. *Decision of 12 April 1989*, BISD 36S/61. *See* § 4.23.

[40]Montreal Rules ¶ G.3.

CHAPTER EIGHT

Remedies

§ 8.01 OVERVIEW

Public international law has long recognized the duty of governments to repair or remedy damage they have caused. The Permanent Court of International Justice stated the principal in the *Factory at Chorzów* case: "Reparation must, as far as possible, wipe out all the consequences of the illegal act and re-establish the situation which would, in all probability, have existed if that act had not been committed."[1] In its first decision, the *Corfu Channel* case, the International Court of Justice awarded damages to the United Kingdom.[2] GATT/WTO practice with regard to remedy, however, is, for the most part, very different.

§ 8.02 GATT PRACTICE

Practice under the GATT with regard to remedies was inconsistent. For the most part, the recommendations were to bring the offending measure into conformity with the relevant provision of the General Agreement or the relevant Tokyo Round code. This remedy is prospective only, providing no relief from damages suffered.

---

[1] P.C.I.J. (ser. A) No. 17 at 47-48.

[2] ICJ Reports at 4. The government of the respondent, Albania, refused to pay the damages. It was not until the change in regime and the resumption of diplomatic relations between Albania and the United Kingdom, in 1992, that the damages were paid in full. *See*, Shabtai Rosenne, The World Court 44 (Martinus Nijhoff 5th ed. 1995).

In a number of instances, however, in cases involving antidumping duties, GATT panels recommended reimbursement of duties paid pursuant to a non-conforming antidumping measure. The Panel in *Electrical Transformers from Finland*, for example, stated:

> The Panel proposes to the Council that it addresses to New Zealand a recommendation to revoke the anti-dumping determination and to reimburse the antidumping duty paid.[3]

However, the United States has consistently opposed reimbursement, and refused to adopt the report in *Stainless Steel Hollow Products from Sweden* for this reason.[4] There a panel established by the Committee on Anti-Dumping Practices recommended that the United States "revoke the anti-dumping duties imposed" and "reimburse the anti-dumping duties paid."[5] In *Cement from Mexico*, also unadopted, the panel was even more specific:

> The Panel recommends that the Committee request the United States to revoke the anti-dumping duty order on grey portland cement and cement clinker from Mexico and to reimburse any anti-dumping duties paid or deposited under this order.[6]

The EU appears to agree with the United States on this issue. As complaining party before a countervailing duty panel conducted under the Tokyo Round Subsidies Code, the EU originally asked for reimbursement and then, mid-proceeding, changed its position.[7]

---

[3]*New Zealand - Imports of Electrical Transformers from Finland*, BISD 32S/55 at 70, ¶ 4:11. This and the other reports recommending reimbursement are discussed by Ernst-Ulrich Petersmann in *GATT Dispute Settlement Proceedings in the Field of Antidumping Law*, 28 COMMON MARKET LAW REVIEW 69 (1991).

[4]*United States - Imposition of Anti-Dumping Duties on Imports of Seamless Stainless Steel Hollow Products from Sweden*, ADP/47 (20 August 1990) (Unadopted). The U.S. took the position that correction of the error prospectively would suffice. *See*, ROBERT E. HUDEC, ENFORCING INTERNATIONAL TRADE LAW: THE EVOLUTION OF THE MODERN GATT LEGAL SYSTEM 253-4 (Butterworth 1993).

[5]*Id.* ¶ 5.24.

[6]*United States - Anti-Dumping Duties on Gray Portland Cement and Cement Clinker from Mexico*, ADP/82 (9 July 1992), ¶ 6.2.

[7]*Brazil - Imposition of Provisional and Definitive Countervailing Duties on Milk Powder and Certain Types of Milk from the European Economic Community*, BISD 41S/467 (27 December 1993) (Adopted 28 April 1994), ¶ 200: "The EEC initially re-

A particularly difficult issue with regard to remedy arose in the *Trondheim Case*, which involved the Tokyo Round Government Procurement Agreement.[8] The panel found that, in awarding the contract for an electronic and mainly unmanned toll collection system for the city of Trondheim, the Government of Norway had not complied with its obligations under the Agreement. However, by the time the panel ruled, performance of the contract had been completed. Faced with a *fait accompli*, the panel observed that the only way "that Norway could bring the Trondheim procurement into line with its obligations under the Agreement would be by annulling the contract and recommencing the procurement process. The Panel did not consider it appropriate to make such a recommendation."[9]

The United States, the complaining party, explicitly stated that it was not asking the panel to recommend negotiation of compensation for past losses.[10] The panel recommended that the Government Procurement Committee request Norway to take the measures necessary to ensure that future procurements were conducted in accordance with its substantive findings.[11]

§ 8.03 WTO PRACTICE

[1] General

When a panel or the Appellate Body concludes that a measure is inconsistent with a covered agreement, the DSU directs the panel or Appellate Body simply to recommend that the Member concerned bring the measure

---

quested that the Panel also recommend that Brazil reimburse any provisional and definitive countervailing duties levied on these imports. Subsequently, the EEC indicated that it was no longer seeking such a recommendation, on the ground that it should generally be left to a signatory found to have acted inconsistently with its obligations under the Agreement to determine the means by which to bring its measure into conformity with its obligations."

[8]*Norway - Procurement of Toll Collection Equipment for the City of Trondheim*, BISD 40S/319 (Adopted 13 May 1992).

[9]*Id.* ¶ 4.17.

[10]*Id.* ¶ 4.20.

[11]*Id.* ¶ 5.2. For a detailed analysis of the remedies issue in this case, *see* Petros C. Mavroidis, *Government Procurement Agreement: The Trondheim Case*, 49 AUSSENWIRTSCHAFT 77 (1993).

into conformity with that agreement.[12] This is consistent with most prior GATT practice. Both the panel and the Appellate Body, however, may suggest ways in which their recommendations may be implemented.[13] The recommendation to bring the measure into conformity and the possible suggestion as to how this might be done constitute the only available remedies that may be offered by panels or the Appellate Body. Compensation and suspension of concessions are potential default remedies only if an adopted report's recommendations are not implemented.[14]

[2] "Suggested steps"

With regard to suggested steps, it is not presently clear how far panels and the Appellate Body may go. In *Guatemala –Anti-Dumping Investigation Regarding Portland Cement from Mexico*, the complainant, Mexico, requested the panel to recommend that Guatemala revoke the measure and also "refund those anti-dumping duties already collected."[15] The panel declined, noting that Article 19.1 of the DSU confines panels to recommending that the Member concerned bring the measure into conformity.[16] However, the panel did note that Article 19.1 authorized it to "suggest" ways in which the Member concerned could bring its measure into conformity.

With regard to Mexico's request concerning revocation, the panel stated that, since it had concluded that the entire investigation rested on an insufficient basis and therefore never should have been initiated, "we suggest that Guatemala revoke the existing anti-dumping measure on imports of Mexican cement, because, in our view, this is the only appropriate means of implementing our recommendation."[17] However, the panel made no suggestion regarding Mexico's request for reimbursement. In a narrow sense,

---

[12]DSU Art. 19.1.

[13]*Id. United States - Restrictions on Imports of Cotton and Man-Made Fibre Underwear*, WT/DS24/R (8 November 1996) (Adopted as Modified by the Appellate Body 25 February 1997) ¶¶ 8.1 - 8.3; *India - Patent Protection for Pharmaceutical and Agricultural Chemical Products*, WT/DS50/R (5 September 1997) (Adopted as Modified by the Appellate Body 16 January 1998) ¶ 8.2.

[14]*See* § 8.04.

[15] WT/DS60/R (19 June 1998) ¶8.1.

[16] *Id.* ¶ 8.2.

[17] *Id.* ¶ 8.6.

the panel addressed Mexico's request for a "recommendation" for reimbursement by explaining why it declined to do so. But it did not explain why it declined to "suggest" the requested remedy. If the investigation never should have been initiated in the first place, as the panel concluded, and if revocation is the only appropriate means of bringing the measure into conformity, as it also concluded, then reimbursement of the illegally-collected duties would seem to follow rather logically.

It is possible that the panel, in conformity with the WTO's generally prospective system of relief, contemplated revocation effective after adoption of the report, rather than revocation effective as of the date of the initiation of the investigation by Guatemala. But if this was the panel's contemplation, it did not say so, and it would seem to be at odds with its conclusion that "the entire investigation rested on an insufficient basis."[18]

Mexico's request was unusual not only because it asked for more than the panel could give – a recommendation of revocation and reimbursement – but also because it asked for more than a simple recommendation that the Member concerned bring its measure into conformity. Clearly, the Members of the WTO have evinced a preference for such recommendations, rather than for being made whole for damages sustained. No doubt this preference reflects the fact that payment of damages based on trade volumes lost can present political difficulties to the Member called upon to pay, and the recognition of Members that today's complainant may be tomorrow's respondent.

[2] Adequacy of implementation

Article 19.1 of the DSU, in the words of the *Guatemala – Cement* panel, leaves the "modalities of implementation of a panel, or Appellate Body, report" to the Member concerned.[19] However, as the panel recognized, the remedy selected by the Member concerned may not, in the view of the prevailing complainant, in fact bring the measure into conformity. This could lead to further litigation. Article 21.5 of the DSU provides that where there is disagreement as to whether the steps taken to comply with an

[18] *Id.*

[19] *Id.* ¶ 8.3.

adopted recommendation or ruling in fact do so, the matter shall be decided "through recourse to these dispute settlement procedures." Whenever possible, the matter will be referred to the original panel, which is instructed by Article 21.5 to circulate its report within 90 days after the date of referral of the matter. A prevailing complainant also might not agree that a remedy suggested by a panel was adequate to bring a measure into conformity. However, if a Member implements the remedy suggested by the panel or the Appellate Body in an adopted report, that action would appear to have a presumption of legality that would not attach to implemention of a remedy selected by the Member.

§ 8.04 OVERVIEW: COMPENSATION AND SUSPENSION OF CONCESSIONS

Compensation and suspension of concessions or other WTO obligations — "sanctions" or "retaliation" — are the aspects of WTO dispute settlement that have received the most public attention. Some supporters of the WTO see the possibility of compensation and suspension of concessions as the threat in the background that makes the system work. Many critics see them as potential infringements of national sovereignty that unwisely limit the flexibility of governments to deal with the complexities of the modern world. Both views are likely exaggerated.

There are many "threats" other than the ultimate potential of trade retaliation that lead Members to adhere to their WTO obligations, the chief one being, in most cases, the fact that to do otherwise would damage a system that Members value. Many losing parties no doubt regret the necessity of changing or eliminating offending measures, but not as much as they would regret the resulting incapacity of the WTO were they to do otherwise. Similarly, while Members of the WTO have agreed to limit the exercise of their sovereign powers, they have agreed to do so in ways they find mutually advantageous and, for all practical purposes, not all that limiting. The core "constitutional" obligations of the WTO remain what they were under GATT: national treatment and most-favored nation treatment, both, particularly the latter, with many exceptions. Nevertheless, the compensation and suspension of concessions provisions in the WTO are far more explicit and, therefore, are potentially far more effective than they were under GATT.

The term "compensation" in a GATT/WTO context does not conform to common usage. It does not refer to payment for trade lost because of an inconsistent measure, but to a re-balancing of trade concessions. Of course, a calculation of the trade involved, and of the trade loss is, in reality, necessary to determine the degree to which a negotiated concession has been nullified or impaired. But the outlook is prospective: to rebalance the benefits and restore the parties to parity for the future with regard to their trade agreements. The same is true of suspension of concessions, should the dispute reach that point.

§ 8.05 NEGOTIATIONS ON COMPENSATION

Both compensation and suspension of concessions or other obligations are considered to be temporary measures, employed only when recommendations and rulings in adopted reports are not implemented within a reasonable period of time.[20] The DSB will continue to keep under surveillance the implementation of adopted reports even when compensation has been agreed to and provided or when concessions or other obligations have been suspended. Surveillance will continue until the recommendations and rulings of the adopted report are implemented or until a settlement is rendered.[21]

If the Member concerned fails to comply with the recommendations and rulings of an adopted report within the reasonable period of time allowed,[22] the Member shall, if requested — and no later than the expiration of the reasonable period of time — enter into negotiations with any party having invoked the dispute settlement procedures, with a view to agreeing on compensation.[23] Any compensation agreed upon must conform to the requirements of the covered agreements which includes the most-favored-nation requirements of the agreements.[24]

---

[20]DSU Art. 22.1.

[21]DSU Art. 22.8. *See* § 7.06 and *also Japan - Taxes on Alcoholic Beverages, Mutually Acceptable Solution on Modalities for Implementation*, WT/DS8/17, WT/DS10/17, WT/DS11/15 (30 July 1997).

[22]*See* § 7.04.

[23]DSU Art. 22.2.

[24]DSU Art. 22.1.

§ 8.06 SUSPENSION OF CONCESSIONS

In the nearly half a century of GATT's existence, the CONTRACTING PARTIES authorized retaliatory suspension of concessions only once. Thus, there was little institutional experience in determining the appropriate level of suspension in particular cases that GATT could pass to the WTO. In the single GATT instance, the Netherlands was authorized to limit imports of wheat flour from the United States to 60,000 tons, based on a Working Party's determination -

> 1. that the measure proposed by the Netherlands Government is appropriate in character, and
> 2. that, having regard to
>   (i) the value of the trade involved,
>   (ii) the broader elements in the impairment suffered by the Netherlands, and
>   (iii) the statement of the Netherlands Government that its principal objective in proposing the measure in question is to contribute to the eventual solution of the matter in accordance with the objectives and spirit of the General Agreement . . .[25]

Perhaps one reason why GATT had so little experience in considering appropriate levels for the suspension of concessions or other obligations was its consensus requirement. For example, both the United States and the European Communities blocked consensus on proposals that could have lead to consideration of appropriate levels for suspension of concessions.[26] A contributing reason might be the fact that the single instance of authorized retaliation did not, in actual practice, lead to any action. The Netherlands ultimately realized the fundamental economic truth, sometimes lost in the mercantilistic world of GATT and the WTO, that the real benefit of trade is imports, not exports.[27] As Prof. Robert Hudec has observed, "The symbolic purpose of retaliation is largely fulfilled by the fanfare which surrounds the

---

[25]*Netherlands Measures of Suspension of Obligations to the United States*, BISD 1S/32-33.

[26]C/M/236 at 21; C/M/237 at 11-12; C/M/259 at 35, 49.

[27]Robert E. Hudec, The GATT Legal System and World Trade Diplomacy 196-97 (Butterworth 2d ed. 1990).

formal decision authorizing it. Actual implementation of the retaliatory measures tends to be something of an anticlimax."[28]

[1] Request for authorization to suspend concessions

If compensation is not agreed upon within 20 days after the expiration of the reasonable period of time, any party that invoked the dispute settlement procedures may request authorization of the DSB to suspend the application to the Member concerned of concessions or other obligations under the covered agreements. The request would specify the concessions or obligations to be suspended. These are limited to the level of the nullification and impairment, a standard that conforms to the principle of proportionality recently recognized by the International Court of Justice.[29]

The DSU sets out principles and procedures the complaining party should follow in preparing its request.

[2] Principles and procedures governing suspension

The WTO, covering services and intellectual property, is a far broader agreement than was GATT. This breadth is reflected in the principles the DSU establishes for the suspension of concessions.

The first principle is that the complaining party initially should seek to suspend concessions or other obligations with respect to the same sector or sectors as that in which the adopted report has found nullification and impairment.[30] Next, if the complaining party considers that it is not practicable or effective to suspend concessions or other obligations with respect to the same sector or sectors, it may seek to do so in other sectors under the

---

[28] *Id.*

[29] DSU Art. 22.4. "[A]n important consideration is that the effects of a countermeasure must be commensurate with the injury suffered;" this is "the proportionality which is required by international law." *Case Concerning the Gabcíkovo-Nagymaros Project (Hungary/Slovakia)*, 1997 ICJ No. 92, ¶ 85, (Judgment of 25 September 1997).

[30] DSU Art. 22.3(a).

same agreement.[31] Finally, if the complaining party considers that it is not practicable or effective to suspend concessions or other obligations with respect to other sectors under the same agreement, and that the circumstances are serious enough, it may seek to suspend concessions or other obligations under another covered agreement.[32] The term "sector" is defined

(i) with respect to goods, to include all goods;
(ii) with respect to services, those identified in the current version of the "Services Sectoral Classification List." Eleven services sectors were so identified in the Uruguay Round: business, communication, construction and related engineering, distribution, educational, environmental, financial, health and related social services, tourism and travel related services; recreational, cultural and sporting; and transport.[33]
(iii) with respect to trade-related intellectual property rights, each of the categories covered in the first seven sections of Part II of the TRIPS Agreement: copyright and related rights, trademarks, geographical indications, industrial designs, patents, lay-out designs (topographies) of integrated circuits, and protection of undisclosed information; the enforcement obligations of Part III of the TRIPS Agreement, and the obligations of Part IV, dealing with the acquisition and maintenance of intellectual property rights and related *inter partes* procedures.[34]

If a party decides to request authorization other than in the same sector in which the adopted report has found a violation or other nullification and impairment, i.e., "cross-retaliate," it must state its reasons in its request. At the same time that the request is forwarded to the DSB, it must also be forwarded to the Councils or sectoral bodies concerned.[35]

The *Agreement on Government Procurement* is an exception to the cross-retaliation provision. Concessions or other obligations under the GPA may not be suspended as a result of obligations under other agree-

[31]DSU Art. 22.3(b).
[32]DSU Art. 22.3(c).
[33]*Services Sectoral Classification List*, MTN.GNS/W/120.
[34]DSU Art. 22.3(f).
[35]DSU Art. 22.3(e).

ments, and disputes involving the GPA may not lead to the suspension of concessions or other obligations under other agreements.[36]

[3] Objection to suspension and referral to arbitration

The Member concerned may object to the level of the proposed suspension, or may claim that the principles and procedures provided by the DSU have not been followed with regard to suspension either in other sectors under the same agreement or under another covered agreement. In either event, the matter shall be referred to arbitration by the original panel, if the members are available, or by an arbitrator (individual or group) appointed by the Director-General. The arbitration shall be completed no later than 60 days after the expiration of the reasonable period of time. Suspension may not occur during the course of the arbitration.[37]

If the objection of the Member concerned is that the level of suspension is not equivalent to the level of the nullification or impairment, the arbitrator may not examine the nature of the concessions or other obligations to be suspended. Rather, the arbitrator is confined to examining the level of the proposed suspension. The arbitrator may also determine if the proposed suspension is permitted under the covered agreement.[38]

If the objection includes a claim that the principles and procedures governing suspension in another sector or under another agreement have not been followed, the arbitrator shall examine the substance of the claim. If the arbitrator determines that the principles and procedures have not been followed, the complaining party shall apply them consistent with Article 22.3. The parties are required to accept the arbitrator's decision as final, and may not seek a second arbitration.[39]

The DSB will be notified promptly of the arbitrator's decision and shall, upon request, grant authorization to suspend concessions or other obligations where the request is consistent with the decision of the arbitrator, unless, by consensus, the DSB decides to reject the request.[40]

---

[36] GPA Art. XXII:7.

[37] DSU Art. 22.6.

[38] DSU Art. 22.7.

[39] *Id.*

[40] *Id.*

§ 8.07 PROHIBITED AND ACTIONABLE SUBSIDIES

Panel recommendations concerning prohibited subsidies include a statement of the time-period within which the measure must be withdrawn.[41] This substitutes for the reasonable period of time for implementation decided by the DSB in most other matters. If the recommendation of the DSB concerning withdrawal of a prohibited subsidy is not followed within the time specified by the panel in its report, which commences with the report's adoption, the DSB shall authorize the complaining Member to take appropriate countermeasures, unless the DSB decides by consensus to reject the request.[42] The issue of whether the countermeasures are "appropriate" may be arbitrated in accordance with the provisions of Article 22 of the DSU.[43]

If, within six months from the date on which the report is adopted, a Member has not withdrawn an actionable subsidy, or has not taken steps to remove its adverse effects, the DSB shall, in the absence of an agreement on compensation, authorize the complaining Member to take countermeasures, unless the DSB decides by consensus to reject the request.[44] Countermeasures must be commensurate with the degree and nature of the adverse effects determined to exist.[45] In the event of dispute concerning whether the countermeasures are commensurate with the adverse effects, the question is submitted to arbitration in accordance with Article 22.6 of the DSU.

§ 8.08 "OTHER SITUATION" REPORTS

The implementation of recommendations and rulings regarding "other situation" reports involving Article XXIII:1(c) of GATT are governed by the Montreal Rules.[46] The implications of the Montreal Rules for remedy in "other situation" disputes are not clear. If a developing country is involved, the Montreal Rules,[47] in turn, provide that any action taken conform

---

[41] SCM Agreement Art. 4.7.

[42] SCM Agreement Art. 4.10.

[43] SCM Agreement Art. 4.11.

[44] SCM Agreement Art. 7.9.

[45] *Id.*

[46] *Decision of 12 April 1989*, BISD 36S/61. *See* §§ 4.23 and 7.08.

[47] Montreal Rules ¶ I.4.

to the provisions of paragraphs 21 and 23 of the 1979 *Understanding Regarding Notification, Consultation, Dispute Settlement and Surveillance.*[48] Again, the implications of the 1979 *Understanding* for remedy are not clear. Given the dearth of cases under this provision during GATT's 47 years, and the retention, via the Montreal Rules, of GATT's positive consensus requirement, early clarification seems unlikely.

[48]BISD 26S/210, 214.

CHAPTER NINE

Conclusion

The World Trade Organization's Dispute Settlement Understanding represents, in the words of Amb. Celso Lafer, a former chairman of the Dispute Settlement Body, a "thickening of legality."[1] In the "symbiosis of diplomacy and litigation," the DSU represents a decided move of the GATT/WTO dispute settlement system toward litigation.[2]

But this move does not diminish the importance of diplomacy. Diplomacy and the negotiations that characterize it will, of necessity, remain central to any international organization composed of governments. Diplomacy, indeed, is the process by which international rules, including WTO rules, are established. Litigation is simply the application of those negotiated rules. The possibility of litigation and the foreseeability of outcomes based on agreed rules become part of the diplomatic process itself, factors that diplomats take into account in their dealings with one another.

A case may go forward because the outcome of the application of the rules to the facts of a particular dispute is not clear in advance. Or it may go forward even though the outcome is clear because a government may wish to show a domestic constituency that it did all that it could, or because it may wish to show a parochial ministry the consequences of not considering international commitments before acting.

---

[1]Celso Lafer, The World Trade Organization Dispute Settlement System 11 (1996 Gilberto Amado Memorial Lecture, United Nations 1996).

[2]The term is that former World Court President Naendra Singh, quoted in Shabtai Rosenne, The World Court 259 (Martinus Nijhoff 5th ed. 1995).

Often, however, the cases will be settled. A negotiated solution will be reached, even "on the court house steps." When this happens it is a triumph both for diplomacy and for the rules-based litigation system that contributed to the outcome, if only by making the litigated outcome more or less apparent.

How far the system has come from its diplomatic origins, how thick has become the layer of legality in the WTO, can be seen by considering the kinds of issues dealt with today by panels and the Appellate Body, described in this book, and comparing the reports dealing with those issues with the report of the first dispute settled in GATT. That occurred on 24 August 1948, before the institution of panels or even working parties to deal with disputes.[3] The Netherlands complained that Cuba was applying a five percent consular tax to imports from some countries and a two percent tax to imports from others. The issue was whether consular taxes were covered by the "charges of any kind" language of Article I:1. The Chairman of the session ruled that they were. That ruling — that first dispute settlement report — states, in its entirety:

> In response to a request for an interpretation of the phrase "charges of any kind" in paragraph 1 of Article I with respect to consular taxes, the Chairman ruled that such taxes would be covered by the phrase "charges of any kind."[4]

If this process and the ruling to which it led was not genuine litigation, it was not simple diplomacy either. It was the resolution of a dispute in a way that put down GATT's first, thin layer of legality. The addition of a multitude of layers over the years has established today's rather remarkably thick system of legality as the basis for settling international commercial disputes.

---

[3]*See* Hudec, Robert E., The GATT Legal System and World Trade Diplomacy (Butterworth 2d ed. 1990).

[4]BISD II/12.

Table of Cases

WTO APPELLATE BODY REPORTS

WTO PANEL REPORTS

WTO ARBITRATOR'S REPORTS

GATT PANEL REPORTS

Australia — Subsidy on Ammonium Sulphate, BISD II/188 (Adopted 3 April 1950), 94

Brazil — Imposition of Provisional and Definitive Countervailing Duties on Milk Powder and Certain Types of Milk from the European Economic Community, SCM/179 (27 December 1993) (Adopted 28 April 1994), 162

Canada — Import Restrictions on Ice Cream and Yoghurt, BISD 36S/68 (Adopted 5 December 1989), 51

Canada — Administration of the Foreign Investment Review Act, BISD 30S/140 (Adopted 7 February 1984), 19

EEC — Restrictions on Imports of Apples — Complaint by the United States, BISD 36S/135 (Adopted 22 June 1989), 51

EEC — Quantitative Restrictions against Import of Certain Products from Hong Kong, BISD 30S/129 (Adopted 12 July 1983), 87

EEC — Restrictions on Imports of Apples from Chile, BISD 27S/98 (Adopted 10 November 1980), 28

EEC — Measures on Animal Feed Proteins, BISD 25S/49 (Adopted 14 March 1978), 28

European Economic Community — Regulation on Imports of Parts and Components, BISD 37S/132 (Adopted 16 May 1990), 24, 26, 87

European Communities — Payments and Subsidies Paid to Processors and Producers of Oilseeds and Related Animal Feed Proteins, BISD 37S/86 (Adopted 25 January 1990), 94

European Economic Community — Restrictions on Imports of Dessert Apples, Complaint by Chile, BISD 36S/93 (Adopted 22 June 1989), 28, 42

Germany — Imports of Sardines, BISD IS/53 (Adopted 31 October 1952), 94

Germany — Import Duties on Starch and Potato Flour, BISD 3S/77 (Noted 16 February 1955), 94

Japan — Trade in Semiconductors, BISD 35S/116 (Adopted 4 May 1988), 74

Japan — Restrictions on Imports of Certain Agricultural Products, BISD 35S/163 (Adopted 22 March 1988), 51

Japanese Imports of Leather, BISD 31S/94 (Adopted 16 May 1984), 87

New Zealand — Imports of Electrical Transformers from Finland, BISD 32S/55 (Adopted 18 July 1985), 43, 162

Norway — Procurement of Toll Collection Equipment for the City of Trondhiem, BISD 40S/319 (Adopted 13 May 1992), 83

Norway — Restrictions on Imports of Certain Textile Products, BISD 27S/119 (Adopted 18 June 1980), 21, 27

United States — Measures Affecting the Importation, Internal Sale and Use of Tobacco, BISD 41S/131. (Adopted 4 October 1994), 25

United States — Restrictions on Imports of Tuna, DS33/1, 10 June 1994 ("Tuna II") 33 I.L.M. 839 (1994) (Unadopted), 21, 26, 56

United States — Imposition of Anti-Dumping Duties on Imports of Fresh and Chilled Atlantic Salmon from Norway, BISD 41S/229 (30 November 1992) (Adopted 27 April 1994), 30, 109

United States — Measures Affecting Imports of Softwood Lumber from Canada, BISD 40S/358 (Adopted 27 October 1993), 51, 107

United States — Denial of Most-Favoured-Nation Treatment as to Non-Rubber Footwear from Brazil, BISD 39S/128 (Adopted 19 June 1992), 24, 63

United States — Measures Affecting Alcoholic and Malt Beverages, BISD 39S/206 (Adopted 19 June 1992), 49, 83

United States — Imposition of Anti-Dumping Duties on Imports of Seamless Stainless Steel Hollow Products from Sweden, ADP/47 (20 August 1990) (Unadopted), 162

United States — Section 337 of the Tariff Act of 1930, BISD 36S/345 (Adopted 7 November 1989), 24, 26

United States — Taxes on Petroleum and Certain Imported Substances, BISD 34S/136 (Adopted 17 June 1987), 24–25

United States — Prohibition of Imports of Tuna and Tuna Products from Canada, BISD 29S/91 (Adopted 22 February 1982), 27

US — Imports of Sugar from Nicaragua, BISD 31S/67 (Adopted 13 March 1984), 87

GATT ARBITRATOR'S REPORTS

Canada/European Communities Article XXVIII Rights, Award by the Arbitrator, BISD 37S/80, 55

DECISIONS OF THE INTERNATIONAL COURT OF JUSTICE

Case Concerning the Gabcíkovo-Nagymaros Project (Hungary/Slovakia), 1997 ICJ No. 92 (Judgment of 25 September 1997), 43, 51, 169

DECISIONS OF THE UNITED STATES SUPREME COURT

NAFTA PANEL REPORTS

Bibliography

BOOKS

Brownlie, Ian, Principles of Public International Law (4th ed., Oxford, 1990).

Carter, Barry E. & Trimble, Philip R., International Law (2d ed., Little Brown, 1994).

Chayes, Abram & Chayes, Antonia Handler, The New Sovereignty: Compliance with International Regulatory Agreements (Harvard 1995).

Croome, John, Reshaping the World Trading System: A History of the Uruguay Round (World Trade Organization 1995).

David, Rene, French Law: Its Structure, Sources, and Methodology (Michael Kindred, trans.) (Louisiana State University Press 1972).

Fitzmaurice, Gerald, The Law and Procedure Of The International Court Of Justice (Cambridge1986)

Franck, Thomas, Fairness in International Law And Institutions (Clarendon Press 1995).

Gardner, Richard N., Sterling-Dollar Diplomacy in Current Perspective: The Origins and Prospects of Our International Economic Order (Columbia Univ. Press ed., 1980).

Gaskin, Richard H., Burdens of Proof in Modern Discourse (Yale 1992).

HIGGINS, ROSALYN, PROBLEMS & PROCESS: INTERNATIONAL LAW AND HOW WE USE IT (Oxford 1994).

HOEKMAN, BERNARD & KOSTECKI, MICHEL, THE POLITICAL ECONOMY OF THE WORLD TRADING SYSTEM: FROM GATT TO THE WTO (Oxford 1995).

HUDEC, ROBERT E., THE GATT LEGAL SYSTEM AND WORLD TRADE DIPLOMACY (Butterworth 2d ed. 1990).

HUDEC, ROBERT E., ENFORCING INTERNATIONAL TRADE LAW: THE EVOLUTION OF THE MODERN GATT LEGAL SYSTEM (Butterworth 1993).

HUDEC, ROBERT E., GATT AND THE DEVELOPING COUNTRIES (Trade Policy Research Centre 1988).

JACKSON, JOHN H., WORLD TRADE AND THE LAW OF GATT (Bobbs-Merrill, 1969)

JACKSON, JOHN H., THE WORLD TRADING SYSTEM (MIT Press 2d ed. 1997).

KAZAZI, MOJTABA, BURDEN OF PROOF AND RELATED ISSUES: A STUDY ON EVIDENCE BEFORE INTERNATIONAL TRIBUNALS (Kluwer 1996).

LONG, OLIVIER, LAW AND ITS LIMITATIONS IN THE GATT MULTILATERAL TRADE SYSTEM (Martinus Nijhoff, 1985).

MESSERLIN, PATRICK, LA NOUVELLE OMC (Dunod 1995).

PAEMEN, HUGO & BENSCH, ALEXANDRA, FROM THE GATT TO THE WTO: THE EUROPEAN COMMUNITY IN THE URUGUAY ROUND (Leuven University Press 1995).

PETERSMANN, ERNST-ULRICH (ED.), INTERNATIONAL TRADE AND THE GATT/WTO DISPUTE SETTLEMENT SYSTEM (Kluwer 1997).

PREEG, ERNEST H., TRADERS IN A BRAVE NEW WORLD: THE URUGUAY ROUND AND THE FUTURE OF THE INTERNATIONAL TRADING SYSTEM (Chicago 1995).

ROSENNE, SHABTAI, THE WORLD COURT (5TH ED. 1995, Martinus Nijhoff).

SANDS, PHILLIPE, PRINCIPLES OF INTERNATIONAL ENVIRONMENTAL LAW, (Manchester Univ. Press 1995).

SCHOTT, JEFFREY J., THE URUGUAY ROUND: AN ASSESSMENT (Institute for International Economics 1994).

SHAHABUDDEEN, MOHAMED, PRECEDENT IN THE WORLD COURT (Grotius, Cambridge 1996).

SHAW, MALCOLM N., INTERNATIONAL LAW (Grotius, Cambridge 1991).

WORLD TRADE ORGANIZATION, ANALYTICAL INDEX, GUIDE TO GATT LAW AND PRACTICE (1995).

MONOGRAPHS

LAFER, CELSO, THE WORLD TRADE ORGANIZATION DISPUTE SETTLEMENT SYSTEM(1996 Gilberto Amado Memorial Lecture, United Nations 1996)

ARTICLES

Croley, Steven P. & Jackson, John H., *WTO Dispute Procedures, Standard of Review, and Deference to National Governments*, 90 AMERICAN JOURNAL OF INTERNATIONAL LAW 193 (April 1996).

Davey, William J., *Dispute Settlement in GATT*, 11 FORDHAM INTERNATIONAL LAW JOURNAL 51 (1987).

Long, Russell, *United States Law and the International Antidumping Code*, 3 INTERNATIONAL LAWYER 464 (1969).

Martha, Rutsel Silvestre J., *Presumptions and Burden of Proof in World Trade Law*, 14 JOURNAL OF INTERNATIONAL ARBITRATION No. 1, (March 1997).

Martha, Rutsel Silvestre J., *World Trade Dispute Settlement and the Exhaustion of Local Remedies Rule*, 30 JOURNAL OF WORLD TRADE No. 4, (August 1996).

Mattoo, Aaditya & Mavroidis, Petros C., *Trade, Environment and the WTO: How Real is the Conflict?*, in ERNST-ULRICH PETERSMANN (ed.), INTERNATIONAL TRADE LAW AND THE GATT/WTO DISPUTE SETTLEMENT SYSTEM (Kluwer, 1997).

Mavroidis, Petros C., *Government Procurement Agreement: The Trondheim Case*, 49 AUSSENWIRTSCHAFT 77 (1993).

Palmeter, David, *The WTO Appellate Body Needs Remand Authority*, 32 JOURNAL OF WORLD TRADE No. 1 (February 1998).

Palmeter, David *The WTO Appellate Body's First Decision*, 9 LEIDEN JOURNAL OF INTERNATIONAL LAW 337, (1996).

Palmeter, David, *Section 337 and the WTO Agreements: Still in Violation?*, 20 WORLD COMPETITION No. 1, (Sept. 1996).

Petersmann, Ernst-Ulrich, *The Dispute Settlement System of the World Trade Organization and the Evolution of the GATT Dispute Settlement System Since 1948*, 31 COMMON MARKET LAW REVIEW 1157 1994.

Petersmann, Ernst-Ulrich, *GATT Dispute Settlement Proceedings in the Field of Antidumping Law*, 28 COMMON MARKET LAW REVIEW 69 (1991).

Thomas, J.C., *The Need for Due Process in WTO Proceedings*, 31 JOURNAL OF WORLD TRADE, No. 1 (February 1997).

Appendix A

Understanding on Rules and Procedures Governing the Settlement of Disputes

Members hereby *agree* as follows:

Article 1

Coverage and Application

1. The rules and procedures of this Understanding shall apply to disputes brought pursuant to the consultation and dispute settlement provisions of the agreements listed in Appendix 1 to this Understanding (referred to in this Understanding as the "covered agreements"). The rules and procedures of this Understanding shall also apply to consultations and the settlement of disputes between Members concerning their rights and obligations under the provisions of the Agreement Establishing the World Trade Organization (referred to in this Understanding as the "WTO Agreement") and of this Understanding taken in isolation or in combination with any other covered agreement.

2. The rules and procedures of this Understanding shall apply subject to such special or additional rules and procedures on dispute settlement contained in the covered agreements as are identified in Appendix 2 to this Understanding. To the extent that there is a difference between the rules and procedures of this Understanding and the special or additional rules and procedures set forth in Appendix 2, the special or additional rules and procedures in Appendix 2 shall prevail. In disputes involving rules and procedures under more than one covered agreement, if there is a conflict between special or additional rules and procedures of such agreements under review, and where the parties to the dispute cannot agree on rules and procedures within 20 days of the establishment of the panel, the Chairman of the Dispute Settlement Body provided for in paragraph 1 of Article 2 (referred to in this Understanding as the "DSB"), in consultation with the parties to the dispute, shall determine the rules and procedures to be followed within 10 days after a request by either Member. The Chairman shall be guided by the principle that special or additional rules and procedures should be used where possible, and the rules and procedures set out in this Understanding should be used to the extent necessary to avoid conflict.

Article 2

Administration

1. The Dispute Settlement Body is hereby established to administer these rules and procedures and, except as otherwise provided in a covered agreement, the consultation and dispute settlement provisions of the covered agreements. Accordingly, the DSB shall have the authority to establish panels, adopt panel and Appellate Body reports, maintain surveillance of implementation of rulings and recommendations, and authorize suspension of concessions and other obligations under the covered agreements. With respect to disputes arising under a covered agreement which is a Plurilateral Trade Agreement, the term "Member" as used herein shall refer only to those Members that are parties to the relevant Plurilateral Trade Agreement. Where the DSB administers the dispute settlement provisions of a Plurilateral Trade Agreement, only those Members that are parties to that Agreement may participate in decisions or actions taken by the DSB with respect to that dispute.

2. The DSB shall inform the relevant WTO Councils and Committees of any developments in disputes related to provisions of the respective covered agreements.

3. The DSB shall meet as often as necessary to carry out its functions within the time-frames provided in this Understanding.

4. Where the rules and procedures of this Understanding provide for the DSB to take a decision, it shall do so by consensus.[1]

Article 3

General Provisions

1. Members affirm their adherence to the principles for the management of disputes heretofore applied under Articles XXII and XXIII of GATT 1947, and the rules and procedures as further elaborated and modified herein.

2. The dispute settlement system of the WTO is a central element in providing security and predictability to the multilateral trading system. The Members recognize that it serves to preserve the rights and obligations of Members under the covered agreements, and to clarify the existing provisions of those agreements in accordance with customary

---

[1]The DSB shall be deemed to have decided by consensus on a matter submitted for its consideration, if no Member, present at the meeting of the DSB when the decision is taken, formally objects to the proposed decision.

rules of interpretation of public international law. Recommendations and rulings of the DSB cannot add to or diminish the rights and obligations provided in the covered agreements.

3. The prompt settlement of situations in which a Member considers that any benefits accruing to it directly or indirectly under the covered agreements are being impaired by measures taken by another Member is essential to the effective functioning of the WTO and the maintenance of a proper balance between the rights and obligations of Members.

4. Recommendations or rulings made by the DSB shall be aimed at achieving a satisfactory settlement of the matter in accordance with the rights and obligations under this Understanding and under the covered agreements.

5. All solutions to matters formally raised under the consultation and dispute settlement provisions of the covered agreements, including arbitration awards, shall be consistent with those agreements and shall not nullify or impair benefits accruing to any Member under those agreements, nor impede the attainment of any objective of those agreements.

6. Mutually agreed solutions to matters formally raised under the consultation and dispute settlement provisions of the covered agreements shall be notified to the DSB and the relevant Councils and Committees, where any Member may raise any point relating thereto.

7. Before bringing a case, a Member shall exercise its judgement as to whether action under these procedures would be fruitful. The aim of the dispute settlement mechanism is to secure a positive solution to a dispute. A solution mutually acceptable to the parties to a dispute and consistent with the covered agreements is clearly to be preferred. In the absence of a mutually agreed solution, the first objective of the dispute settlement mechanism is usually to secure the withdrawal of the measures concerned if these are found to be inconsistent with the provisions of any of the covered agreements. The provision of compensation should be resorted to only if the immediate withdrawal of the measure is impracticable and as a temporary measure pending the withdrawal of the measure which is inconsistent with a covered agreement. The last resort which this Understanding provides to the Member invoking the dispute settlement procedures is the possibility of suspending the application of concessions or other obligations under the covered agreements on a discriminatory basis vis-à-vis the other Member, subject to authorization by the DSB of such measures.

8. In cases where there is an infringement of the obligations assumed under a covered agreement, the action is considered *prima facie* to constitute a case of nullification or impairment. This means that there is normally a presumption that a breach of the rules has an adverse impact on other Members parties to that covered agreement, and in such

cases, it shall be up to the Member against whom the complaint has been brought to rebut the charge.

9. The provisions of this Understanding are without prejudice to the rights of Members to seek authoritative interpretation of provisions of a covered agreement through decision-making under the WTO Agreement or a covered agreement which is a Plurilateral Trade Agreement.

10. It is understood that requests for conciliation and the use of the dispute settlement procedures should not be intended or considered as contentious acts and that, if a dispute arises, all Members will engage in these procedures in good faith in an effort to resolve the dispute. It is also understood that complaints and counter-complaints in regard to distinct matters should not be linked.

11. This Understanding shall be applied only with respect to new requests for consultations under the consultation provisions of the covered agreements made on or after the date of entry into force of the WTO Agreement. With respect to disputes for which the request for consultations was made under GATT 1947 or under any other predecessor agreement to the covered agreements before the date of entry into force of the WTO Agreement, the relevant dispute settlement rules and procedures in effect immediately prior to the date of entry into force of the WTO Agreement shall continue to apply.[2]

12. Notwithstanding paragraph 11, if a complaint based on any of the covered agreements is brought by a developing country Member against a developed country Member, the complaining party shall have the right to invoke, as an alternative to the provisions contained in Articles 4, 5, 6 and 12 of this Understanding, the corresponding provisions of the Decision of 5 April 1966 (BISD 14S/18), except that where the Panel considers that the time-frame provided for in paragraph 7 of that Decision is insufficient to provide its report and with the agreement of the complaining party, that time-frame may be extended. To the extent that there is a difference between the rules and procedures of Articles 4, 5, 6 and 12 and the corresponding rules and procedures of the Decision, the latter shall prevail.

Article 4

Consultations

1. Members affirm their resolve to strengthen and improve the effectiveness of the consultation procedures employed by Members.

---

[2]This paragraph shall also be applied to disputes on which panel reports have not been adopted or fully implemented.

2. Each Member undertakes to accord sympathetic consideration to and afford adequate opportunity for consultation regarding any representations made by another Member concerning measures affecting the operation of any covered agreement taken within the territory of the former.[3]

3. If a request for consultations is made pursuant to a covered agreement, the Member to which the request is made shall, unless otherwise mutually agreed, reply to the request within 10 days after the date of its receipt and shall enter into consultations in good faith within a period of no more than 30 days after the date of receipt of the request, with a view to reaching a mutually satisfactory solution. If the Member does not respond within 10 days after the date of receipt of the request, or does not enter into consultations within a period of no more than 30 days, or a period otherwise mutually agreed, after the date of receipt of the request, then the Member that requested the holding of consultations may proceed directly to request the establishment of a panel.

4. All such requests for consultations shall be notified to the DSB and the relevant Councils and Committees by the Member which requests consultations. Any request for consultations shall be submitted in writing and shall give the reasons for the request, including identification of the measures at issue and an indication of the legal basis for the complaint.

5. In the course of consultations in accordance with the provisions of a covered agreement, before resorting to further action under this Understanding, Members should attempt to obtain satisfactory adjustment of the matter.

6. Consultations shall be confidential, and without prejudice to the rights of any Member in any further proceedings.

7. If the consultations fail to settle a dispute within 60 days after the date of receipt of the request for consultations, the complaining party may request the establishment of a panel. The complaining party may request a panel during the 60-day period if the consulting parties jointly consider that consultations have failed to settle the dispute.

8. In cases of urgency, including those which concern perishable goods, Members shall enter into consultations within a period of no more than 10 days after the date of receipt of the request. If the consultations have failed to settle the dispute within a period of 20 days after the date of receipt of the request, the complaining party may request the establishment of a panel.

---

[3]Where the provisions of any other covered agreement concerning measures taken by regional or local governments or authorities within the territory of a Member contain provisions different from the provisions of this paragraph, the provisions of such other covered agreement shall prevail.

9. In cases of urgency, including those which concern perishable goods, the parties to the dispute, panels and the Appellate Body shall make every effort to accelerate the proceedings to the greatest extent possible.

10. During consultations Members should give special attention to the particular problems and interests of developing country Members.

11. Whenever a Member other than the consulting Members considers that it has a substantial trade interest in consultations being held pursuant to paragraph 1 of Article XXII of GATT 1994, paragraph 1 of Article XXII of GATS, or the corresponding provisions in other covered agreements[4], such Member may notify the consulting Members and the DSB, within 10 days after the date of the circulation of the request for consultations under said Article, of its desire to be joined in the consultations. Such Member shall be joined in the consultations, provided that the Member to which the request for consultations was addressed agrees that the claim of substantial interest is well-founded. In that event they shall so inform the DSB. If the request to be joined in the consultations is not accepted, the applicant Member shall be free to request consultations under paragraph 1 of Article XXII or paragraph 1 of Article XXIII of GATT 1994, paragraph 1 of Article XXII or paragraph 1 of Article XXIII of GATS, or the corresponding provisions in other covered agreements.

Article 5

Good Offices, Conciliation and Mediation

1. Good offices, conciliation and mediation are procedures that are undertaken voluntarily if the parties to the dispute so agree.

---

[4]The corresponding consultation provisions in the covered agreements are listed hereunder: Agreement on Agriculture, Article 19: Agreement on the Application of Sanitary and Phytosanitary Measures, paragraph 1 of Article 11: Agreement on Textiles and Clothing, paragraph 4 of Article 8: Agreement on Technical Barriers to Trade, paragraph 1 of Article 14: Agreement on Trade-Related Investment Measures, Article 8: Agreement on Implementation of Article VI of GATT 1994, paragraph 2 of Article 17: Agreement on Implementation of Article VII of GATT 1994, paragraph 2 of Article 19: Agreement on Preshipment Inspection, Article 7: Agreement on Rules of Origin, Article 7: Agreement on Import Licensing Procedures, Article 6: Agreement on Subsidies and Countervailing Measures, Article 30: Agreement on Safeguards, Article 14: Agreement on Trade-Related Aspects of Intellectual Property Rights, Article 64.1; and any corresponding consultation provisions in Plurilateral Trade Agreements as determined by the competent bodies of each Agreement and as notified to the DSB.

2. Proceedings involving good offices, conciliation and mediation, and in particular positions taken by the parties to the dispute during these proceedings, shall be confidential, and without prejudice to the rights of either party in any further proceedings under these procedures.

3. Good offices, conciliation or mediation may be requested at any time by any party to a dispute. They may begin at any time and be terminated at any time. Once procedures for good offices, conciliation or mediation are terminated, a complaining party may then proceed with a request for the establishment of a panel.

4. When good offices, conciliation or mediation are entered into within 60 days after the date of receipt of a request for consultations, the complaining party must allow a period of 60 days after the date of receipt of the request for consultations before requesting the establishment of a panel. The complaining party may request the establishment of a panel during the 60-day period if the parties to the dispute jointly consider that the good offices, conciliation or mediation process has failed to settle the dispute.

5. If the parties to a dispute agree, procedures for good offices, conciliation or mediation may continue while the panel process proceeds.

6. The Director-General may, acting in an *ex officio* capacity, offer good offices, conciliation or mediation with the view to assisting Members to settle a dispute.

Article 6

Establishment of Panels

1. If the complaining party so requests, a panel shall be established at the latest at the DSB meeting following that at which the request first appears as an item on the DSB's agenda, unless at that meeting the DSB decides by consensus not to establish a panel.[5]

2. The request for the establishment of a panel shall be made in writing. It shall indicate whether consultations were held, identify the specific measures at issue and provide a brief summary of the legal basis of the complaint sufficient to present the problem clearly. In case the applicant requests the establishment of a panel with other than standard terms of reference, the written request shall include the proposed text of special terms of reference.

[5]If the complaining party so requests, a meeting of the DSB shall be convened for this purpose within 15 days of the request, provided that at least 10 days' advance notice of the meeting is given.

Article 7

Terms of Reference of Panels

1. Panels shall have the following terms of reference unless the parties to the dispute agree otherwise within 20 days from the establishment of the panel:

> "To examine, in the light of the relevant provisions in (name of the covered agreement(s) cited by the parties to the dispute), the matter referred to the DSB by (name of party) in document . . . and to make such findings as will assist the DSB in making the recommendations or in giving the rulings provided for in that/those agreement(s)."

2. Panels shall address the relevant provisions in any covered agreement or agreements cited by the parties to the dispute.

3. In establishing a panel, the DSB may authorize its Chairman to draw up the terms of reference of the panel in consultation with the parties to the dispute, subject to the provisions of paragraph 1. The terms of reference thus drawn up shall be circulated to all Members. If other than standard terms of reference are agreed upon, any Member may raise any point relating thereto in the DSB.

Article 8

Composition of Panels

1. Panels shall be composed of well-qualified governmental and/or non-governmental individuals, including persons who have served on or presented a case to a panel, served as a representative of a Member or of a contracting party to GATT 1947 or as a representative to the Council or Committee of any covered agreement or its predecessor agreement, or in the Secretariat, taught or published on international trade law or policy, or served as a senior trade policy official of a Member.

2. Panel members should be selected with a view to ensuring the independence of the members, a sufficiently diverse background and a wide spectrum of experience.

3. Citizens of Members whose governments[6] are parties to the dispute or third parties as defined in paragraph 2 of Article 10 shall not serve on a panel concerned with that dispute, unless the parties to the dispute agree otherwise.

---

[6]In the case where customs unions or common markets are parties to a dispute, this provision applies to citizens of all member countries of the customs unions or common markets.

4. To assist in the selection of panelists, the Secretariat shall maintain an indicative list of governmental and non-governmental individuals possessing the qualifications outlined in paragraph 1, from which panelists may be drawn as appropriate. That list shall include the roster of non-governmental panelists established on 30 November 1984 (BISD 31S/9), and other rosters and indicative lists established under any of the covered agreements, and shall retain the names of persons on those rosters and indicative lists at the time of entry into force of the WTO Agreement. Members may periodically suggest names of governmental and non-governmental individuals for inclusion on the indicative list, providing relevant information on their knowledge of international trade and of the sectors or subject matter of the covered agreements, and those names shall be added to the list upon approval by the DSB. For each of the individuals on the list, the list shall indicate specific areas of experience or expertise of the individuals in the sectors or subject matter of the covered agreements.

5. Panels shall be composed of three panelists unless the parties to the dispute agree, within 10 days from the establishment of the panel, to a panel composed of five panelists. Members shall be informed promptly of the composition of the panel.

6. The Secretariat shall propose nominations for the panel to the parties to the dispute. The parties to the dispute shall not oppose nominations except for compelling reasons.

7. If there is no agreement on the panelists within 20 days after the date of the establishment of a panel, at the request of either party, the Director-General, in consultation with the Chairman of the DSB and the Chairman of the relevant Council or Committee, shall determine the composition of the panel by appointing the panelists whom the Director-General considers most appropriate in accordance with any relevant special or additional rules or procedures of the covered agreement or covered agreements which are at issue in the dispute, after consulting with the parties to the dispute. The Chairman of the DSB shall inform the Members of the composition of the panel thus formed no later than 10 days after the date the Chairman receives such a request.

8. Members shall undertake, as a general rule, to permit their officials to serve as panelists.

9. Panelists shall serve in their individual capacities and not as government representatives, nor as representatives of any organization. Members shall therefore not give them instructions nor seek to influence them as individuals with regard to matters before a panel.

10. When a dispute is between a developing country Member and a developed country Member the panel shall, if the developing country Member so requests, include at least one panelist from a developing country Member.

11. Panelists' expenses, including travel and subsistence allowance, shall be met from the WTO budget in accordance with criteria to be adopted by the General Council, based on recommendations of the Committee on Budget, Finance and Administration.

Article 9

Procedures for Multiple Complainants

1. Where more than one Member requests the establishment of a panel related to the same matter, a single panel may be established to examine these complaints taking into account the rights of all Members concerned. A single panel should be established to examine such complaints whenever feasible.

2. The single panel shall organize its examination and present its findings to the DSB in such a manner that the rights which the parties to the dispute would have enjoyed had separate panels examined the complaints are in no way impaired. If one of the parties to the dispute so requests, the panel shall submit separate reports on the dispute concerned. The written submissions by each of the complainants shall be made available to the other complainants, and each complainant shall have the right to be present when any one of the other complainants presents its views to the panel.

3. If more than one panel is established to examine the complaints related to the same matter, to the greatest extent possible the same persons shall serve as panelists on each of the separate panels and the timetable for the panel process in such disputes shall be harmonized.

Article 10

Third Parties

1. The interests of the parties to a dispute and those of other Members under a covered agreement at issue in the dispute shall be fully taken into account during the panel process.

2. Any Member having a substantial interest in a matter before a panel and having notified its interest to the DSB (referred to in this Understanding as a "third party") shall have an opportunity to be heard by the panel and to make written submissions to the panel. These submissions shall also be given to the parties to the dispute and shall be reflected in the panel report.

3. Third parties shall receive the submissions of the parties to the dispute to the first meeting of the panel.

4. If a third party considers that a measure already the subject of a panel proceeding nullifies or impairs benefits accruing to it under any covered agreement, that Member may have recourse to normal dispute settlement procedures under this Understanding. Such a dispute shall be referred to the original panel wherever possible.

Article 11

Function of Panels

The function of panels is to assist the DSB in discharging its responsibilities under this Understanding and the covered agreements. Accordingly, a panel should make an objective assessment of the matter before it, including an objective assessment of the facts of the case and the applicability of and conformity with the relevant covered agreements, and make such other findings as will assist the DSB in making the recommendations or in giving the rulings provided for in the covered agreements. Panels should consult regularly with the parties to the dispute and give them adequate opportunity to develop a mutually satisfactory solution.

Article 12

Panel Procedures

1. Panels shall follow the Working Procedures in Appendix 3 unless the panel decides otherwise after consulting the parties to the dispute.

2. Panel procedures should provide sufficient flexibility so as to ensure high-quality panel reports, while not unduly delaying the panel process.

3. After consulting the parties to the dispute, the panelists shall, as soon as practicable and whenever possible within one week after the composition and terms of reference of the panel have been agreed upon, fix the timetable for the panel process, taking into account the provisions of paragraph 9 of Article 4, if relevant.

4. In determining the timetable for the panel process, the panel shall provide sufficient time for the parties to the dispute to prepare their submissions.

5. Panels should set precise deadlines for written submissions by the parties and the parties should respect those deadlines.

6. Each party to the dispute shall deposit its written submissions with the Secretariat for immediate transmission to the panel and to the other party or parties to the dispute.

The complaining party shall submit its first submission in advance of the responding party's first submission unless the panel decides, in fixing the timetable referred to in paragraph 3 and after consultations with the parties to the dispute, that the parties should submit their first submissions simultaneously. When there are sequential arrangements for the deposit of first submissions, the panel shall establish a firm time period for receipt of the responding party's submission. Any subsequent written submissions shall be submitted simultaneously.

7. Where the parties to the dispute have failed to develop a mutually satisfactory solution, the panel shall submit its findings in the form of a written report to the DSB. In such cases, the report of a panel shall set out the findings of fact, the applicability of relevant provisions and the basic rationale behind any findings and recommendations that it makes. Where a settlement of the matter among the parties to the dispute has been found, the report of the panel shall be confined to a brief description of the case and to reporting that a solution has been reached.

8. In order to make the procedures more efficient, the period in which the panel shall conduct its examination, from the date that the composition and terms of reference of the panel have been agreed upon until the date the final report is issued to the parties to the dispute, shall, as a general rule, not exceed six months. In cases of urgency, including those relating to perishable goods, the panel shall aim to issue its report to the parties to the dispute within three months.

9. When the panel considers that it cannot issue its report within six months, or within three months in cases of urgency, it shall inform the DSB in writing of the reasons for the delay together with an estimate of the period within which it will issue its report. In no case should the period from the establishment of the panel to the circulation of the report to the Members exceed nine months.

10. In the context of consultations involving a measure taken by a developing country Member, the parties may agree to extend the periods established in paragraphs 7 and 8 of Article 4. If, after the relevant period has elapsed, the consulting parties cannot agree that the consultations have concluded, the Chairman of the DSB shall decide, after consultation with the parties, whether to extend the relevant period and, if so, for how long. In addition, in examining a complaint against a developing country Member, the panel shall accord sufficient time for the developing country Member to prepare and present its argumentation. The provisions of paragraph 1 of Article 20 and paragraph 4 of Article 21 are not affected by any action pursuant to this paragraph.

11. Where one or more of the parties is a developing country Member, the panel's report shall explicitly indicate the form in which account has been taken of relevant provisions on differential and more-favourable treatment for developing country Members

that form part of the covered agreements which have been raised by the developing country Member in the course of the dispute settlement procedures.

12. The panel may suspend its work at any time at the request of the complaining party for a period not to exceed 12 months. In the event of such a suspension, the time-frames set out in paragraphs 8 and 9 of this Article, paragraph 1 of Article 20, and paragraph 4 of Article 21 shall be extended by the amount of time that the work was suspended. If the work of the panel has been suspended for more than 12 months, the authority for establishment of the panel shall lapse.

Article 13

Right to Seek Information

1. Each panel shall have the right to seek information and technical advice from any individual or body which it deems appropriate. However, before a panel seeks such information or advice from any individual or body within the jurisdiction of a Member it shall inform the authorities of that Member. A Member should respond promptly and fully to any request by a panel for such information as the panel considers necessary and appropriate. Confidential information which is provided shall not be revealed without formal authorization from the individual, body, or authorities of the Member providing the information.

2. Panels may seek information from any relevant source and may consult experts to obtain their opinion on certain aspects of the matter. With respect to a factual issue concerning a scientific or other technical matter raised by a party to a dispute, a panel may request an advisory report in writing from an expert review group. Rules for the establishment of such a group and its procedures are set forth in Appendix 4.

Article 14

Confidentiality

1. Panel deliberations shall be confidential.

2. The reports of panels shall be drafted without the presence of the parties to the dispute in the light of the information provided and the statements made.

3. Opinions expressed in the panel report by individual panelists shall be anonymous.

Article 15

Interim Review Stage

1. Following the consideration of rebuttal submissions and oral arguments, the panel shall issue the descriptive (factual and argument) sections of its draft report to the parties to the dispute. Within a period of time set by the panel, the parties shall submit their comments in writing.

2. Following the expiration of the set period of time for receipt of comments from the parties to the dispute, the panel shall issue an interim report to the parties, including both the descriptive sections and the panel's findings and conclusions. Within a period of time set by the panel, a party may submit a written request for the panel to review precise aspects of the interim report prior to circulation of the final report to the Members. At the request of a party, the panel shall hold a further meeting with the parties on the issues identified in the written comments. If no comments are received from any party within the comment period, the interim report shall be considered the final panel report and circulated promptly to the Members.

3. The findings of the final panel report shall include a discussion of the arguments made at the interim review stage. The interim review stage shall be conducted within the time period set out in paragraph 8 of Article 12.

Article 16

Adoption of Panel Reports

1. In order to provide sufficient time for the Members to consider panel reports, the reports shall not be considered for adoption by the DSB until 20 days after the date they have been circulated to the Members.

2. Members having objections to a panel report shall give written reasons to explain their objections for circulation at least 10 days prior to the DSB meeting at which the panel report will be considered.

3. The parties to a dispute shall have the right to participate fully in the consideration of the panel report by the DSB, and their views shall be fully recorded.

4. Within 60 days after the date of circulation of a panel report to the Members, the report shall be adopted at a DSB meeting[7] unless a party to the dispute formally notifies

[7]If a meeting of the DSB is not scheduled within this period at a time that enables the

the DSB of its decision to appeal or the DSB decides by consensus not to adopt the report. If a party has notified its decision to appeal, the report by the panel shall not be considered for adoption by the DSB until after completion of the appeal. This adoption procedure is without prejudice to the right of Members to express their views on a panel report.

Article 17

Appellate Review
Standing Appellate Body

1. A standing Appellate Body shall be established by the DSB. The Appellate Body shall hear appeals from panel cases. It shall be composed of seven persons, three of whom shall serve on any one case. Persons serving on the Appellate Body shall serve in rotation. Such rotation shall be determined in the working procedures of the Appellate Body.

2. The DSB shall appoint persons to serve on the Appellate Body for a four-year term, and each person may be reappointed once. However, the terms of three of the seven persons appointed immediately after the entry into force of the WTO Agreement shall expire at the end of two years, to be determined by lot. Vacancies shall be filled as they arise. A person appointed to replace a person whose term of office has not expired shall hold office for the remainder of the predecessor's term.

3. The Appellate Body shall comprise persons of recognized authority, with demonstrated expertise in law, international trade and the subject matter of the covered agreements generally. They shall be unaffiliated with any government. The Appellate Body membership shall be broadly representative of membership in the WTO. All persons serving on the Appellate Body shall be available at all times and on short notice, and shall stay abreast of dispute settlement activities and other relevant activities of the WTO. They shall not participate in the consideration of any disputes that would create a direct or indirect conflict of interest.

4. Only parties to the dispute, not third parties, may appeal a panel report. Third parties which have notified the DSB of a substantial interest in the matter pursuant to paragraph 2 of Article 10 may make written submissions to, and be given an opportunity to be heard by, the Appellate Body.

---

requirements of paragraphs 1 and 4 of Article 16 to be met, a meeting of the DSB shall be held for this purpose.

5. As a general rule, the proceedings shall not exceed 60 days from the date a party to the dispute formally notifies its decision to appeal to the date the Appellate Body circulates its report. In fixing its timetable the Appellate Body shall take into account the provisions of paragraph 9 of Article 4, if relevant. When the Appellate Body considers that it cannot provide its report within 60 days, it shall inform the DSB in writing of the reasons for the delay together with an estimate of the period within which it will submit its report. In no case shall the proceedings exceed 90 days.

6. An appeal shall be limited to issues of law covered in the panel report and legal interpretations developed by the panel.

7. The Appellate Body shall be provided with appropriate administrative and legal support as it requires.

8. The expenses of persons serving on the Appellate Body, including travel and subsistence allowance, shall be met from the WTO budget in accordance with criteria to be adopted by the General Council, based on recommendations of the Committee on Budget, Finance and Administration.

Procedures for Appellate Review

9. Working procedures shall be drawn up by the Appellate Body in consultation with the Chairman of the DSB and the Director-General, and communicated to the Members for their information.

10. The proceedings of the Appellate Body shall be confidential. The reports of the Appellate Body shall be drafted without the presence of the parties to the dispute and in the light of the information provided and the statements made.

11. Opinions expressed in the Appellate Body report by individuals serving on the Appellate Body shall be anonymous.

12. The Appellate Body shall address each of the issues raised in accordance with paragraph 6 during the appellate proceeding.

13. The Appellate Body may uphold, modify or reverse the legal findings and conclusions of the panel.

Adoption of Appellate Body Reports

14. An Appellate Body report shall be adopted by the DSB and unconditionally accepted by the parties to the dispute unless the DSB decides by consensus not to adopt the

Appellate Body report within 30 days following its circulation to the Members.[8] This adoption procedure is without prejudice to the right of Members to express their views on an Appellate Body report.

Article 18

Communications with the Panel or Appellate Body

1. There shall be no *ex parte* communications with the panel or Appellate Body concerning matters under consideration by the panel or Appellate Body.

2. Written submissions to the panel or the Appellate Body shall be treated as confidential, but shall be made available to the parties to the dispute. Nothing in this Understanding shall preclude a party to a dispute from disclosing statements of its own positions to the public. Members shall treat as confidential information submitted by another Member to the panel or the Appellate Body which that Member has designated as confidential. A party to a dispute shall also, upon request of a Member, provide a non-confidential summary of the information contained in its written submissions that could be disclosed to the public.

Article 19

Panel and Appellate Body Recommendations

1. Where a panel or the Appellate Body concludes that a measure is inconsistent with a covered agreement, it shall recommend that the Member concerned[9] bring the measure into conformity with that agreement.[10] In addition to its recommendations, the panel or Appellate Body may suggest ways in which the Member concerned could implement the recommendations.

2. In accordance with paragraph 2 of Article 3, in their findings and recommendations, the panel and Appellate Body cannot add to or diminish the rights and obligations provided in the covered agreements.

---

[8] If a meeting of the DSB is not scheduled during this period, such a meeting of the DSB shall be held for this purpose.

[9] The "Member concerned" is the party to the dispute to which the panel or Appellate Body recommendations are directed.

[10] With respect to recommendations in cases not involving a violation of GATT 1994 or any other covered agreement, see Article 26.

Article 20

Time-frame for DSB Decisions

Unless otherwise agreed to by the parties to the dispute, the period from the date of establishment of the panel by the DSB until the date the DSB considers the panel or appellate report for adoption shall as a general rule not exceed nine months where the panel report is not appealed or 12 months where the report is appealed. Where either the panel or the Appellate Body has acted, pursuant to paragraph 9 of Article 12 or paragraph 5 of Article 17, to extend the time for providing its report, the additional time taken shall be added to the above periods.

Article 21

Surveillance of Implementation of Recommendations and Rulings

1. Prompt compliance with recommendations or rulings of the DSB is essential in order to ensure effective resolution of disputes to the benefit of all Members.

2. Particular attention should be paid to matters affecting the interests of developing country Members with respect to measures which have been subject to dispute settlement.

3. At a DSB meeting held within 30 days[11] after the date of adoption of the panel or Appellate Body report, the Member concerned shall inform the DSB of its intentions in respect of implementation of the recommendations and rulings of the DSB. If it is impracticable to comply immediately with the recommendations and rulings, the Member concerned shall have a reasonable period of time in which to do so. The reasonable period of time shall be:

(a) the period of time proposed by the Member concerned, provided that such period is approved by the DSB: or, in the absence of such approval,
(b) a period of time mutually agreed by the parties to the dispute with in 45 days after the date of adoption of the recommendations and rulings; or, in the absence of such agreement,
(c) a period of time determined through binding arbitration within 90 days after the date of adoption of the recommendations and rulings.[12] In such

[11]If a meeting of the DSB is not scheduled during this period, such a meeting of the DSB shall be held for this purpose.

[12]If the parties cannot agree on an arbitrator within 10 days after referring the matter to arbitration, the arbitrator shall be appointed by the Director-General within 10 days, after consulting the parties.

arbitration, a guideline for the arbitrator[13] should be that the reasonable period of time to implement panel or Appellate Body recommendations should not exceed 15 months from the date of adoption of a panel or Appellate Body report. However, that time may be shorter or longer, depending upon the particular circumstances.

4. Except where the panel or the Appellate Body has extended, pursuant to paragraph 9 of Article 12 or paragraph 5 of Article 17, the time of providing its report, the period from the date of establishment of the panel by the DSB until the date of determination of the reasonable period of time shall not exceed 15 months unless the parties to the dispute agree otherwise. Where either the panel or the Appellate Body has acted to extend the time of providing its report, the additional time taken shall be added to the 15-month period; provided that unless the parties to the dispute agree that there are exceptional circumstances, the total time shall not exceed 18 months.

5. Where there is disagreement as to the existence or consistency with a covered agreement of measures taken to comply with the recommendations and rulings such dispute shall be decided through recourse to these dispute settlement procedures, including wherever possible resort to the original panel. The panel shall circulate its report within 90 days after the date of referral of the matter to it. When the panel considers that it cannot provide its report within this time frame, it shall inform the DSB in writing of the reasons for the delay together with an estimate of the period within which it will submit its report.

6. The DSB shall keep under surveillance the implementation of adopted recommendations or rulings. The issue of implementation of the recommendations or rulings may be raised at the DSB by any Member at any time following their adoption. Unless the DSB decides otherwise, the issue of implementation of the recommendations or rulings shall be placed on the agenda of the DSB meeting after six months following the date of establishment of the reasonable period of time pursuant to paragraph 3 and shall remain on the DSB's agenda until the issue is resolved. At least 10 days prior to each such DSB meeting, the Member concerned shall provide the DSB with a status report in writing of its progress in the implementation of the recommendations or rulings.

7. If the matter is one which has been raised by a developing country Member, the DSB shall consider what further action it might take which would be appropriate to the circumstances.

8. If the case is one brought by a developing country Member, in considering what appropriate action might be taken, the DSB shall take into account not only the trade cov-

[13]The expression "arbitrator" shall be interpreted as referring either to an individual or a group.

erage of measures complained of, but also their impact on the economy of developing country Members concerned.

Article 22

Compensation and the Suspension of Concessions

1. Compensation and the suspension of concessions or other obligations are temporary measures available in the event that the recommendations and rulings are not implemented within a reasonable period of time. However, neither compensation nor the suspension of concessions or other obligations is preferred to full implementation of a recommendation to bring a measure into conformity with the covered agreements. Compensation is voluntary and, if granted, shall be consistent with the covered agreements.

2. If the Member concerned fails to bring the measure found to be inconsistent with a covered agreement into compliance therewith or otherwise comply with the recommendations and rulings within the reasonable period of time determined pursuant to paragraph 3 of Article 21, such Member shall, if so requested, and no later than the expiry of the reasonable period of time, enter into negotiations with any party having invoked the dispute settlement procedures, with a view to developing mutually acceptable compensation. If no satisfactory compensation has been agreed within 20 days after the date of expiry of the reasonable period of time, any party having invoked the dispute settlement procedures may request authorization from the DSB to suspend the application to the Member concerned of concessions or other obligations under the covered agreements.

3. In considering what concessions or other obligations to suspend, the complaining party shall apply the following principles and procedures:

(a) the general principle is that the complaining party should first seek to suspend concessions or other obligations with respect to the same sector(s) as that in which the panel or Appellate Body has found a violation or other nullification or impairment;
(b) if that party considers that it is not practicable or effective to suspend concessions or other obligations with respect to the same sector(s), it may seek to suspend concessions or other obligations in other sectors under the same agreement;
(c) if that party considers that it is not practicable or effective to suspend concessions or other obligations with respect to other sectors under the same agreement, and that the circumstances are serious enough, it may seek to suspend concessions or other obligations under another covered agreement;

(d) in applying the above principles, that party shall take into account:
   (i) the trade in the sector or under the agreement under which the panel or Appellate Body has found a violation or other nullification or impairment, and the importance of such trade to that party;
   (ii) the broader economic elements related to the nullification or impairment and the broader economic consequences of the suspension of concessions or other obligations;

(e) if that party decides to request authorization to suspend concessions or other obligations pursuant to subparagraphs (b) or (c), it shall state the reasons therefor in its request. At the same time as the request is forwarded to the DSB, it also shall be forwarded to the relevant Councils and also, in the case of a request pursuant to subparagraph (b), the relevant sectoral bodies;

(f) for purposes of this paragraph, "sector" means:
   (i) with respect to goods, all goods;
   (ii) with respect to services, a principal sector as identified in the current "Services Sectoral Classification List" which identifies such sectors;[14]
   (iii) with respect to trade-related intellectual property rights, each of the categories of intellectual property rights covered in Section 1, or Section 2, or Section 3, or Section 4, or Section 5, or Section 6, or Section 7 of Part II, or the obligations under Part III, or Part IV of the Agreement on TRIPS;

(g) for purposes of this paragraph, "agreement" means:
   (i) with respect to goods, the agreements listed in Annex 1A of the WTO Agreement, taken as a whole as well as the Plurilateral Trade Agreements in so far as the relevant parties to the dispute are parties to these agreements;
   (ii) with respect to services, the GATS;
   (iii) with respect to intellectual property rights, the Agreement on TRIPS.

4. The level of the suspension of concessions or other obligations authorized by the DSB shall be equivalent to the level of the nullification or impairment.

5. The DSB shall not authorize suspension of concessions or other obligations if a covered agreement prohibits such suspension.

6. When the situation described in paragraph 2 occurs, the DSB, upon request, shall grant authorization to suspend concessions or other obligations within 30 days of the expiry of the reasonable period of time unless the DSB decides by consensus to reject the

[14]The list in document MTN.GNS/W/120 identifies 11 sectors.

request. However, if the Member concerned objects to the level of suspension proposed, or claims that the principles and procedures set forth in paragraph 3 have not been followed where a complaining party has requested authorization to suspend concessions or other obligations pursuant to paragraph 3(b) or (c), the matter shall be referred to arbitration. Such arbitration shall be carried out by the original panel, if members are available, or by an arbitrator[15] appointed by the Director-General and shall be completed within 60 days after the date of expiry of the reasonable period of time. Concessions or other obligations shall not be suspended during the course of the arbitration.

7. The arbitrator[16] acting pursuant to paragraph 6 shall not examine the nature of the concessions or other obligations to be suspended but shall determine whether the level of such suspension is equivalent to the level of nullification or impairment. The arbitrator may also determine if the proposed suspension of concessions or other obligations is allowed under the covered agreement. However, if the matter referred to arbitration includes a claim that the principles and procedures set forth in paragraph 3 have not been followed, the arbitrator shall examine that claim. In the event the arbitrator determines that those principles and procedures have not been followed, the complaining party shall apply them consistent with paragraph 3. The parties shall accept the arbitrator's decision as final and the parties concerned shall not seek a second arbitration. The DSB shall be informed promptly of the decision of the arbitrator and shall upon request, grant authorization to suspend concessions or other obligations where the request is consistent with the decision of the arbitrator, unless the DSB decides by consensus to reject the request.

8. The suspension of concessions or other obligations shall be temporary and shall only be applied until such time as the measure found to be inconsistent with a covered agreement has been removed, or the Member that must implement recommendations or rulings provides a solution to the nullification or impairment of benefits, or a mutually satisfactory solution is reached. In accordance with paragraph 6 of Article 21, the DSB shall continue to keep under surveillance the implementation of adopted recommendations or rulings, including those cases where compensation has been provided or concessions or other obligations have been suspended but the recommendations to bring a measure into conformity with the covered agreements have not been implemented.

9. The dispute settlement provisions of the covered agreements may be invoked in respect of measures affecting their observance taken by regional or local governments or authorities within the territory of a Member. When the DSB has ruled that a provision

[15]The expression "arbitrator" shall be interpreted as referring either to an individual or a group.

[16]The expression "arbitrator" shall be interpreted as referring either to an individual or a group or to the members of the original panel when serving in the capacity of arbitrator.

of a covered agreement has not been observed, the responsible Member shall take such reasonable measures as may be available to it to ensure its observance. The provisions of the covered agreements and this Understanding relating to compensation and suspension of concessions or other obligations apply in cases where it has not been possible to secure such observance.[17]

Article 23

Strengthening of the Multilateral System

1. When Members seek the redress of a violation of obligations or other nullification or impairment of benefits under the covered agreements or an impediment to the attainment of any objective of the covered agreements, they shall have recourse to, and abide by, the rules and procedures of this Understanding.

2. In such cases, Members shall:

(a) not make a determination to the effect that a violation has occurred, that benefits have been nullified or impaired or that the attainment of any objective of the covered agreements has been impeded, except through recourse to dispute settlement in accordance with the rules and procedures of this Understanding, and shall make any such determination consistent with the findings contained in the panel or Appellate Body report adopted by the DSB or an arbitration award rendered under this Understanding;

(b) follow the procedures set forth in Article 21 to determine the reasonable period of time for the Member concerned to implement the recommendations and rulings; and

(c) follow the procedures set forth in Article 22 to determine the level of suspension of concessions or other obligations and obtain DSB authorization in accordance with those procedures before suspending concessions or other obligations under the covered agreements in response to the failure of the Member concerned to implement the recommendations and rulings within that reasonable period of time.

---

[17]Where the provisions of any covered agreement concerning measures taken by regional or local governments or authorities within the territory of a Member contain provisions different from the provisions of this paragraph, the provisions of such covered agreement shall prevail.

Article 24

Special Procedures Involving Least-Developed Country Members

1. At all stages of the determination of the causes of a dispute and of dispute settlement procedures involving a least-developed country Member, particular consideration shall be given to the special situation of least-developed country Members. In this regard, Members shall exercise due restraint in raising matters under these procedures involving a least-developed country Member. If nullification or impairment is found to result from a measure taken by a least-developed country Member, complaining parties shall exercise due restraint in asking for compensation or seeking authorization to suspend the application of concessions or other obligations pursuant to these procedures.

2. In dispute settlement cases involving a least-developed country Member, where a satisfactory solution has not been found in the course of consultations the Director-General or the Chairman of the DSB shall, upon request by a least-developed country Member offer their good offices, conciliation and mediation with a view to assisting the parties to settle the dispute, before a request for a panel is made. The Director-General or the Chairman of the DSB, in providing the above assistance, may consult any source which either deems appropriate.

Article 25

Arbitration

1. Expeditious arbitration within the WTO as an alternative means of dispute settlement can facilitate the solution of certain disputes that concern issues that are clearly defined by both parties.

2. Except as otherwise provided in this Understanding, resort to arbitration shall be subject to mutual agreement of the parties which shall agree on the procedures to be followed. Agreements to resort to arbitration shall be notified to all Members sufficiently in advance of the actual commencement of the arbitration process.

3. Other Members may become party to an arbitration proceeding only upon the agreement of the parties which have agreed to have recourse to arbitration. The parties to the proceeding shall agree to abide by the arbitration award. Arbitration awards shall be notified to the DSB and the Council or Committee of any relevant agreement where any Member may raise any point relating thereto.

4. Articles 21 and 22 of this Understanding shall apply *mutatis mutandis* to arbitration awards.

Article 26

Non-Violation Complaints of the Type Described in Paragraph 1(b) of Article XXIII of GATT 1994

1. Where the provisions of paragraph 1(b) of Article XXIII of GATT 1994 are applicable to a covered agreement, a panel or the Appellate Body may only make rulings and recommendations where a party to the dispute considers that any benefit accruing to it directly or indirectly under the relevant covered agreement is being nullified or impaired or the attainment of any objective of that Agreement is being impeded as a result of the application by a Member of any measure, whether or not it conflicts with the provisions of that Agreement. Where and to the extent that such party considers and a panel or the Appellate Body determines that a case concerns a measure that does not conflict with the provisions of a covered agreement to which the provisions of paragraph 1(b) of Article XXIII of GATT 1994 are applicable, the procedures in this Understanding shall apply, subject to the following:

(a) the complaining party shall present a detailed justification in support of any complaint relating to a measure which does not conflict with the relevant covered agreement;
(b) where a measure has been found to nullify or impair benefits under, or impede the attainment of objectives, of the relevant covered agreement without violation thereof, there is no obligation to withdraw the measure. However, in such cases, the panel or the Appellate Body shall recommend that the Member concerned make a mutually satisfactory adjustment;
(c) notwithstanding the provisions of Article 21, the arbitration provided for in paragraph 3 of Article 21, upon request of either party, may include a determination of the level of benefits which have been nullified or impaired, and may also suggest ways and means of reaching a mutually satisfactory adjustment: such suggestions shall not be binding upon the parties to the dispute;
(d) notwithstanding the provisions of paragraph 1 of Article 22, compensation may be part of a mutually satisfactory adjustment as final settlement of the dispute.

2. *Complaints of the Type Described in Paragraph 1(c) of Article XXIII of GATT 1994*

Where the provisions of paragraph 1(c) of Article XXIII of GATT 1994 are applicable to a covered agreement, a panel may only make rulings and recommendations where a party considers that any benefit accruing to it directly or indirectly under the relevant covered agreement is being nullified or impaired or the attainment of any objective of that Agreement is being impeded as a result of the existence of any situation other than those to which the provisions of paragraphs 1(a) and 1(b) of Article XXIII of GATT 1994 are applicable. Where and to the extent that such party considers and a panel determines that the matter is covered by this paragraph, the procedures of this

Understanding shall apply only up to and including the point in the proceedings where the panel report has been circulated to the Members. The dispute settlement rules and procedures contained in the Decision of 12 April 1989 (BISD 36S/61-67) shall apply to consideration for adoption, and surveillance and implementation of recommendations and rulings. The following shall also apply:

(a) the complaining party shall present a detailed justification in support of any argument made with respect to issues covered under this paragraph;

(b) in cases involving matters covered by this paragraph, if a panel finds that cases also involve dispute settlement matters other than those covered by this paragraph, the panel shall circulate a report to the DSB addressing any such matters and a separate report on matters falling under this paragraph.

Article 27

Responsibilities of the Secretariat

1. The Secretariat shall have the responsibility of assisting panels, especially on the legal, historical and procedural aspects of the matters dealt with, and of providing secretarial and technical support.

2. While the Secretariat assists Members in respect of dispute settlement at their request, there may also be a need to provide additional legal advice and assistance in respect of dispute settlement to developing country Members. To this end, the Secretariat shall make available a qualified legal expert from the WTO technical cooperation services to any developing country Member which so requests. This expert shall assist the developing country Member in a manner ensuring the continued impartiality of the Secretariat.

3. The Secretariat shall conduct special training courses for interested Members concerning these dispute settlement procedures and practices so as to enable Members' experts to be better informed in this regard.

Appendix 1

Agreements Covered by the Understanding

(A) Agreement Establishing the World Trade Organization
(B) Multilateral Trade Agreements

Annex 1A: Multilateral Agreements on Trade in Goods
Annex 1B: General Agreement on Trade in Services
Annex 1C: Agreement on Trade-Related Aspects of Intellectual Property Rights
Annex 2: Understanding on Rules and Procedures Governing the Settlement of Disputes

(C) Plurilateral Trade Agreements

Annex 4: Agreement on Trade in Civil Aircraft
Agreement on Government Procurement
International Dairy Agreement
International Bovine Meat Agreement

The applicability of this Understanding to the Plurilateral Trade Agreements shall be subject to the adoption of a decision by the parties to each agreement setting out the terms for the application of the Understanding to the individual agreement, including any special or additional rules or procedures for inclusion in Appendix 2, as notified to the DSB.

Appendix 2

Special or Additional Rules and Procedures Contained in the Covered Agreements

Agreement	Rules and Procedures
Agreement on the Application of Sanitary and Phytosanitary Measures	11.2
Agreement on Textiles and Clothing	2.14, 2.21, 4.4, 5.2, 5.4, 5.6, 6.9, 6.10, 6.11, 8.1 through 8.12
Agreement on Technical Barriers to Trade	14.2 through 14.4, Annex 2
Agreement on Implementation of Article VI of GATT 1994	17.4 through 17.7
Agreement on Implementation of Article VII of GATT 1994	19.3 through 19.5, Annex II.2(f), 3, 9, 21
Agreement on Subsidies and Countervailing Measures	4.2 through 4.12, 6.6, 7.2 through 7.10, 8.5, footnote 35, 24.4, 27.7, Annex V
General Agreement on Trade in Services	XXII:3, XXIII:3
Annex on Financial Services	4
Annex on Air Transport Services	4
Decision on Certain Dispute Settlement Procedures for the GATS	1 through 5

The list of rules and procedures in this Appendix includes provisions where only a part of the provision may be relevant in this context.

Any special or additional rules or procedures in the Plurilateral Trade Agreements as determined by the competent bodies of each agreement and as notified to the DSB.

Appendix 3

Working Procedures

1. In its proceedings the panel shall follow the relevant provisions of this Understanding. In addition, the following working procedures shall apply.

2. The panel shall meet in closed session. The parties to the dispute, and interested parties, shall be present at the meetings only when invited by the panel to appear before it.

3. The deliberations of the panel and the documents submitted to it shall be kept confidential. Nothing in this Understanding shall preclude a party to a dispute from disclosing statements of its own positions to the public. Members shall treat as confidential information submitted by another Member to the panel which that Member has designated as confidential. Where a party to a dispute submits a confidential version of its written submissions to the panel, it shall also, upon request of a Member, provide a non-confidential summary of the information contained in its submissions that could be disclosed to the public.

4. Before the first substantive meeting of the panel with the parties, the parties to the dispute shall transmit to the panel written submissions in which they present the facts of the case and their arguments.

5. At its first substantive meeting with the parties, the panel shall ask the party which has brought the complaint to present its case. Subsequently, and still at the same meeting, the party against which the complaint has been brought shall be asked to present its point of view.

6. All third parties which have notified their interest in the dispute to the DSB shall be invited in writing to present their views during a session of the first substantive meeting of the panel set aside for that purpose. All such third parties may be present during the entirety of this session.

7. Formal rebuttals shall be made at a second substantive meeting of the panel. The party complained against shall have the right to take the floor first to be followed by

the complaining party. The parties shall submit, prior to that meeting, written rebuttals to the panel.

8. The panel may at any time put questions to the parties and ask them for explanations either in the course of a meeting with the parties or in writing.

9. The parties to the dispute and any third party invited to present its views in accordance with Article 10 shall make available to the panel a written version of their oral statements.

10. In the interest of full transparency, the presentations, rebuttals and statements referred to in paragraphs 5 to 9 shall be made in the presence of the parties. Moreover, each party's written submissions, including any comments on the descriptive part of the report and responses to questions put by the panel, shall be made available to the other party or parties.

11. Any additional procedures specific to the panel.

12. Proposed timetable for panel work:

(a)	Receipt of first written submissions of the parties:		
	(1) complaining Party:	_______	3-6 weeks
	(2) Party complained against:	_______	2-3 weeks
(b)	Date, time and place of first substantive meeting with the parties: third party session:	_______	1-2 weeks
(c)	Receipt of written rebuttals of the parties:	_______	2-3 weeks
(d)	Date, time and place of second substantive meeting with the parties:	_______	1-2 weeks
(e)	Issuance of descriptive part of the report to the parties:	_______	2-4 weeks
(f)	Receipt of comments by the parties on the descriptive part of the report:	_______	2 weeks
(g)	Issuance of the interim report, including the findings and conclusions, to the parties:	_______	2-4 weeks
(h)	Deadline for party to request review of part(s) of report:	_______	1 week
(i)	Period of review by panel, including possible additional meeting with parties:	_______	2 weeks
(j)	Issuance of final report to parties to dispute:	_______	2 weeks

(k) Circulation of the final report to the Members: _______ 3 weeks

The above calendar may be changed in the light of unforeseen developments. Additional meetings with the parties shall be scheduled if required.

Appendix 4

Expert Review Groups

The following rules and procedures shall apply to expert review groups established in accordance with the provisions of paragraph 2 of Article 13.

1. Expert review groups are under the panel's authority. Their terms of reference and detailed working procedures shall be decided by the panel, and they shall report to the panel.

2. Participation in expert review groups shall be restricted to persons of professional standing and experience in the field in question.

3. Citizens of parties to the dispute shall not serve on an expert review group without the joint agreement of the parties to the dispute, except in exceptional circumstances when the panel considers that the need for specialized scientific expertise cannot be fulfilled otherwise. Government officials of parties to the dispute shall not serve on an expert review group. Members of expert review groups shall serve in their individual capacities and not as government representatives, nor as representatives of any organization. Governments or organizations shall therefore not give them instructions with regard to matters before an expert review group.

4. Expert review groups may consult and seek information and technical advice from any source they deem appropriate. Before an expert review group seeks such information or advice from a source within the jurisdiction of a Member, it shall inform the government of that Member. Any Member shall respond promptly and fully to any request by an expert review group for such information as the expert review group considers necessary and appropriate.

5. The parties to a dispute shall have access to all relevant information provided to an expert review group, unless it is of a confidential nature. Confidential information provided to the expert review group shall not be released without formal authorization from the government, organization or person providing the information. Where such information is requested from the expert review group but release of such information

by the expert review group is not authorized, a non-confidential summary of the information will be provided by the government, organization or person supplying the information.

6. The expert review group shall submit a draft report to the parties to the dispute with a view to obtaining their comments, and taking them into account, as appropriate, in the final report, which shall also be issued to the parties to the dispute when it is submitted to the panel. The final report of the expert review group shall be advisory only.

Appendix B

Working Procedures for Appellate Review

Definitions

I. In these *Working Procedures for Appellate Review,*

"appellant"

means any party to the dispute that has filed a Notice of Appeal pursuant to Rule 20 or has filed a submission pursuant to paragraph 1 of Rule 23;

"appellate report"

means an Appellate Body report as described in Article 17 of the *DSU*;

"appellee"

means any party to the dispute that has filed a submission pursuant to Rule 22 or paragraph 3 of Rule 23;

"consensus"

a decision is deemed to be made by consensus if no Member formally objects to it;

"covered agreements"

has the same meaning as "covered agreements" in paragraph 1 of Article 1 of the *DSU*;

"division"

means the three Members who are selected to serve on any one appeal in accordance with paragraph 1 of Article 17 of the *DSU* and paragraph 2 of Rule 6;

"documents"

means the Notice of Appeal and the submissions and other written statements presented by the participants;

"DSB"

means the Dispute Settlement Body established under Article 2 of the *DSU*;

"DSU"

means the *Understanding on Rules and Procedures Governing the Settlement of Disputes* which is Annex 2 to the *WTO Agreement*;

"Member"

means a Member of the Appellate Body who has been appointed by the DSB in accordance with Article 17 of the *DSU*;

"participant"

means any party to the dispute that has filed a Notice of Appeal pursuant to Rule 20 or a submission pursuant to Rule 22 or paragraphs 1 or 3 of Rule 23;

"party to the dispute"

means any WTO Member who was a complaining or defending party in the panel dispute, but does not include a third party;

"proof of service"

means a letter or other written acknowledgement that a document has been delivered, as required, to the parties to the dispute, participants, third parties or third participants, as the case may be;

"Rules"

means these *Working Procedures for Appellate Review*;

"Rules of Conduct"

means the *Rules of Conduct for the Understanding on Rules and Procedures Governing the Settlement of Disputes* as attached in Annex II to these Rules;

"SCM Agreement"

means the *Agreement on Subsidies and Countervailing Measures* which is in Annex 1A to the *WTO Agreement*;

"Secretariat"

means the Appellate Body Secretariat;

"service address"

means the address of the party to the dispute, participant, third party or third participant as generally used in WTO dispute settlement proceedings, unless the party to the dispute, participant, third party or third participant has clearly indicated another address;

"third participant"
means any third party that has filed a submission pursuant to Rule 24;

"third party"
means any WTO Member who has notified the DSB of its substantial interest in the matter before the panel pursuant to paragraph 2 of Article 10 of the *DSU*;

"WTO"
means the World Trade Organization;

"*WTO Agreement*"
means the *Marrakesh Agreement Establishing the World Trade Organization*, done at Marrakesh, Morocco on 15 April 1994;

"WTO Member"
means any State or separate customs territory possessing full autonomy in the conduct of its external commercial relations that has accepted or acceded to the WTO in accordance with Articles XI, XII or XIV of the *WTO Agreement*; and

"WTO Secretariat"
means the Secretariat of the World Trade Organization.

Part I
Members

Duties and Responsibilities

II. (1) A Member shall abide by the terms and conditions of the *DSU*, these Rules and any decisions of the DSB affecting the Appellate Body.

(2) During his/her term, a Member shall not accept any employment nor pursue any professional activity that is inconsistent with his/her duties and responsibilities.

(3) A Member shall exercise his/her office without accepting or seeking instructions from any international, governmental, or non-governmental organization or any private source.

(4) A Member shall be available at all times and on short notice and, to this end, shall keep the Secretariat informed of his/her whereabouts at all times.

Decision-Making

III. (1) In accordance with paragraph 1 of Article 17 of the *DSU*, decisions relating to an appeal shall be taken solely by the division assigned to that appeal. Other decisions shall be taken by the Appellate Body as a whole.

(2) The Appellate Body and its divisions shall make every effort to take their decisions by consensus. Where, nevertheless, a decision cannot be arrived at by consensus, the matter at issue shall be decided by a majority vote.

Collegiality

IV. (1) To ensure consistency and coherence in decision-making, and to draw on the individual and collective expertise of the Members, the Members shall convene on a regular basis to discuss matters of policy, practice and procedure.

(2) The Members shall stay abreast of dispute settlement activities and other relevant activities of the WTO and, in particular, each Member shall receive all documents filed in an appeal.

(3) In accordance with the objectives set out in paragraph 1, the division responsible for deciding each appeal shall exchange views with the other Members before the division finalizes the appellate report for circulation to the WTO Members. This paragraph is subject to paragraphs 2 and 3 of Rule 11.

(4) Nothing in these Rules shall be interpreted as interfering with a division's full authority and freedom to hear and decide an appeal assigned to it in accordance with paragraph 1 of Article 17 of the *DSU*.

Chairman

V. (1) There shall be a Chairman of the Appellate Body who shall be elected by the Members.

(2) The first Chairman of the Appellate Body shall have a term of office of two years. Thereafter, the term of office of the Chairman shall be one year. In order to ensure rotation of the Chairmanship, no Member shall serve as Chairman for more than one term consecutively.

(3) The Chairman shall be responsible for the overall direction of the Appellate Body business, and in particular, his/her responsibilities shall include:

(a) the supervision of the internal functioning of the Appellate Body; and

(b) any such other duties as the Members may agree to entrust to him/her.

(4) Where the office of the Chairman becomes vacant due to permanent incapacity as a result of illness or death or by resignation or expiration of his/her term, the Members shall elect a new Chairman who shall serve a full term in accordance with paragraph 2.

(5) In the event of a temporary absence or incapacity of the Chairman, the Appellate Body shall authorize another Member to act as Chairman *ad interim*, and the Member so authorized shall temporarily exercise all the powers, duties and functions of the Chairman until the Chairman is capable of resuming his/her functions.

Divisions

VI. (1) In accordance with paragraph 1 of Article 17 of the *DSU*, a division consisting of three Members shall be established to hear and decide an appeal.

(2) The Members constituting a division shall be selected on the basis of rotation, while taking into account the principles of random selection, unpredictability and opportunity for all Members to serve regardless of their national origin.

(3) A Member selected pursuant to paragraph 2 to serve on a division shall serve on that division, unless:

(i) he/she is excused from that division pursuant to Rules 9 or 10;
(ii) he/she has notified the Chairman and the Presiding Member that he/she is prevented from serving on the division because of illness or other serious reasons pursuant to Rule 12; or
(iii) he/she has notified his/her intentions to resign pursuant to Rule 14.

Presiding Member of the Division

VII. (1) Each division shall have a Presiding Member, who shall be elected by the Members of that division.

(2) The responsibilities of the Presiding Member shall include:

(a) coordinating the overall conduct of the appeal proceeding;
(b) chairing all oral hearings and meetings related to that appeal; and
(c) coordinating the drafting of the appellate report.

(3) In the event that a Presiding Member becomes incapable of performing his/her duties, the other Members serving on that division and the Member selected as a replacement pursuant to Rule 13 shall elect one of their number to act as the Presiding Member.

Rules of Conduct

VIII. (1) On a provisional basis, the Appellate Body adopts those provisions of the *Rules of Conduct for the Understanding on Rules and Procedures Governing the Settlement of Disputes*, attached in Annex II to these Rules, which are applicable to it, until *Rules of Conduct* are approved by the DSB.

(2) Upon approval of *Rules of Conduct* by the DSB, such *Rules of Conduct* shall be directly incorporated and become part of these Rules and shall supersede Annex II.

IX. (1) Upon the filing of a Notice of Appeal, each Member shall take the steps set out in Article VI:4(b)(i) of Annex II, and a Member may consult with the other Members prior to completing the disclosure form.

(2) Upon the filing of a Notice of Appeal, the professional staff of the Secretariat assigned to that appeal shall take the steps set out in Article VI:4(b)(ii) of Annex II.

(3) Where information has been submitted pursuant to Article VI:4(b)(i) or (ii) of Annex II, the Appellate Body shall consider whether further action is necessary.

(4) As a result of the Appellate Body's consideration of the matter pursuant to paragraph 3, the Member or the professional staff member concerned may continue to be assigned to the division or may be excused from the division.

X. (1) Where evidence of a material violation is filed by a participant pursuant to Article VIII of Annex II, such evidence shall be confidential and shall be supported by affidavits made by persons having actual knowledge or a reasonable belief as to the truth of the facts stated.

(2) Any evidence filed pursuant to Article VIII:1 of Annex II shall be filed at the earliest practicable time: that is, forthwith after the participant submitting it knew or reasonably could have known of the facts supporting it. In no case shall such evidence be filed after the appellate report is circulated to the WTO Members.

(3) Where a participant fails to submit such evidence at the earliest practicable time, it shall file an explanation in writing of the reasons why it did not do so earlier, and the Appellate Body may decide to consider or not to consider such evidence, as appropriate.

(4) While taking fully into account paragraph 5 of Article 17 of the *DSU*, where evidence has been filed pursuant to Article VIII of Annex II, an appeal shall be suspended for fifteen days or until the procedure referred to in Article VIII:14-16 of Annex II is completed, whichever is earlier.

(5) As a result of the procedure referred to in Article VIII:14-16 of Annex II, the Appellate Body may decide to dismiss the allegation, to excuse the Member or professional staff member concerned from being assigned to the division or make such other order as it deems necessary in accordance with Article VIII of Annex II.

XI. (1) A Member who has submitted a disclosure form with information attached pursuant to Article VI:4(b)(i) or is the subject of evidence of a material violation pursuant to Article VIII:1 of Annex II, shall not participate in any decision taken pursuant to paragraph 4 of Rule 9 or paragraph 5 of Rule 10.

(2) A Member who is excused from a division pursuant to paragraph 4 of Rule 9 or paragraph 5 of Rule 10 shall not take part in the exchange of views conducted in that appeal pursuant to paragraph 3 of Rule 4.

(3) A Member who, had he/she been a Member of a division, would have been excused from that division pursuant to paragraph 4 of Rule 9, shall not take part in the exchange of views conducted in that appeal pursuant to paragraph 3 of Rule 4.

Incapacity

XII. (1) A Member who is prevented from serving on a division by illness or for other serious reasons shall give notice and duly explain such reasons to the Chairman and to the Presiding Member.

(2) Upon receiving such notice, the Chairman and the Presiding Member shall forthwith inform the Appellate Body.

Replacement

XIII. Where a Member is unable to serve on a division for a reason set out in paragraph 3 of Rule 6, another Member shall be selected forthwith pursuant to paragraph 2 of Rule 6 to replace the Member originally selected for that division.

Resignation

XIV. (1) A Member who intends to resign from his/her office shall notify his/her intentions in writing to the Chairman of the Appellate Body who shall immediately inform the Chairman of the DSB, the Director-General and the other Members of the Appellate Body.

(2) The resignation shall take effect 90 days after the notification has been made pursuant to paragraph 1, unless the DSB, in consultation with the Appellate Body, decides otherwise.

Transition

XV. A person who ceases to be a Member of the Appellate Body may, with the authorization of the Appellate Body and upon notification to the DSB, complete the disposition of any appeal to which that person was assigned while a Member, and that person shall, for that purpose only, be deemed to continue to be a Member of the Appellate Body.

Part II
Process

General Provisions

XVI. (1) In the interests of fairness and orderly procedure in the conduct of an appeal, where a procedural question arises that is not covered by these Rules, a division may adopt an appropriate procedure for the purposes of that appeal only, provided that it is not inconsistent with the *DSU*, the other covered agreements and these Rules. Where such a procedure is adopted, the Division shall immediately notify the participants and third participants in the appeal as well as the other Members of the Appellate Body.

(2) In exceptional circumstances, where strict adherence to a time period set out in these Rules would result in a manifest unfairness, a party to the dispute, a participant, a third party or a third participant may request that a division modify a time period set out in these Rules for the filing of documents or the date set out in the working schedule for the oral hearing. Where such a request is granted by a division, any modification of time shall be notified to the parties to the dispute, participants, third parties and third participants in a revised working schedule.

XVII. (1) Unless the DSB decides otherwise, in computing any time period stipulated in the *DSU* or in the special or additional provisions of the covered agreements, or in these Rules, within which a communication must be made or an action taken by a WTO Member to exercise or preserve its rights, the day from which the time period begins to run shall be excluded and, subject to paragraph 2, the last day of the time-period shall be included.

(2) The DSB Decision on "Expiration of Time-Periods in the *DSU*", WT/DSB/M/7, shall apply to appeals heard by divisions of the Appellate Body.

Documents

XVIII. (1) No document is considered filed with the Appellate Body unless the document is received by the Secretariat within the time period set out for filing in accordance with these Rules.

(2) Except as otherwise provided in these Rules, every document filed by a party to the dispute, a participant, a third party or a third participant shall be served on each of the other parties to the dispute, participants, third parties and third participants in the appeal.

(3) A proof of service on the other parties to the dispute, participants, third parties and third participants shall appear on, or be affixed to, each document filed with the Secretariat under paragraph 1 above.

(4) A document shall be served by the most expeditious means of delivery or communication available, including by:

(a) delivering a copy of the document to the service address of the party to the dispute, participant, third party or third participant; or

(b) sending a copy of the document to the service address of the party to the dispute, participant, third party or third participant by facsimile transmission, expedited delivery courier or expedited mail service.

(5) Upon authorization by the division, a participant or a third participant may correct clerical errors in any of its submissions. Such correction shall be made within 3 days of the filing of the original submission and a copy of the revised version shall be filed with the Secretariat and served upon the other participants and third participants.

Ex Parte Communications

XIX. (1) Neither a division nor any of its Members shall meet with or contact one participant or third participant in the absence of the other participants and third participants.

(2) No Member of the division may discuss any aspect of the subject matter of an appeal with any participant or third participant in the absence of the other Members of the division.

(3) A Member who is not assigned to the division hearing the appeal shall not discuss any aspect of the subject matter of the appeal with any participant or third participant.

Commencement of Appeal

XX. (1) An appeal shall be commenced by notification in writing to the DSB in accordance with paragraph 4 of Article 16 of the *DSU* and simultaneous filing of a Notice of Appeal with the Secretariat.

(2) A Notice of Appeal shall include the following information:

(a) the title of the panel report under appeal;
(b) the name of the party to the dispute filing the Notice of Appeal;
(c) the service address, telephone and facsimile numbers of the party to the dispute; and
(d) a brief statement of the nature of the appeal, including the allegations of errors in the issues of law covered in the panel report and legal interpretations developed by the panel.

Appellant's Submission

XXI. (1) The appellant shall, within 10 days after the date of the filing of the Notice of Appeal, file with the Secretariat a written submission prepared in accordance with paragraph 2 and serve a copy of the submission on the other parties to the dispute and third parties.

(2) A written submission referred to in paragraph 1 shall

(a) be dated and signed by the appellant; and
(b) set out

(i) a precise statement of the grounds for the appeal, including the specific allegations of errors in the issues of law covered in the panel report and legal interpretations developed by the panel, and the legal arguments in support thereof;
(ii) a precise statement of the provisions of the covered agreements and other legal sources relied on; and
(iii) the nature of the decision or ruling sought.

Appellee's Submission

XXII. (1) Any party to the dispute that wishes to respond to allegations raised in an appellant's submission filed pursuant to Rule 21 may, within 25 days after the date of the filing of the Notice of Appeal, file with the Secretariat a written submission prepared in accordance with paragraph 2 and serve a copy of the submission on the appellant, other parties to the dispute and third parties.

(2) A written submission referred to in paragraph 1 shall

(a) be dated and signed by the appellee; and
(b) set out

(i) a precise statement of the grounds for opposing the specific allegations of errors in the issues of law covered in the panel report and legal interpretations developed by the panel raised in the appellant's submission, and the legal arguments in support thereof;
(ii) an acceptance of, or opposition to, each ground set out in the appellant's submission;

(iii) a precise statement of the provisions of the covered agreements and other legal sources relied on; and

(iv) the nature of the decision or ruling sought.

Multiple Appeals

XXIII. (1) Within 15 days after the date of the filing of the Notice of Appeal, a party to the dispute other than the original appellant may join in that appeal or appeal on the basis of other alleged errors in the issues of law covered in the panel report and legal interpretations developed by the panel.

(2) Any written submission made pursuant to paragraph 1 shall be in the format required by paragraph 2 of Rule 21.

(3) The appellant, any appellee and any other party to the dispute that wishes to respond to a submission filed pursuant to paragraph 1 may file a written submission within 25 days after the date of the filing of the Notice of Appeal, and any such submission shall be in the format required by paragraph 2 of Rule 22.

(4) This Rule does not preclude a party to the dispute which has not filed a submission under Rule 21 or paragraph 1 of this Rule from exercising its right of appeal pursuant to paragraph 4 of Article 16 of the *DSU*.

(5) Where a party to the dispute which has not filed a submission under Rule 21 or paragraph 1 of this Rule exercises its right to appeal as set out in paragraph 4, a single division shall examine the appeals.

Third Participants

XXIV. Any third party may file a written submission, stating its intention to participate as a third participant in the appeal and containing the grounds and legal arguments in support of its position, within 25 days after the date of the filing of the Notice of Appeal.

Transmittal of Record

XXV. (1) Upon the filing of a Notice of Appeal, the Director-General of the WTO shall transmit forthwith to the Appellate Body the complete record of the panel proceeding.

(2) The complete record of the panel proceeding includes, but is not limited to:

(i) written submissions, rebuttal submissions, and supporting evidence attached thereto by the parties to the dispute and the third parties;

(ii) written arguments submitted at the panel meetings with the parties to the dispute and the third parties, the recordings of such panel meetings, and any written answers to questions posed at such panel meetings;

(iii) the correspondence relating to the panel dispute between the panel or the WTO Secretariat and the parties to the dispute or the third parties; and

(iv) any other documentation submitted to the panel.

Working Schedule

XXVI. (1) Forthwith after the commencement of an appeal, the division shall draw up an appropriate working schedule for that appeal in accordance with the time periods stipulated in these Rules.

(2) The working schedule shall set forth precise dates for the filing of documents and a timetable for the division's work, including where possible, the date for the oral hearing.

(3) In accordance with paragraph 9 of Article 4 of the *DSU*, in appeals of urgency, including those which concern perishable goods, the Appellate Body shall make every effort to accelerate the appellate proceedings to the greatest extent possible. A division shall take this into account in drawing up its working schedule for that appeal.

(4) The Secretariat shall serve forthwith a copy of the working schedule on the appellant, the parties to the dispute and any third parties.

Oral Hearing

XXVII. (1) A division shall hold an oral hearing, which shall be held, as a general rule, 30 days after the date of the filing of the Notice of Appeal.

(2) Where possible in the working schedule or otherwise at the earliest possible date, the Secretariat shall notify all parties to the dispute, participants, third parties and third participants of the date for the oral hearing.

(3) Any third participant who has filed a submission pursuant to Rule 24 may appear to make oral arguments or presentations at the oral hearing.

(4) The Presiding Member may, as necessary, set time-limits for oral arguments and presentations.

Written Responses

XXVIII. (1) At any time during the appellate proceeding, including, in particular, during the oral hearing, the division may address questions orally or in writing to, or request additional memoranda from, any participant or third participant, and specify the time periods by which written responses or memoranda shall be received.

(2) Any such questions, responses or memoranda shall be made available to the other participants and third participants in the appeal, who shall be given an opportunity to respond.

Failure to Appear

XXIX. Where a participant fails to file a submission within the required time periods or fails to appear at the oral hearing, the division shall, after hearing the views of the participants, issue such order, including dismissal of the appeal, as it deems appropriate.

Withdrawal of Appeal

XXX. (1) At any time during an appeal, the appellant may withdraw its appeal by notifying the Appellate Body, which shall forthwith notify the DSB.

(2) Where a mutually agreed solution to a dispute which is the subject of an appeal has been notified to the DSB pursuant to paragraph 6 of Article 3 of the *DSU*, it shall be notified to the Appellate Body.

Prohibited Subsidies

XXXI. (1) Subject to Article 4 of the *SCM Agreement*, the general provisions of these Rules shall apply to appeals relating to panel reports concerning prohibited subsidies under Part II of that *Agreement*.

(2) The working schedule for an appeal involving prohibited subsidies under Part II of the *SCM Agreement* shall be as set out in Annex I to these Rules.

Entry into Force and Amendment

XXXII. (1) These Rules shall enter into force on 15 February 1996.

(2) The Appellate Body may amend these Rules in compliance with the procedures set forth in paragraph 9 of Article 17 of the *DSU*.

(3) Whenever there is an amendment to the *DSU* or to the special or additional rules and procedures of the covered agreements, the Appellate Body shall examine whether amendments to these Rules are necessary.

ANNEX I

TIMETABLE FOR APPEALS

	General Appeals Day	*Prohibited Subsidies Appeals* Day
Notice of Appeal[1]	0	0
Appellant's Submission[2]	10	5
Other Appellant(s) Submission(s)[3]	15	7
Appellee(s) Submission(s)[4]	25	12
Third Participant(s) Submission(s)[5]	25	12
Oral Hearing[6]	30	15
Circulation of Appellate Report	60–90[7]	30–60[8]
DSB Meeting for Adoption	90–120[9]	50–80[10]

ANNEX II

RULES OF CONDUCT FOR THE UNDERSTANDING ON RULES AND PROCEDURES GOVERNING THE SETTLEMENT OF DISPUTES

I. Preamble

Members,

Recalling that on 15 April 1994 in Marrakesh, Ministers welcomed the stronger and clearer legal framework they had adopted for the conduct of international trade, including a more effective and reliable dispute settlement mechanism;

Recognizing the importance of full adherence to the Understanding on Rules and Procedures Governing the Settlement of Disputes ("DSU") and the principles for the

[1]Rule XX.

[2]Rule XXI.

[3]Rule XXIII(1).

[4]Rules XXII and XXIII(3).

[5]Rule XXIV.

[6]Rule XXVII.

[7]Article 17:5, *DSU.*

[8]Article 4:9, *SCM Agreement.*

[9]Article 17:14, *DSU.*

[10]Article 4:9, *SCM Agreement.*

management of disputes applied under Articles XXII and XXIII of GATT 1947, as further elaborated and modified by the DSU;

Affirming that the operation of the DSU would be strengthened by rules of conduct designed to maintain the integrity, impartiality and confidentiality of proceedings conducted under the DSU thereby enhancing confidence in the new dispute settlement mechanism;

Hereby establish the following Rules of Conduct.

II. Governing Principle

1. Each person covered by these Rules (as defined in paragraph 1 of Section IV below and hereinafter called "covered person") shall be independent and impartial, shall avoid direct or indirect conflicts of interest and shall respect the confidentiality of proceedings of bodies pursuant to the dispute settlement mechanism, so that through the observance of such standards of conduct the integrity and impartiality of that mechanism are preserved. These Rules shall in no way modify the rights and obligations of Members under the DSU nor the rules and procedures therein.

III. Observance of the Governing Principle

1. To ensure the observance of the Governing Principle of these Rules, each covered person is expected (1) to adhere strictly to the provisions of the DSU; (2) to disclose the existence or development of any interest, relationship or matter that that person could reasonably be expected to know and that is likely to affect, or give rise to justifiable doubts as to, that person's independence or impartiality; and (3) to take due care in the performance of their duties to fulfil these expectations, including through avoidance of any direct or indirect conflicts of interest in respect of the subject matter of the proceedings.

2. Pursuant to the Governing Principle, each covered person, shall be independent and impartial, and shall maintain confidentiality. Moreover, such persons shall consider only issues raised in, and necessary to fulfil their responsibilities within, the dispute settlement proceeding and shall not delegate this responsibility to any other person. Such person shall not incur any obligation or accept any benefit that would in anyway interfere with, or which could give rise to, justifiable doubts as to the proper performance of that person's dispute settlement duties.

IV. Scope

1. These Rules shall apply, as specified in the text, to each person serving: (a) on a panel; (b) on the Standing Appellate Body; (c) as an arbitrator pursuant to the provisions mentioned in Annex "1a"; or (d) as an expert participating in the dispute settlement mechanism pursuant to the provisions mentioned in Annex "1b". These Rules

shall also apply, as specified in this text and the relevant provisions of the Staff Regulations, to those members of the Secretariat called upon to assist the panel in accordance with Article 27.1 of the DSU or to assist in formal arbitration proceedings pursuant to Annex "1a"; to the Chairman of the Textiles Monitoring Body (hereinafter called "TMB") and other members of the TMB Secretariat called upon to assist the TMB in formulating recommendations, findings or observations pursuant to the WTO Agreement on Textiles and Clothing; and to Standing Appellate Body support staff called upon to provide the Standing Appellate Body with administrative or legal support in accordance with Article 17.7 of the DSU (hereinafter "Member of the Secretariat or Standing Appellate Body support staff"), reflecting their acceptance of established norms regulating the conduct of such persons as international civil servants and the Governing Principle of these Rules.

2. The application of these Rules shall not in any way impede the Secretariat's discharge of its responsibility to continue to respond to Members' requests for assistance and information.

3. These Rules shall apply to the members of the TMB to the extent prescribed in Section V.

V. Textiles Monitoring Body

1. Members of the TMB shall discharge their functions on an *ad personam* basis, in accordance with the requirement of Article 8.1 of the Agreement on Textiles and Clothing, as further elaborated in the working procedures of the TMB, so as to preserve the integrity and impartiality of its proceedings.[11]

[11] These working procedures, as adopted by the TMB on 26 July 1995 (G/TMB/R/1), currently include, *inter alia*, the following language in paragraph 1.4: "In discharging their functions in accordance with paragraph 1.1 above, the TMB members and alternates shall undertake not to solicit, accept or act upon instructions from governments, nor to be influenced by any other organisations or undue extraneous factors. They shall disclose to the Chairman any information that they may consider likely to impede their capacity to discharge their functions on an *ad personam* basis. Should serious doubts arise during the deliberations of the TMB regarding the ability of a TMB member to act on an *ad personam* basis, they shall be communicated to the Chairman. The Chairman shall deal with the particular matter as necessary".

VI. *Self-Disclosure Requirements by Covered Persons*

1. (a) Each person requested to serve on a panel, on the Standing Appellate Body, as an arbitrator, or as an expert shall, at the time of the request, receive from the Secretariat these Rules, which include an Illustrative List (Annex 2) of examples of the matters subject to disclosure.

   (b) Any member of the Secretariat described in paragraph IV:1, who may expect to be called upon to assist in a dispute, and Standing Appellate Body support staff, shall be familiar with these Rules.

2. As set out in paragraph VI:4 below, all covered persons described in paragraph VI.1(a) and VI.1(b) shall disclose any information that could reasonably be expected to be known to them at the time which, coming within the scope of the Governing Principle of these Rules, is likely to affect or give rise to justifiable doubts as to their independence or impartiality. These disclosures include the type of information described in the Illustrative List, if relevant.

3. These disclosure requirements shall not extend to the identification of matters whose relevance to the issues to be considered in the proceedings would be insignificant. They shall take into account the need to respect the personal privacy of those to whom these Rules apply and shall not be so administratively burdensome as to make it impracticable for otherwise qualified persons to serve on panels, the Standing Appellate Body, or in other dispute settlement roles.

4. (a) All panelists, arbitrators and experts, prior to confirmation of their appointment, shall complete the form at Annex 3 of these Rules. Such information would be disclosed to the Chair of the Dispute Settlement Body ("DSB") for consideration by the parties to the dispute.

   (b) (i) Persons serving on the Standing Appellate Body who, through rotation, are selected to hear the appeal of a particular panel case, shall review the factual portion of the Panel report and complete the form at Annex 3. Such information would be disclosed to the Standing Appellate Body for its consideration whether the member concerned should hear a particular appeal.

   (ii) Standing Appellate Body support staff shall disclose any relevant matter to the Standing Appellate Body, for its consideration in deciding on the assignment of staff to assist in a particular appeal.

   (c) When considered to assist in a dispute, members of the Secretariat shall disclose to the Director-General of the WTO the information required under paragraph VI:2 of these Rules and any other relevant information required under the Staff Regulations, including the information described in the footnote.**

5. During a dispute, each covered person shall also disclose any new information relevant to paragraph VI:2 above at the earliest time they become aware of it.

6. The Chair of the DSB, the Secretariat, parties to the dispute, and other individuals involved in the dispute settlement mechanism shall maintain the confidentiality of any information revealed through this disclosure process, even after the panel process and its enforcement procedures, if any, are completed.

VII. Confidentiality

1. Each covered person shall at all times maintain the confidentiality of dispute settlement deliberations and proceedings together with any information identified by a party as confidential. No covered person shall at any time use such information acquired during such deliberations and proceedings to gain personal advantage or advantage for others.

2. During the proceedings, no covered person shall engage in *ex parte* contacts concerning matters under consideration. Subject to paragraph VII:1, no covered person shall make any statements on such proceedings or the issues in dispute in which that person is participating, until the report of the panel or the Standing Appellate Body has been derestricted.

**Pending adoption of the Staff Regulations, members of the Secretariat shall make disclosures to the Director-General in accordance with the following draft provision to be included in the Staff Regulations:

"When paragraph VI:4(c) of the Rules of Conduct for the DSU is applicable, members of the Secretariat would disclose to the Director-General of the WTO the information required in paragraph VI:2 of those Rules, as well as any information regarding their participation in earlier formal consideration of the specific measure at issue in a dispute under any provisions of the WTO Agreement, including through formal legal advice under Article 27.2 of the DSU, as well as any involvement with the dispute as an official of a WTO Member government or otherwise professionally, before having joined the Secretariat.

The Director-General shall consider any such disclosures in deciding on the assignment of members of the Secretariat to assist in a dispute.

When the Director-General, in the light of his consideration, including of available Secretariat resources, decides that a potential conflict of interest is not sufficiently material to warrant non-assignment of a particular member of the Secretariat to assist in a dispute, the Director-General shall inform the panel of his decision and of the relevant supporting information."

VIII. Procedures Concerning Subsequent Disclosure and Possible Material Violations

1. Any party to a dispute, conducted pursuant to the WTO Agreement, who possesses or comes into possession of evidence of a material violation of the obligations of independence, impartiality or confidentiality or the avoidance of direct or indirect conflicts of interest by covered persons which may impair the integrity, impartiality or confidentiality of the dispute settlement mechanism, shall at the earliest possible time and on a confidential basis, submit such evidence to the Chair of the DSB, the Director-General or the Standing Appellate Body, as appropriate according to the respective procedures detailed in paragraphs VIII:5 to VIII:17 below, in a written statement specifying the relevant facts and circumstances. Other Members who possess or come into possession of such evidence, may provide such evidence to the parties to the dispute in the interest of maintaining the integrity and impartiality of the dispute settlement mechanism.

2. When evidence as described in paragraph VIII:1 is based on an alleged failure of a covered person to disclose a relevant interest, relationship or matter, that failure to disclose, as such, shall not be a sufficient ground for disqualification unless there is also evidence of a material violation of the obligations of independence, impartiality, confidentiality or the avoidance of direct or indirect conflicts of interests and that the integrity, impartiality or confidentiality of the dispute settlement mechanism would be impaired thereby.

3. When such evidence is not provided at the earliest practicable time, the party submitting the evidence shall explain why it did not do so earlier and this explanation shall be taken into account in the procedures initiated in paragraph VIII:1.

4. Following the submission of such evidence to the Chair of the DSB, the Director-General of the WTO or the Standing Appellate Body, as specified below, the procedures outlined in paragraphs VIII:5 to VIII:17 below shall be completed within fifteen working days.

Panelists, Arbitrators, Experts

5. If the covered person who is the subject of the evidence is a panelist, an arbitrator or an expert, the party shall provide such evidence to the Chair of the DSB.

6. Upon receipt of the evidence referred to in paragraphs VIII:1 and VIII:2, the Chair of the DSB shall forthwith provide the evidence to the person who is the subject of such evidence, for consideration by the latter.

7. If, after having consulted with the person concerned, the matter is not resolved, the Chair of the DSB shall forthwith provide all the evidence, and any additional informa-

tion from the person concerned, to the parties to the dispute. If the person concerned resigns, the Chair of the DSB shall inform the parties to the dispute and, as the case may be, the panelists, the arbitrator(s) or experts.

8. In all cases, the Chair of the DSB, in consultation with the Director-General and a sufficient number of Chairs of the relevant Council or Councils to provide an odd number, and after having provided a reasonable opportunity for the views of the person concerned and the parties to the dispute to be heard, would decide whether a material violation of these Rules as referred to in paragraphs VIII:1 and VIII:2 above has occurred. Where the parties agree that a material violation of these Rules has occurred, it would be expected that, consistent with maintaining the integrity of the dispute settlement mechanism, the disqualification of the person concerned would be confirmed.

9. The person who is the subject of the evidence shall continue to participate in the consideration of the dispute unless it is decided that a material violation of these Rules has occurred.

10. The Chair of the DSB shall thereafter take the necessary steps for the appointment of the person who is the subject of the evidence to be formally revoked, or excused from the dispute as the case may be, as of that time.

Secretariat

11. If the covered person who is the subject of the evidence is a member of the Secretariat, the party shall only provide the evidence to the Director-General of the WTO, who shall forthwith provide the evidence to the person who is the subject of such evidence and shall further inform the other party or parties to the dispute and the panel.

12. It shall be for the Director-General to take any appropriate action in accordance with the Staff Regulations.***

13. The Director-General shall inform the parties to the dispute, the panel and the Chair of the DSB of his decision, together with relevant supporting information.

***Pending adoption of the Staff Regulations, the Director-General would act in accordance with the following draft provision for the Staff Regulations: "If paragraph VIII:11 of the Rules of Conduct for the DSU governing the settlement of disputes is invoked, the Director-General shall consult with the person who is the subject of the evidence and the panel and shall, if necessary, take appropriate disciplinary action".

Standing Appellate Body

14. If the covered person who is the subject of the evidence is a member of the Standing Appellate Body or of the Standing Appellate Body support staff, the party shall provide the evidence to the other party to the dispute and the evidence shall thereafter be provided to the Standing Appellate Body.

15. Upon receipt of the evidence referred to in paragraphs VIII:1 and VIII:2 above, the Standing Appellate Body shall forthwith provide it to the person who is the subject of such evidence, for consideration by the latter.

16. It shall be for the Standing Appellate Body to take any appropriate action after having provided a reasonable opportunity for the views of the person concerned and the parties to the dispute to be heard.

17. The Standing Appellate Body shall inform the parties to the dispute and the Chair of the DSB of its decision, together with relevant supporting information.

***

18. Following completion of the procedures in paragraphs VIII:5 to VIII:17, if the appointment of a covered person, other than a member of the Standing Appellate Body, is revoked or that person is excused or resigns, the procedures specified in the DSU for initial appointment shall be followed for appointment of a replacement, but the time periods shall be half those specified in the DSU.****The member of the Standing Appellate Body who, under that Body's rules, would next be selected through rotation to consider the dispute, would automatically be assigned to the appeal. The panel, members of the Standing Appellate Body hearing the appeal, or the arbitrator, as the case may be, may then decide after consulting with the parties to the dispute, on any necessary modifications to their working procedures or proposed timetable.

19. All covered persons and Members concerned shall resolve matters involving possible material violations of these Rules as expeditiously as possible so as not to delay the completion of proceedings, as provided in the DSU.

20. Except to the extent strictly necessary to carry out this decision, all information concerning possible or actual material violations of these Rules shall be kept confidential.

****Appropriate adjustments would be made in the case of appointments pursuant to the Agreement on Subsidies and Countervailing Measures.

IX. Review

1. These Rules of Conduct shall be reviewed within two years of their adoption and a decision shall be taken by the DSB as to whether to continue, modify or terminate these Rules.

ANNEX 1a

Arbitrators acting pursuant to the following provisions:

- Articles 21.3(c); 22.6 and 22.7; 26.1(c) and 25 of the DSU;
- Article 8.5 of the Agreement on Subsidies and Countervailing Measures;
- Articles XXI.3 and XXII.3 of the General Agreement on Trade in Services.

ANNEX 1b

Experts advising or providing information pursuant to the following provisions:

- Article 13.1; 13.2 of the DSU;
- Article 4.5 of the Agreement on Subsidies and Countervailing Measures;
- Article 11.2 of the Agreement on the Application of Sanitary and Phytosanitary Measures;
- Article 14.2; 14.3 of the Agreement on Technical Barriers to Trade.

ANNEX 2

ILLUSTRATIVE LIST OF INFORMATION TO BE DISCLOSED

This list contains examples of information of the type that a person called upon to serve in a dispute should disclose pursuant to the Rules of Conduct for the Understanding on Rules and Procedures Governing the Settlement of Disputes.

Each covered person, as defined in Section IV:1 of these Rules of Conduct has a continuing duty to disclose the information described in Section VI:2 of these Rules which may include the following:

(a) financial interests (e.g. investments, loans, shares, interests, other debts); business interests (e.g. directorship or other contractual interests); and property interests relevant to the dispute in question;

(b) professional interests (e.g. a past or present relationship with private clients, or any interests the person may have in domestic or international proceedings, and their implications, where these involve issues similar to those addressed in the dispute in question);
(c) other active interests (e.g. active participation in public interest groups or other organisations which may have a declared agenda relevant to the dispute in question);
(d) considered statements of personal opinion on issues relevant to the dispute in question (e.g. publications, public statements);
(e) employment or family interests (e.g. the possibility of any indirect advantage or any likelihood of pressure which could arise from their employer, business associates or immediate family members).

ANNEX 3

Dispute Number: ________

WORLD TRADE ORGANIZATION
DISCLOSURE FORM

I have read the Understanding on Rules and Procedures Governing the Settlement of Disputes (DSU) and the Rules of Conduct for the DSU. I understand my continuing duty, while participating in the dispute settlement mechanism, and until such time as the Dispute Settlement Body (DSB) makes a decision on adoption of a report relating to the proceeding or notes its settlement, to disclose herewith and in future any information likely to affect my independence or impartiality, or which could give rise to justifiable doubts as to the integrity and impartiality of the dispute settlement mechanism; and to respect my obligations regarding the confidentiality of dispute settlement proceedings.

Signed: Dated:

Appendix C

Draft Rules of Procedure for the Permanent Group of Experts

Revision

As indicated by the Chairman at the last meeting of the Committee on Subsidies and Countervailing Measures, the Permanent Group of Experts prepared a revised draft Rules of Procedure and requested that it be circulated in view of the meeting of the Committee on 26 July 1996.

DRAFT RULES OF PROCEDURE
FOR THE PERMANENT GROUP OF EXPERTS

PART I
DEFINITIONS

I. In these Rules of Procedure for the Permanent Group of Experts,

"SCM Agreement" means the Agreement on Subsidies and Countervailing Measures which is in Annex 1A to the WTO Agreement;

"SCM Committee" means the Committee on Subsidies and Countervailing Measures established by Article 24.1 of the SCM Agreement;

"DSB" means the Dispute Settlement Body established under Article 2 of the DSU;

"DSU" means the Understanding on Rules and Procedures Governing the Settlement of Disputes which is Annex 2 to the WTO Agreement;

"Expert" means a person elected by the SCM Committee to serve on the PGE in accordance with Article 24.3 of the SCM Agreement;

"party to the dispute" means any WTO Member who is a complaining or defending party in the panel dispute, but does not include a third party;

"PGE" means the Permanent Group of Experts established by the SCM Committee pursuant to Article 24.3 of the SCM Agreement;

"Rules" means these Rules of Procedure for the PGE;

"Secretariat" means the Secretariat of the World Trade Organization;

"third party" means any WTO Member who has notified the DSB of its substantial interest in the matter before the panel pursuant to paragraph 2 of Article 10 of the DSU;

"WTO" means the World Trade Organization;

"WTO Agreement" means the Marrakesh Agreement Establishing the World Trade Organization, done at Marrakesh, Morocco, on 15 April 1994;

~~"WTO Member" means any State or separate customs territory possessing full autonomy in the conduct of its external commercial relations that has accepted or acceded to the WTO in accordance with Articles XI, XII or XIV of the WTO Agreement.~~

PART II
EXPERTS

Duties and Responsibilities

II. (1) An Expert shall abide by the terms and conditions of the SCM Agreement, these Rules and any decisions of the SCM Committee affecting the PGE.

(2) An Expert shall exercise his/her office without accepting or seeking instructions from any international, governmental, or non-governmental organization or any private source.

(3) Whenever an Expert considers that his/her family relationships and/or past or present professional or financial activities are incompatible with his/her independent participation in a particular proceeding before the PGE, he/she shall immediately inform the Chairman of the PGE. The Chairman of the PGE shall exclude the Expert for that particular proceeding.

(4) Whenever an Expert has reasons to believe that his/her family relationships and/or past or present professional or financial activities may be incompatible with his/her independent participation in a particular proceeding before the PGE, he/she shall immediately inform the Chairman of the PGE. The Chairman of the PGE may, after consultation with the other Experts, excuse the Expert for that particular proceeding.

(5) An Expert shall keep the Secretariat informed on how to contact him/ ~~or~~ her.

(6) An Expert shall not communicate to any person or entity any unpublished information made known to him/her in the course of performing his/her duties as a member of the PGE, except upon authorization by the Director General of the WTO.

Chairman of the PGE

III. (1) There shall be a Chairman of the PGE who shall be elected by the Experts.

(2) The term of office of the Chairman of the PGE shall be one year. In order to ensure rotation of the Chairmanship, no Expert shall serve as Chairman for more than one term consecutively.

(3) The Chairman of the PGE shall be responsible for the overall direction of PGE business, and in particular, his/her responsibilities shall include:

(a) the supervision of the internal functioning of the PGE;

(b) such duties as are assigned to him/her under these Rules; and

(c) any other duties the Experts may agree to entrust to him/her.

(4) Where the office of the Chairman of the PGE becomes vacant due to permanent incapacity as a result of illness or death or by resignation or expiration of his/her term, the Experts shall elect a new Chairman who shall serve a full term in accordance with paragraph 2, but not exceeding the term of that Expert.

(5) In the event of a temporary unavailability or incapacity of the Chairman of the PGE, the PGE shall authorize another Expert to act as Chairman *ad interim*, and the Expert so authorized shall temporarily exercise all the powers, duties and functions of the Chairman of the PGE until the Chairman is capable of resuming his/her functions.

Incapacity

IV. (1) An Expert who is prevented from serving by reason of illness or for other serious reasons shall give notice and duly explain such reasons to the Chairman of the PGE.

(2) Upon receiving such notice, the Chairman of the PGE shall forthwith inform the SCM Committee.

Resignation

V. (1) An Expert who intends to resign from his/her office shall notify his/her intentions in writing to the Chairman of the PGE who shall immediately inform the Chairman of the SCM Committee and the other Experts.

(2) The resignation shall take effect 90 days after the notification has been made pursuant to paragraph 1, unless the SCM Committee decides otherwise.

PART III
ASSISTANCE TO PANELS

Commencement of Procedure

VI. (1) The PGE shall provide assistance at the request of a panel with respect to whether a measure is a prohibited subsidy, as provided in Article 4.5 of the SCM Agreement.

(2) The request for assistance should be made in writing, within ~~fourteen (14)~~ ten (10) days of the date of composition and establishment of the terms of reference of the panel, and should be directed to the Chairman of the PGE through the Secretariat.[1]

(3) The request should identify the measure(s) with respect to which the panel seeks the assistance of the PGE.

(4) The request should be accompanied by any relevant documentation, including any correspondence relating to the panel dispute between the panel or the WTO Secretariat and the parties to the dispute or the third parties and any other documentation submitted to the panel. It should also include the service address of each party to the dispute and third party, as notified to the Secretariat.

[1]The panel should immediately inform the parties to the dispute and third parties as well as the SCM Committee of its request for assistance to the PGE.

Collegiality

VII. (1) All conclusions shall be rendered on behalf of the PGE. Except where an Expert is excluded or excused pursuant to Rules 2(3), 2(4) or 19, conclusions of the PGE shall be deemed to be prepared and rendered collegially by the five Experts.

(2) Except where an Expert is excluded or excused pursuant to Rules 2(3) or 2(4), all five Experts shall contribute to the conclusions of the PGE on each request for assistance. However, where ~~appropriate~~ necessary, the Chairman of the PGE may, in ~~consultation~~ agreement with the other Experts, select three Experts to examine and respond to a request for assistance from a panel.

(3) The three Experts selected pursuant to paragraph 2 shall be selected on a basis which shall ensure, to the maximum extent possible, that the composition of each group of three Experts will not be predictable. The Chairman of the PGE may serve as one of the three Experts.

(4) An Expert selected pursuant to paragraph 2 ~~above~~ shall make best endeavours to be available for that service. In the event an Expert is prevented from serving on the basis of nationality pursuant to Rule 19, due to incapacity or resignation under Rules 4 and 5, or is otherwise unavailable to serve, the Chairman of the PGE will assign the next Expert on the basis set forth in paragraph 3.

(5) Where three Experts have been selected by the Chairman of the PGE pursuant to paragraph 2 or 4, they shall, in the interests of consistency and coherence, consult with the other Expert~~s~~(s) regarding the matter under review and shall circulate the report to the other Experts for comments before presenting it to the panel. Experts excused or excluded pursuant to Rules 2(3), ~~or~~ 2(4) or 19 shall not be consulted.

Presiding Member

VIII. (1) For each proceeding, the PGE or ~~E~~each group of three Experts appointed pursuant to Rule 7(2) above shall have a Presiding Member, who shall be elected by the members of the PGE or the members of the group of three Experts as the case may be ~~three Experts~~.

(2) The responsibilities of the Presiding Member shall include:

(a) coordinating the overall conduct of the proceeding;

(b) chairing all oral hearings and meetings related to that proceeding; and

(c) coordinating the drafting of the report.

(3) When a matter is referred to a group of three Experts, ~~I~~in the event that a Presiding Member becomes incapable of performing his/her duties, the other members ~~of the group of three Experts~~ and the member selected as a replacement pursuant to Rule 7(4) shall elect one of their number as Presiding Member.

Written Submissions

IX. (1) The parties to the dispute and any third parties so desiring shall, within seven (7) days after the date of a request for assistance, make a written submission to the PGE through the Secretariat and serve a copy of the submission on the other parties to the dispute and on any third parties.

(2) A written submission referred to in paragraph 1 shall address the issue whether the measure identified by the panel in its request for assistance is a prohibited subsidy. It shall contain any relevant information regarding the measure including any legislation, regulations or other documentation relating to the establishment and operation of the measure.

(3) Any parties to the dispute so desiring, but not third parties, may, within fourteen (14) days after the date of a request for assistance, make a written rebuttal submission to the PGE through the Secretariat and shall serve a copy of any such submission on the other parties to the dispute and on any third parties.

Oral Hearing

X. (1) The PGE or the group of three Experts selected pursuant to Rule 7~~(2)~~, as the case may be, may hold one oral hearing at the request of at least one of the parties to the dispute or on its own initiative. This hearing should be held, as a general rule, twenty-one (21) days after the request of the panel for assistance.

(2) The parties to the dispute shall, in the written submissions submitted pursuant to Rule 9(1), specify whether they request the PGE to hold an oral hear-

ing. When an oral hearing is to be held pursuant to paragraph 1, ~~requested or when the PGE or the group of three Experts decides of its own initiative to hold an oral hearing, the Chairman or~~ the Presiding Member ~~of a group of three Experts~~ shall, at the earliest possible date, notify all parties to the dispute and third parties of the date and place for the oral hearing.

(3) Any party to the dispute or third party who has made a submission pursuant to Rule 9(1) may appear to make an oral ~~arguments or~~ presentation~~s~~ at the oral hearing.

(4) During the oral hearing, each party to the dispute or third party referred to under paragraph 3 shall be entitled to make one ~~single~~ oral presentation ~~or submission of oral arguments~~ in the presence of the other parties to the dispute. The complaining party(ies) before the panel shall make its/their oral ~~arguments or~~ presentation(s) first. Third parties may attend the oral hearing only for the duration of their oral presentations ~~or submissions of oral arguments~~. The ~~Chairman or the~~ Presiding Member, with the agreement of the other members of the PGE or of the other members of the group of three Experts as the case may be, ~~of a group of three Experts, as the case may be,~~ may, as ~~necessary~~ appropriate, ~~set time limits~~ adapt the rules for oral ~~arguments and~~ presentations.

Written Responses

XI. (1) At any time during the proceeding, including during any oral hearing, the PGE or the group of three experts may address questions orally or in writing to any party to the dispute or third party, and specify the time periods within which written responses shall be received.

(2) Any such written questions and responses shall be ~~made available~~ served on ~~to~~ the other parties to the dispute, who shall be given an opportunity to respond.

Conclusions of the PGE

XII. (1) Except under the circumstances contemplated under Rule 13(1) or unless otherwise requested by the panel pursuant to Article 4.5 of the SCM Agreement, the PGE should present its conclusions to the panel within forty-~~two (42)~~ six (46) days of the request for assistance.

(2) The PGE's conclusions shall be presented in a written report. Pursuant to Article 4.5 of the SCM Agreement, t~~T~~he conclusions shall be restricted to a determination whether the measure in question is a prohibited subsidy.

(3) The PGE's report shall also set out a summary of the arguments presented by the parties and third parties, the findings of fact, the applicability of relevant provisions and the basic rationale behind its conclusions.

(4) When applicable, the PGE's report shall also specify whether one or more Experts were excused or excluded for the proceeding pursuant to Rules 2(3), ~~or~~ 2(4), or 19.

General Provisions

XIII. (1) In exceptional circumstances, where strict adherence to a time period set out in these Rules would result in a manifest unfairness, the PGE or the group of three Experts as the case may be may, at the request of a party to the dispute, modify a time period set out in these Rules for the filing of documents or the date set out in the working schedule for the oral hearing. Where such a request is granted, any modification of time shall be notified to the parties to the dispute and to third parties in a revised working schedule. Under those circumstances, the ~~Chairman of the PGE~~ Presiding Member may postpone the date of presentation of the report to the panel by a number of days to be agreed with the panel.

(2) In computing any time period stipulated in these Rules, within which a communication must be made or an action taken by a WTO Member to exercise or preserve its rights, the day from which the time period begins to run shall be excluded and, subject to paragraph 1, the last day of the time-period shall be included.

(3) The PGE or the group of three Experts, as the case may be, may extend the time periods provided for in Rules 6, 9, 10 and 12 with the consent of the parties to the dispute and the panel.

(~~3~~4) The DSB Decision on "Expiration of Time-Periods in the DSU", WT/DSB/M/7, shall apply *mutatis mutandis* to matters considered by the PGE.

Working Procedures and Schedule

XIV. (1) Forthwith after being requested to assist a panel, the PGE or the group of three Experts, as the case may be, shall draw up an appropriate working schedule in accordance with the time periods stipulated in these Rules.

(2) The working schedule shall set forth precise dates for the submission of documents and a timetable for the PGE's work including, where possible, the date when the oral hearing would be held, should one of the parties to the dispute request one or should the PGE or the group of three Experts, as the case may be, decide to have one.

(3) The Secretariat shall promptly provide a copy of the working schedule to the panel, the parties to the dispute and any third parties.

Documents

XV. (1) The PGE or the group of three Experts, as the case may be, may disregard any submission not received by the Secretariat within the time period as set out in these Rules or in the working schedule referred to in Rule 14, unless the PGE or the group of three Experts determines that there is good cause for accepting the submission after the expiration of the relevant time period.

(2) Except as otherwise provided in these Rules, every document filed by a party to the dispute or a third party shall be served on each of the other parties to the dispute and on third parties.

(3) A document shall be served by the most expeditious means of delivery or communication available, including by:

(a) delivering a copy of the document to the service address of the party to the dispute or third party; or

(b) sending a copy of the document to the service address of the party to the dispute or third party by facsimile transmission, expedited delivery courier or expedited mail service.

Decision-Making

XVI. (1) The PGE or the group of three Experts, as the case may be, shall make every effort to take decisions by consensus. Where, nevertheless, a decision cannot be arrived at by consensus, the matter at issue shall be decided by a majority vote. Individual opinions shall not be disclosed.

(2) Whenever a request for assistance to a panel has not been assigned by the Chairman of the PGE to a group of three Experts and it appears in the course of the proceeding that, for reasons foreseen under Rules 2 and 4, only four Experts can take part in the decision-making process, the Chairman of the PGE shall immediately select a group of three Experts to examine and respond to the request for assistance.

Confidentiality

XVII. (1) PGE deliberations shall be confidential. The PGE report shall remain confidential until released by the panel.

(2) The report of the PGE shall be drafted without the presence of the parties to the dispute in the light of the information provided and the ~~statements~~ presentations made.

~~(3) Except as otherwise provided in these Rules, no Expert may discuss the subject matter of a request for assistance to a panel with the representatives of any WTO Member.~~

Ex Parte Communications

XVIII. (1) Neither the PGE nor any of its Experts shall discuss any aspect of the subject matter of a request for assistance with any party to the dispute or third party in the absence of the other party(ies) to the dispute until the report of the panel is adopted or, in case of appeal, until the report of the Appellate Body is adopted.

(2) No Expert may discuss any aspect of the subject matter of a request for assistance with any party to the dispute or third party in the absence of the other members of the PGE or of the other members of the group of three

Experts, as the case may be, until the report of the panel is adopted or, in case of appeal, until the report of the Appellate Body is adopted.

Nationals of Parties to the Dispute

XIX. (1) Unless a party to the dispute objects, Experts who are nationals of WTO Members[2] parties to the dispute may contribute to the decision-making process in accordance with Rule 16, may be selected as members of a group of three Experts ~~and may contribute to the decision-making process in accordance with Rule 16~~ or may make comments pursuant to Rule 7(5).

(2) No objections under paragraph 1 shall be considered ~~made~~ where such objections would lead, by themselves or in addition to other factors ~~such as exclusion, excuse, incapacity or non-availability of one or more Experts~~, to a situation where ~~less~~ fewer than three Experts could contribute to the decision-making process.

(3) Any objection under paragraph 1 shall be communicated to the Chairman of the PGE within two (2) days after the date of a request for assistance.

Transition

XX. (1) A person who ceases to be an Expert may, subject to the provisions of Rules 2(3) and 2(4), with the authorization of the Chairman of the PGE and upon notification to the SCM Committee, complete the disposition of any pending request for assistance from a panel, and that person shall, for that purpose only, be deemed to continue to be an Expert.

(2) Any newly elected Expert shall serve only in proceedings initiated after his/her election, unless decided otherwise by the Chairman of the PGE in agreement with the other Experts.

[2]In the case where customs unions or common markets are parties to a dispute, this provision applies to nationals of all member countries of the customs unions or common markets.

PART IV
ADVISORY OPINIONS TO WTO MEMBERS

Request for Advisory Opinion

XXI. (1) Pursuant to Article 24.4 of the SCM Agreement, a~~A~~ WTO Member may request an advisory opinion from the PGE on the nature of any subsidy proposed to be introduced or currently maintained by that WTO Member.

(2) A request for an advisory opinion shall be made in writing. The request shall contain the following:

(a) A clear statement of the ~~issue~~ matter the WTO Member requests the PGE to address;

(b) A detailed description of the programme or measure, addressing any points relevant to the nature of the subsidy;

(c) A copy of any legislation, regulations or other relevant documents establishing the programme or measure and/or governing its operation;

(d) Any other relevant information.

(3) The request shall be submitted to the Chairman of the PGE through the Secretariat. The Chairman of the PGE shall review the request to determine whether it contains the information identified in paragraph 2. If the Chairman of the PGE considers that the request is not complete, he/she shall so indicate to the WTO Member and shall identify the additional information required.

Preparation of the Advisory Opinion

XXII. (1) The PGE or the group of three Experts selected pursuant to Rule 23(2) may, as necessary, in writing or at an oral hearing if any, request further information from, or may pose questions to, the WTO Member requesting an advisory opinion.

(2) The PGE shall make its best efforts to provide its opinion at the earliest date possible.

(~~2~~3) Unless otherwise requested by the WTO Member seeking an advisory opinion, an advisory opinion shall be provided in writing. The advisory opinion shall include the relevant facts on which the PGE based its opinion, the applicability of relevant provisions and the basic rationale behind its conclusions.

(~~3~~4) When applicable, the PGE's advisory opinion shall also specify whether one or more Experts were excused or excluded for the proceeding pursuant to Rules 2(3) or 2(4).

Collegiality

XXIII. (1) All advisory opinions shall be rendered on behalf of the PGE. Except where an Expert is excluded or excused pursuant to Rules 2(3) or 2(4), advisory opinions of the PGE shall be deemed to be prepared and rendered collegially by the five Experts.

(2) Except where an Expert is excluded or excused pursuant to Rules 2(3) or 2(4), all five Experts shall contribute to the advisory opinion of the PGE on each request for such an opinion. However, where ~~appropriate~~ necessary, the Chairman of the PGE may, in ~~consultation~~ agreement with the other Experts, select three Experts to examine and respond to a request for an advisory opinion from a WTO Member.

(3) The three Experts shall be selected on a basis which shall ensure, to the maximum extent possible, that the composition of each group of three Experts will not be predictable. The Chairman of the PGE may serve as one of the three Experts.

(4) An Expert selected pursuant to paragraph 2 above shall make best endeavours to be available for that service. In the event an Expert is prevented from serving due to incapacity or resignation under Rules 4 and 5, or is otherwise unavailable to serve, the Chairman of the PGE will assign the next Expert on the basis set forth in paragraph 3.

(5) Where three Experts have been appointed by the Chairman of the PGE pursuant to paragraph 2, they shall, in the interests of consistency and coherence, consult with the other Experts regarding the matter under review and shall circulate the advisory opinion to the other Experts for comments before presenting it to the WTO Member who requested the advisory opinion. Experts excused or excluded pursuant to Rules 2(3) or 2(4) shall not be consulted.

Presiding Member

XXIV. (1) For each proceeding, the PGE or eEach group of three Experts appointed pursuant to Rule 23(2) above shall have a Presiding Member, who shall be elected by the members of the PGE or the members of the group of three Experts as the case may be ~~three Experts~~.

(2) The responsibilities of the Presiding Member shall include:

(a) coordinating the overall conduct of the work of the group of three Experts;

(b) chairing all meetings related to that work; and

(c) coordinating the drafting of the advisory opinion.

(3) When a matter is referred to a group of three Experts, iIn the event that a Presiding Member becomes incapable of performing his/her duties, the other members ~~of the group of three Experts~~ and the member selected as a replacement pursuant to Rule 23(4) shall elect one of their number as Presiding Member.

Decision-Making

XXV. (1) The PGE or the group of three Experts, as the case may be, shall make every effort to take decisions by consensus. Where, nevertheless, a decision cannot be arrived at by consensus, the matter at issue shall be decided by a majority vote. Individual opinions shall not be disclosed.

(2) Whenever a request for an advisory opinion has not been assigned by the Chairman of the PGE to a group of three Experts and it appears in the course of the proceeding that, for reasons foreseen under Rules 2 and 4, only four Experts can take part in the decision-making process, the Chairman of the PGE shall immediately select a group of three Experts to examine and respond to the request for an advisory opinion.

Confidentiality and Status of Advisory Opinions

XXVI. ~~(1)~~ An advisory opinion is for the exclusive use of the WTO Member requesting it. The existence and content of a request for an advisory opinion, and of any advisory opinion, will ~~shall~~ be confidential. ~~Except as provided in paragraph 2,~~ N~~n~~either the PGE nor the WTO Member seeking the advisory opinion shall reveal its existence or content.

~~(2) Advisory opinions may not be invoked in proceedings under the Article 7 of the SCM Agreement. However, where a specific programme or measure that has been the subject of an advisory opinion is at issue in a dispute under Article 4 of the SCM Agreement, the Chairman of the PGE shall promptly inform the panel and the parties to the dispute and shall provide a copy of the advisory opinion of the PGE to the panel and to the parties to the dispute.~~

~~(3) Except as otherwise provided in these Rules, no Expert may discuss the subject matter of an advisory opinion with the representative of any WTO Member.~~

Transition

XXVII. (1) A person who ceases to be an Expert may, subject to the provisions of Rules 2(3) and 2(4), with the authorization of the Chairman of the PGE and upon notification to the SCM Committee, complete the disposition of any pending request for an advisory opinion, and that person shall, for that purpose only, be deemed to continue to be an Expert.

(2) Any newly elected Expert shall serve only in proceedings initiated after his/her election, unless decided otherwise by the Chairman of the PGE in agreement with the other Experts.

PART V
ADVISORY OPINIONS TO THE SCM COMMITTEE

Request for an Advisory Opinion

XXVIII. (1) Pursuant to Article 24.3 of the SCM Agreement, t~~T~~he SCM Committee may seek an advisory opinion on the existence and nature of any subsidy.

(2) A request for an advisory opinion shall be made in writing. The request shall clearly state the ~~issue~~ matter the SCM Committee requests the PGE to address, and should include a copy of any legislation, regulations or

other relevant ~~documents~~ information relating to the measure or programme.

Information

XXIX. (1) The PGE may, as it considers necessary, request information from, or address questions to any WTO Members~~s~~ regarding the measure(s) or programme(s) in question. WTO Members to whom such requests or questions are addressed shall make best endeavours to respond fully and completely to the PGE. Such requests or questions, and any answers thereto, shall be made in writing, and copies shall be provided to the SCM Committee.

(2) Any WTO Member may present, in writing, any information regarding the measure or programme in question and/or its views regarding the issue the SCM Committee has requested the PGE to address. Any such information or views shall be made in writing, and copies shall be provided to the SCM Committee.

(3) All WTO Members shall have an opportunity to comment upon any requests or questions and answers thereto pursuant to paragraph 1, and upon any information and views provided to the PGE pursuant to paragraph 2, above. Any such comment shall be made in writing, and copies shall be provided to the SCM Committee.

Collegiality

XXX. (1) All advisory opinions shall be rendered on behalf of the PGE. Except where an Expert is excluded or excused pursuant to Rules 2(3) or 2(4), advisory opinions of the PGE shall be deemed to be prepared and rendered collegially by the five Experts.

(2) Except where an Expert is excluded or excused pursuant to Rules 2(3) or 2(4), all five Experts shall contribute to the advisory opinion of the PGE on each request for such an opinion. However, where ~~appropriate~~ necessary, the Chairman of the PGE may, in ~~consultation~~ agreement with the other Experts, select three Experts to examine and respond to a request for an advisory opinion from the SCM Committee.

(3) The three Experts shall be selected on a basis which shall ensure, to the maximum extent possible, that the composition of each group of three Experts will not be predictable. The Chairman of the PGE may serve as one of the three Experts.

(4) An Expert selected pursuant to paragraph 2 above shall make best endeavours to be available for that service. In the event an Expert is prevented from serving due to incapacity or resignation under Rules 4 and 5, or is otherwise unavailable to serve, the Chairman of the PGE will assign the next Expert on the basis set forth in paragraph 3.

(5) Where three Experts have been appointed by the Chairman of the PGE pursuant to paragraph 2, they shall, in the interests of consistency and coherence, consult with the other Experts regarding the matter under review and shall circulate the advisory opinion to the other Experts for comments before presenting it to the SCM Committee. Experts excused or excluded pursuant to Rules 2(3) or 2(4) shall not be consulted.

Presiding Member

XXXI. (1) For each proceeding, the PGE or eEach group of three Experts appointed pursuant to Rule 30(2) above shall have a Presiding Member, who shall be elected by the members of the PGE or the members of the group of three Experts as the case may be three Experts.

(2) The responsibilities of the Presiding Member shall include:

(a) coordinating the overall conduct of the work of the group of three Experts;

(b) chairing all meetings related to that work; and

(c) coordinating the drafting of the advisory opinion.

(3) When a matter is referred to a group of three Experts, iIn the event that a Presiding Member becomes incapable of performing his/her duties, the other members of the group of three Experts and the member selected as a replacement pursuant to Rule 30(4) shall elect one of their number as Presiding Member.

The Advisory Opinion

XXXII. (1) Unless otherwise requested by the SCM Committee, the PGE's advisory opinion shall be provided in the form of a written report.

(2) The PGE's report shall also set out the findings of fact, the applicability of relevant provisions and the basic rationale behind its conclusions.

(3) When applicable, the PGE's report shall also specify whether one or more Experts were excused or excluded for the proceeding pursuant to Rules 2(3) or 2(4).

Decision-Making

XXXIII. (1) The PGE or the group of three Experts, as the case may be, shall make every effort to take decisions by consensus. Where, nevertheless, a decision cannot be arrived at by consensus, the matter at issue shall be decided by a majority vote. Individual opinions shall not be disclosed.

(2) Whenever a request for an advisory opinion has not been assigned by the Chairman of the PGE to a group of three Experts and it appears in the course of the proceeding that, for reasons foreseen under Rules 2 and 4, only four Experts can take part in the decision-making process, the Chairman of the PGE shall immediately select a group of three Experts to examine and respond to the request for an advisory opinion.

Confidentiality

XXXIV. ~~(1)~~ PGE deliberations shall be confidential.

~~(2) Except as otherwise provided in these Rules, no Expert may discuss the subject matter of a request for an advisory opinion with the representatives of any WTO Member.~~

Direction of the SCM Committee

XXXV. (1) The status of and use to be made of an advisory opinion is a matter to be determined by the SCM Committee.

(2) Notwithstanding this Part, the SCM Committee may with respect to a given request for an advisory opinion specify, after consultation with the Chairman of the PGE, the procedures to be followed by the PGE.

Transition

XXXVI. (1) A person who ceases to be an Expert may, subject to the provisions of Rules 2(3) and 2(4), with the authorization of the Chairman of the PGE and upon notification to the SCM Committee, complete the disposition of any pending request for an advisory opinion, and that person shall, for that purpose only, be deemed to continue to be an Expert.

(2) Any newly elected Expert shall serve only in proceedings initiated after his/her election, unless decided otherwise by the Chairman of the PGE in agreement with the other Experts.

PART VI
OTHER

Secretariat

XXXVII. The Secretariat shall provide such assistance to the PGE as is necessary and appropriate.

Entry into Force and Amendment

XXXVIII. (1) These Rules shall enter into force upon their approval by the SCM Committee.

(2) The PGE may propose amendments to these Rules in light of experience. Any such amendments shall enter into force upon their approval by the SCM Committee and, unless otherwise agreed by the WTO Member(s) concerned, shall apply only to requests made on or after such date.

(3) Any WTO Member may suggest amendments to these Rules in the light of experience. Any suggested amendment shall be examined by the SCM Committee. After examination, the SCM Committee may forward the suggested amendment to the PGE. The PGE shall review the suggested amendment and may propose amendments to these Rules to the SCM Committee on that basis.

Appendix D

PROCEDURES FOR ARBITRATION UNDER ARTICLE 8.5 OF THE AGREEMENT ON SUBSIDIES AND COUNTERVAILING MEASURES

Adopted by the Committee on 2 June 1998

Introduction

The Committee on Subsidies and Countervailing Measures has discussed at length the provisions contained in Article 8.5 of the Agreement on Subsidies and Countervailing Measures. In view of the importance of these provisions, as well as the limited time specified in Article 8.5 for the completion of arbitration proceedings and the absence of detailed guidance for their conduct, the Committee has developed the following procedures with the aim of facilitating the operation of arbitration proceedings and enhancing transparency and predictability for all Members with respect to the application of Article 8 of the Agreement. The Committee affirms that because arbitration under Article 8.5 determines the status of a notified programme or individual cases of subsidization under Article 8, the results of any such arbitration proceeding are equally applicable to all Members. This is without prejudice to the right of any Member to request arbitration.

The Committee notes that the provisions of Article 8.5 cannot be viewed strictly in isolation, insofar as they form an integrated part of the whole of Part IV of the Agreement. In this regard, the Committee recognizes the importance of the review procedure under Article 8.4 and the seriousness with which Members are expected to treat it. In particular, to the extent that Members may have questions about the consistency of a notified programme with the conditions and criteria provided for in the provisions of Article 8.2, the Committee would expect Members to make full and substantive use of the procedures under Article 8.4 in order to clarify all relevant questions regarding a notified programme. In the same vein, the Committee notes that, pursuant to Article 8.3, a Member which is notifying a programme is required to provide sufficiently precise information to enable other Members to evaluate the consistency of the programme with the relevant conditions and criteria of Article 8.2. The Committee would, therefore, expect notifying Members to cooperate as fully as possible in responding to the questions of other Members in the course of the Article 8.4 review procedure.

In short, the Committee exhorts all Members to participate constructively and in good faith in the notification and review process provided for in paragraphs 3 and 4 of Article 8 so as to resolve any questions and concerns about notified programmes at the earliest opportunity. Where appropriate, it is recognized that such efforts encompass the possibility of concerned Members consulting informally prior to requesting arbitration in order to avoid unnecessary arbitration requests. Finally, without prejudice to Members' rights as provided for under Article 8.5, the Committee notes that: (i) the interests of clarity, predictability and greater legal certainty would be best served if arbitration requests involving Committee determinations under Article 8.4 (or the failure of the Committee to make a determination) were made as soon as practicable following the conclusion of the procedure set forth in Article 8.4; and (ii) arbitration procedures would be facilitated if requesting Members fully identify and describe those issues which were not raised during the Article 8.4 procedure.

Procedures

The Committee on Subsidies and Countervailing Measures hereby decides, pursuant to the decision of the General Council of 31 January 1995 (WT/GC/M/1), to adopt the following procedures for use in binding arbitration conducted pursuant to Article 8.5 of the Agreement on Subsidies and Countervailing Measures. These procedures shall not add to or detract from the existing rights and obligations of Members under the Agreement on Subsidies and Countervailing Measures or under any other WTO Agreement.

I. *Requests for arbitration*

1. Any Member wishing to request arbitration under Article 8.5 shall address a written request to that effect to the Chairman of the Committee on Subsidies and Countervailing Measures ("the Committee"). The request shall include:

(a) the basis for the request, i.e. a determination by the Committee under Article 8.4, a failure by the Committee to make such a determination, and/or the violation in individual cases of subsidization of the conditions set out in a subsidy programme notified under Article 8.3;

(b) the specific questions to be addressed by the arbitration body, as related to requirements under the provisions of Article 8.2, and a statement of the position taken by the Member requesting the arbitration with respect to each such question;

(c) a brief summary of the information on which the request is based.

2. Any request for arbitration shall be circulated immediately to the Members.

3. Without prejudice to the right of any Member to request arbitration, Members should take into account the need to avoid undue multiplication of arbitration proceedings in respect of the same programme, and should therefore avail themselves of the

procedures under paragraph 4 for becoming Parties, or the procedures under paragraph 17 for becoming Third Parties, to an arbitration.

4. In order to become Parties to the arbitration proceeding, other Members shall have a period of 15 days after the date of circulation of the request for arbitration to provide the Chairman of the Committee with a communication which shall conform with the requirements for requests for arbitration set forth in paragraph 1. Any such communication shall be circulated immediately to the Members.

5. During the 30-day period referred to in paragraph 10, Parties also may agree, subject to the provisions of Section VI, to any supplemental or alternative procedures for arbitration under Article 8.5 to those specified herein, provided that such supplemental or alternative procedures are not incompatible with Article 8.5. Any such supplemental or alternative procedures shall be promptly notified to the Members. In the event that there is no agreement by all Parties on such supplemental or alternative procedures, the procedures specified herein shall apply exclusively and in full.

II. *Referral to arbitration*

6. As soon as the composition of the arbitration body has been decided, a notice to that effect shall be circulated promptly to the Members.

7. For purposes of Article 8.5, the date of circulation of the notice under paragraph 6 shall be deemed to be the date on which the matter is referred to the arbitration body.

III. *Parties to the arbitration proceeding*[1]

8. The Parties to the arbitration proceeding shall be the Member which has notified the subsidy programme in question, the Member which requests the arbitration, and any other Member which has become a Party to the arbitration in accordance with paragraph 4.

IV. *Composition of the arbitration body*

9. The arbitration body shall consist of three arbitrators, unless the Parties agree to a different uneven number.

10. The members of the arbitration body and its president shall be appointed by agreement of the Parties. If the Parties do not reach agreement within 30 days after the date of circulation of the request for arbitration, unless the Parties agree on a longer period, any Party may request the Director-General of the WTO to appoint, in consultation with the Chairman of the Committee, the arbitrator or arbitrators not yet appointed. Such appointment shall be made, after consultation with the Parties, within 10 days of the request to the Director-General.

[1]As used throughout this text, the terms "Party" and "Parties" do not encompass the terms "Third Party" and "Third Parties" provided for in Section VI, infra.

11. Except as the Parties otherwise agree, the arbitrators shall not be citizens of any of the Parties or Third Parties to the arbitration proceeding.[2]

12. The arbitrators shall be chosen from among persons with relevant legal, economic, financial or technical expertise, including expertise in the Agreement on Subsidies and Countervailing Measures, with respect to the matter referred to the arbitration body.

13. Based upon nominations put forward by delegations and approved by the Committee, the Secretariat shall maintain an indicative list of qualified persons from which arbitrators may be selected. This list shall include an identification of each person's academic and/or professional background and qualifications.

14. Where a Party to an arbitration is a developing country Member, the arbitration body shall, if the developing country Member so requests, include at least one arbitrator from a developing country Member.

V. *Terms of reference of the arbitration body*[3]

15. If a request for arbitration pertains to a determination of the Committee under Article 8.4, or a failure of the Committee to make such a determination, the arbitration body shall determine, in light of the specific questions raised under paragraphs 1 and 4 by the Parties to the arbitration, whether the subsidy programme notified under Article 8.3 does not meet the conditions and criteria of Article 8.2.

16. If a request for arbitration pertains to alleged violation in individual cases of the conditions set out in a subsidy programme notified under Article 8.3, the arbitration body shall determine, in light of the specific questions raised under paragraphs 1 and 4 by the Parties to the arbitration, whether or not individual cases of subsidization violate the conditions set out in the subsidy programme notified under Article 8.3. If a Party so requested under paragraph 1 or 4, the arbitration body also shall determine whether the programme in question does not meet the conditions and criteria of Article 8.2.

VI. *Third parties*

17. A Member not wishing to become a Party to the arbitration, but wishing instead to participate in the arbitration on a limited basis, shall have a period of 20 days after the date of circulation of the request for arbitration to inform the Chairman of the Committee in writing that it wishes to become a Third Party to the arbitration proceeding. A Third Party may intervene only with respect to specific questions raised by Parties.

18. A Member that has informed the Committee under paragraph 17 of its interest to participate as a Third Party in the arbitration proceeding shall have the right to make a written submission to the arbitration body and to receive copies of written submissions

[2]In the case where a customs union or a common market is a Party or Third Party to an arbitration, this provision applies to citizens of all members of that customs union or common market.

[3]These terms of reference apply equally to requests for second or later arbitrations.

of the Parties to the arbitration proceeding, shall have an opportunity to be heard at meetings of the arbitration body, and shall otherwise have the right to participate in the arbitration proceeding as specified elsewhere in these procedures. A Third Party may not participate in the selection of arbitrators or in the establishment of the arbitration body's working procedures.

VII. *Working procedures*

19. The arbitration proceedings shall be conducted on the basis of written submissions and documents. The Parties and Third Parties to the arbitration proceedings shall make written submissions within time periods to be determined by the arbitration body after consultation with the Parties. The arbitration body shall decide whether further written submissions are necessary and shall fix a period of time for such submissions after consulting the Parties.

20. The arbitration body also may hold meetings with the Parties and shall hold one such meeting if any Party so requests at an appropriate stage of the proceedings. Any such meeting normally shall include Third Parties. If in exceptional circumstances the arbitration body holds a meeting with Parties only, the arbitration body also shall, upon request of a Third Party, hold one session for Third Parties to present their views, at which Parties shall have the right to be present. Written texts of the oral statements made by Parties and Third Parties shall be submitted to the arbitration body, and shall consist only of the information and views actually presented orally.

VIII. *Process*

21. The proceedings of the arbitration body shall be confidential. Written submissions to the arbitration body shall be treated as confidential. The arbitration body and all Parties and Third Parties to a proceeding shall treat as confidential any information submitted to the arbitration body which the submitter has designated as confidential. Nothing in these procedures shall preclude a Party or a Third Party to an arbitration from disclosing statements of its own positions to the public.

22. A Party or Third Party to an arbitration shall make available to all other Parties and Third Parties its written submissions. A Party or a Third Party shall also, upon request of a Member, provide a non-confidential summary of the information contained in its written submissions that could be disclosed to the public. When providing a non-confidential summary, a Party or Third Party will duly take into account the expeditious nature of these proceedings.

23. There shall be no *ex parte* communications with the arbitration body concerning matters under consideration by the arbitration body.

24. Before presenting its conclusions, the arbitration body shall provide to the Parties and Third Parties a written summary of the information on which it intends to base its conclusions. The arbitration body shall provide an opportunity for the Parties and Third Parties to comment, within a time period to be established by the arbitration body, on the written summary. Each Third Party shall have the right to comment only

on those sections of the written summary which pertain to the specific questions that that Third Party has addressed.
25. The arbitration proceedings shall take place at the seat of the World Trade Organization.
26. The WTO Secretariat shall act as Secretariat to the arbitration body, and shall perform all administrative functions necessary to assist the arbitration body, including the receipt and circulation of communications related to arbitration requests, and the maintenance of an organized permanent record for each arbitration proceeding.

IX. *Information before the arbitration body*

27. The arbitration body shall proceed on the basis of the information before it, to include such of the following as exist and are relevant:

(a) the notifications of the subsidy programme in question, and any yearly updates of such notifications;

(b) the findings of the Secretariat, the minutes of the Committee and the determination by the Committee, as recorded during the procedure under Article 8.4;

(c) the documents and arguments submitted to the Secretariat and the Committee in the procedure under Article 8.4;

(d) the record(s) of any previous arbitration(s) related to the same programme;

(e) any information provided to the arbitration body by the Parties and Third Parties under these procedures;

(f) any information or technical advice obtained by the arbitration body under the provisions of paragraphs 28, 29, and 30.

28. A Member should respond promptly and fully to any request by an arbitration body for such information as the arbitration body considers necessary and appropriate.
29. The arbitration body shall have the right to seek information and technical advice from any individual or body which it deems appropriate. However, before an arbitration body seeks such information or technical advice from any individual or body within the jurisdiction of a Member it shall inform the authorities of that Member.
30. The Parties and Third Parties shall have full access to any requests for information or technical advice under this or the preceding two paragraphs, as well as to any information or technical advice obtained thereby. At the time that it requests information or technical advice under this or the preceding two paragraphs, the arbitration body shall obtain the agreement of the individual, body or Member to disclose to the Parties and

Third Parties all such information or technical advice. The Parties and Third Parties shall treat as confidential any information or technical advice that an individual, body or Member has designated as confidential. The arbitration body shall provide an opportunity to the Parties and Third Parties to comment upon any information or technical advice obtained under this or the preceding two paragraphs.

X. *Rules of conduct*

31. As provided in paragraph IV:1 of the Rules of Conduct for the Understanding on Rules and Procedures Governing the Settlement of Disputes, the Rules of Conduct apply to arbitrators acting pursuant to Article 8.5, and to those Members of the Secretariat called upon to assist in arbitration proceedings pursuant to Article 8.5. In addition, the Rules of Conduct shall apply to any individual from whom any information or technical advice is sought under paragraphs 28, 29 and 30 of these procedures.

XI. *Conclusions of the arbitration body*

2. The conclusions of the arbitration body shall consist of a determination, in light of the specific questions raised under paragraphs 1 and 4 by the Parties to the arbitration, of whether the subsidy programme notified under Article 8.3 does not meet the conditions and criteria of Article 8.2, and/or whether or not the individual cases of subsidization violate the conditions set out in the subsidy programme notified under Article 8.3.

33. The arbitration body shall present to the Members its conclusions and the reasons on which those conclusions are based in the form of a single, collegial decision, within 120 days from the date of circulation of the notice under paragraph 6.

34. These conclusions shall be binding in accordance with Article 8.5.

XII. *Review of these procedures*

35. Without prejudice to Article 31 of the Agreement on Subsidies and Countervailing Measures, the Committee shall, no later than five years after the adoption of these procedures, review their operation, and may decide at that time on any modifications to them.

Appendix E

Agreement on the Application of Sanitary and Phytosanitary Measures

Article 11

Consultations and Dispute Settlement

1. The provisions of Articles XXII and XXIII of GATT 1994 as elaborated and applied by the Dispute Settlement Understanding shall apply to consultations and the settlement of disputes under this Agreement, except as otherwise specifically provided herein.

2. In a dispute under this Agreement involving scientific or technical issues, a panel should seek advice from experts chosen by the panel in consultation with the parties to the dispute. To this end, the panel may, when it deems it appropriate, establish an advisory technical experts group, or consult the relevant international organizations, at the request of either party to the dispute or on its own initiative.

3. Nothing in this Agreement shall impair the rights of Members under other international agreements, including the right to resort to the good offices or dispute settlement mechanisms of other international organizations or established under any international agreement.

Appendix F

Agreement on Textiles and Clothing

Article 4

1. Restrictions referred to in Article 2, and those applied under Article 6, shall be administered by the exporting Members. Importing Members shall not be obliged to accept shipments in excess of the restrictions notified under Article 2, or of restrictions applied pursuant to Article 6.

2. Members agree that the introduction of changes, such as changes in practices, rules, procedures and categorization of textile and clothing products, including those changes relating to the Harmonized System, in the implementation or administration of those restrictions notified or applied under this Agreement should not: upset the balance of rights and obligations between the Members concerned under this Agreement; adversely affect the access available to a Member; impede the full utilization of such access; or disrupt trade under this Agreement.

3. If a product which constitutes only part of a restriction is notified for integration pursuant to the provisions of Article 2, Members agree that any change in the level of that restriction shall not upset the balance of rights and obligations between the Members concerned under this Agreement.

4. When changes mentioned in paragraphs 2 and 3 are necessary, however, Members agree that the Member initiating such changes shall inform and, wherever possible, initiate consultations with the affected Member or Members prior to the implementation of such changes, with a view to reaching a mutually acceptable solution regarding appropriate and equitable adjustment. Members further agree that where consultation prior to implementation is not feasible, the Member initiating such changes will, at the request of the affected Member, consult, within 60 days if possible, with the Members concerned with a view to reaching a mutually satisfactory solution regarding appropriate and equitable adjustments. If a mutually satisfactory solution is not reached, any Member involved may refer the matter to the TMB for recommendations as provided in Article 8. Should the TSB not have had the opportunity to review a dispute concerning

such changes introduced prior to the entry into force of the WTO Agreement, it shall be reviewed by the TMB in accordance with the rules and procedures of the MFA applicable for such a review.

Article 5

1. Members agree that circumvention by transshipment, re-routing, false declaration concerning country or place of origin, and falsification of official documents, frustrates the implementation of this Agreement to integrate the textiles and clothing sector into GATT 1994. Accordingly, Members should establish the necessary legal provisions and/or administrative procedures to address and take action against such circumvention. Members further agree that, consistent with their domestic laws and procedures, they will cooperate fully to address problems arising from circumvention.

2. Should any Member believe that this Agreement is being circumvented by transshipment, re-routing, false declaration concerning country or place of origin, or falsification of official documents, and that no, or inadequate, measures are being applied to address and/or to take action against such circumvention, that Member should consult with the Member or Members concerned with a view to seeking a mutually satisfactory solution. Such consultations should be held promptly, and within 30 days when possible. If a mutually satisfactory solution is not reached, the matter may be referred by any Member involved to the TMB for recommendations.

3. Members agree to take necessary action, consistent with their domestic laws and procedures, to prevent, to investigate and, where appropriate, to take legal and/or administrative action against circumvention practices within their territory. Members agree to cooperate fully, consistent with their domestic laws and procedures, in instances of circumvention or alleged circumvention of this Agreement, to establish the relevant facts in the places of import, export and, where applicable, transshipment. It is agreed that such cooperation, consistent with domestic laws and procedures, will include: investigation of circumvention practices which increase restrained exports to the Member maintaining such restraints; exchange of documents, correspondence, reports and other relevant information to the extent available; and facilitation of plant visits and contacts, upon request and on a case-by-case basis. Members should endeavour to clarify the circumstances of any such instances of circumvention or alleged circumvention, including the respective roles of the exporters or importers involved.

4. Where, as a result of investigation, there is sufficient evidence that circumvention has occurred (e.g. where evidence is available concerning the country or place of true origin, and the circumstances of such circumvention), Members agree that appropriate

action, to the extent necessary to address the problem, should be taken. Such action may include the denial of entry of goods or, where goods have entered, having due regard to the actual circumstances and the involvement of the country or place of true origin, the adjustment of charges to restraint levels to reflect the true country or place of origin. Also, where there is evidence of the involvement of the territories of the Members through which the goods have been transshipped, such action may include the introduction of restraints with respect to such Members. Any such actions, together with their timing and scope, may be taken after consultations held with a view to arriving at a mutually satisfactory solution between the concerned Members and shall be notified to the TMB with full justification. The Members concerned may agree on other remedies in consultation. Any such agreement shall also be notified to the TMB, and the TMB may make such recommendations to the Members concerned as it deems appropriate. If a mutually satisfactory solution is not reached, any Member concerned may refer the matter to the TMB for prompt review and recommendations.

5. Members note that some cases of circumvention may involve shipments transiting through countries or places with no changes or alterations made to the goods contained in such shipments in the places of transit. They note that it may not be generally practicable for such places of transit to exercise control over such shipments.

6. Members agree that false declaration concerning fibre content, quantities, description or classification of merchandise also frustrates the objective of this Agreement. Where there is evidence that any such false declaration has been made for purposes of circumvention, Members agree that appropriate measures, consistent with domestic laws and procedures, should be taken against the exporters or importers involved. Should any Member believe that this Agreement is being circumvented by such false declaration and that no, or inadequate, administrative measures are being applied to address and/or to take action against such circumvention, that Member should consult promptly with the Member involved with a view to seeking a mutually satisfactory solution. If such a solution is not reached, the matter may be referred by any Member involved to the TMB for recommendations. This provision is not intended to prevent Members from making technical adjustments when inadvertent errors in declarations have been made.

Article 6

7. The Member proposing to take safeguard action shall seek consultations with the Member or Members which would be affected by such action. The request for consultations shall be accompanied by specific and relevant factual information, as up-to-date as possible, particularly in regard to: (*a*) the factors, referred to in paragraph 3, on which

the Member invoking the action has based its determination of the existence of serious damage or actual threat thereof; and (*b*) the factors, referred to in paragraph 4, on the basis of which it proposes to invoke the safeguard action with respect to the Member or Members concerned. In respect of requests made under this paragraph, the information shall be related, as closely as possible, to identifiable segments of production and to the reference period set out in paragraph 8. The Member invoking the action shall also indicate the specific level at which imports of the product in question from the Member or Members concerned are proposed to be restrained; such level shall not be lower than the level referred to in paragraph 8. The Member seeking consultations shall, at the same time, communicate to the Chairman of the TMB the request for consultations, including all the relevant factual data outlined in paragraphs 3 and 4, together with the proposed restraint level. The Chairman shall inform the members of the TMB of the request for consultations, indicating the requesting Member, the product in question and the Member having received the request. The Member or Members concerned shall respond to this request promptly and the consultations shall be held without delay and normally be completed within 60 days of the date on which the request was received.

8. If, in the consultations, there is mutual understanding that the situation calls for restraint on the exports of the particular product from the Member or Members concerned, the level of such restraint shall be fixed at a level not lower than the actual level of exports or imports from the Member concerned during the 12-month period terminating two months preceding the month in which the request for consultation was made.

9. Details of the agreed restraint measure shall be communicated to the TMB within 60 days from the date of conclusion of the agreement. The TMB shall determine whether the agreement is justified in accordance with the provisions of this Article. In order to make its determination, the TMB shall have available to it the factual data provided to the Chairman of the TMB, referred to in paragraph 7, as well as any other relevant information provided by the Members concerned. The TMB may make such recommendations as it deems appropriate to the Members concerned.

10. If, however, after the expiry of the period of 60 days from the date on which the request for consultations was received, there has been no agreement between the Members, the Member which proposed to take safeguard action may apply the restraint by date of import or date of export, in accordance with the provisions of this Article, within 30 days following the 60-day period for consultations, and at the same time refer the matter to the TMB. It shall be open to either Member to refer the matter to the TMB before the expiry of the period of 60 days. In either case, the TMB shall promptly conduct an examination of the matter, including the determination of serious damage, or actual threat thereof, and its causes, and make appropriate recommendations to the Members concerned within 30 days. In order to conduct such examination, the TMB shall have

available to it the factual data provided to the Chairman of the TMB, referred to in paragraph 7, as well as any other relevant information provided by the Members concerned.

11. In highly unusual and critical circumstances, where delay would cause damage which would be difficult to repair, action under paragraph 10 may be taken provisionally on the condition that the request for consultations and notification to the TMB shall be effected within no more than five working days after taking the action. In the case that consultations do not produce agreement, the TMB shall be notified at the conclusion of consultations, but in any case no later than 60 days from the date of the implementation of the action. The TMB shall promptly conduct an examination of the matter, and make appropriate recommendations to the Members concerned within 30 days. In the case that consultations do produce agreement, Members shall notify the TMB upon conclusion but, in any case, no later than 90 days from the date of the implementation of the action. The TMB may make such recommendations as it deems appropriate to the Members concerned.

Article 8

1. In order to supervise the implementation of this Agreement, to examine all measures taken under this Agreement and their conformity therewith, and to take the actions specifically required of it by this Agreement, the Textiles Monitoring Body ("TMB") is hereby established. The TMB shall consist of a Chairman and 10 members. Its membership shall be balanced and broadly representative of the Members and shall provide for rotation of its members at appropriate intervals. The members shall be appointed by Members designated by the Council for Trade in Goods to serve on the TMB, discharging their function on an *ad personam* basis.

2. The TMB shall develop its own working procedures. It is understood, however, that consensus within the TMB does not require the assent or concurrence of members appointed by Members involved in an unresolved issue under review by the TMB.

3. The TMB shall be considered as a standing body and shall meet as necessary to carry out the functions required of it under this Agreement. It shall rely on notifications and information supplied by the Members under the relevant Articles of this Agreement, supplemented by any additional information or necessary details they may submit or it may decide to seek from them. It may also rely on notifications to and reports from other WTO bodies and from such other sources as it may deem appropriate.

4. Members shall afford to each other adequate opportunity for consultations with respect to any matters affecting the operation of this Agreement.

5. In the absence of any mutually agreed solution in the bilateral consultations provided for in this Agreement, the TMB shall, at the request of either Member, and following a thorough and prompt consideration of the matter, make recommendations to the Members concerned.

6. At the request of any Member, the TMB shall review promptly any particular matter which that Member considers to be detrimental to its interests under this Agreement and where consultations between it and the Member or Members concerned have failed to produce a mutually satisfactory solution. On such matters, the TMB may make such observations as it deems appropriate to the Members concerned and for the purposes of the review provided for in paragraph 11.

7. Before formulating its recommendations or observations, the TMB shall invite participation of such Members as may be directly affected by the matter in question.

8. Whenever the TMB is called upon to make recommendations or findings, it shall do so, preferably within a period of 30 days, unless a different time period is specified in this Agreement. All such recommendations or findings shall be communicated to the Members directly concerned. All such recommendations or findings shall also be communicated to the Council for Trade in Goods for its information.

9. The Members shall endeavour to accept in full the recommendations of the TMB, which shall exercise proper surveillance of the implementation of such recommendations.

10. If a Member considers itself unable to conform with the recommendations of the TMB, it shall provide the TMB with the reasons therefor not later than one month after receipt of such recommendations. Following thorough consideration of the reasons given, the TMB shall issue any further recommendations it considers appropriate forthwith. If, after such further recommendations, the matter remains unresolved, either Member may bring the matter before the Dispute Settlement Body and invoke paragraph 2 of Article XXIII of GATT 1994 and the relevant provisions of the Dispute Settlement Understanding.

11. In order to oversee the implementation of this Agreement, the Council for Trade in Goods shall conduct a major review before the end of each stage of the integration process. To assist in this review, the TMB shall, at least five months before the end of each stage, transmit to the Council for Trade in Goods a comprehensive report on the implementation of this Agreement during the stage under review, in particular in matters with regard to the integration process, the application of the transitional safeguard mechanism, and relating to the application of GATT 1994 rules and disciplines as defined in Articles 2, 3, 6 and 7 respectively. The TMB's comprehensive report may include

any recommendation as deemed appropriate by the TMB to the Council for Trade in Goods.

12. In the light of its review the Council for Trade in Goods shall by consensus take such decisions as it deems appropriate to ensure that the balance of rights and obligations embodied in this Agreement is not being impaired. For the resolution of any disputes that may arise with respect to matters referred to in Article 7, the Dispute Settlement Body may authorize, without prejudice to the final date set out under Article 9, an adjustment to paragraph 14 of Article 2, for the stage subsequent to the review, with respect to any Member found not to be complying with its obligations under this Agreement.

Appendix G

Agreement on Technical Barriers to Trade

Article 14

Consultation and Dispute Settlement

14.1 Consultations and the settlement of disputes with respect to any matter affecting the operation of this Agreement shall take place under the auspices of the Dispute Settlement Body and shall follow, *mutatis mutandis*, the provisions of Articles XXII and XXIII of GATT 1994, as elaborated and applied by the Dispute Settlement Understanding.

14.2 At the request of a party to a dispute, or at its own initiative, a panel may establish a technical expert group to assist in questions of a technical nature, requiring detailed consideration by experts.

14.3 Technical expert groups shall be governed by the procedures of Annex 2.

14.4 The dispute settlement provisions set out above can be invoked in cases where a Member considers that another Member has not achieved satisfactory results under Articles 3, 4, 7, 8 and 9 and its trade interests are significantly affected. In this respect, such results shall be equivalent to those as if the body in question were a Member.

ANNEX 2

TECHNICAL EXPERT GROUPS

The following procedures shall apply to technical expert groups established in accordance with the provisions of Article 14.

1. Technical expert groups are under the panel's authority. Their terms of reference and detailed working procedures shall be decided by the panel, and they shall report to the panel.

2. Participation in technical expert groups shall be restricted to persons of professional standing and experience in the field in question.

3. Citizens of parties to the dispute shall not serve on a technical expert group without the joint agreement of the parties to the dispute, except in exceptional circumstances when the panel considers that the need for specialized scientific expertise cannot be fulfilled otherwise. Government officials of parties to the dispute shall not serve on a technical expert group. Members of technical expert groups shall serve in their individual capacities and not as government representatives, nor as representatives of any organization. Governments or organizations shall therefore not give them instructions with regard to matters before a technical expert group.

4. Technical expert groups may consult and seek information and technical advice from any source they deem appropriate. Before a technical expert group seeks such information or advice from a source within the jurisdiction of a Member, it shall inform the government of that Member. Any Member shall respond promptly and fully to any request by a technical expert group for such information as the technical expert group considers necessary and appropriate.

5. The parties to a dispute shall have access to all relevant information provided to a technical expert group, unless it is of a confidential nature. Confidential information provided to the technical expert group shall not be released without formal authorization from the government, organization or person providing the information. Where such information is requested from the technical expert group but release of such information by the technical expert group is not authorized, a non-confidential summary of the information will be provided by the government, organization or person supplying the information.

6. The technical expert group shall submit a draft report to the Members concerned with a view to obtaining their comments, and taking them into account, as appropriate, in the final report, which shall also be circulated to the Members concerned when it is submitted to the panel.

Appendix H

Agreement on Implementation of Article VI of Gatt 1994

Article 17

Consultation and Dispute Settlement

17.1 Except as otherwise provided herein, the Dispute Settlement Understanding is applicable to consultations and the settlement of disputes under this Agreement.

17.2 Each Member shall afford sympathetic consideration to, and shall afford adequate opportunity for consultation regarding, representations made by another Member with respect to any matter affecting the operation of this Agreement.

17.3 If any Member considers that any benefit accruing to it, directly or indirectly, under this Agreement is being nullified or impaired, or that the achievement of any objective is being impeded, by another Member or Members, it may, with a view to reaching a mutually satisfactory resolution of the matter, request in writing consultations with the Member or Members in question. Each Member shall afford sympathetic consideration to any request from another Member for consultation.

17.4 If the Member that requested consultations considers that the consultations pursuant to paragraph 3 have failed to achieve a mutually agreed solution, and if final action has been taken by the administering authorities of the importing Member to levy definitive anti-dumping duties or to accept price undertakings, it may refer the matter to the Dispute Settlement Body ("DSB"). When a provisional measure has a significant impact and the Member that requested consultations considers that the measure was taken contrary to the provisions of paragraph 1 of Article 7, that Member may also refer such matter to the DSB.

17.5 The DSB shall, at the request of the complaining party, establish a panel to examine the matter based upon:

(i) a written statement of the Member making the request indicating how a benefit accruing to it, directly or indirectly, under this Agreement has been nullified or impaired, or that the achieving of the objectives of the Agreement is being impeded, and

(ii) the facts made available in conformity with appropriate domestic procedures to the authorities of the importing Member.

17.6 In examining the matter referred to in paragraph 5:

(i) in its assessment of the facts of the matter, the panel shall determine whether the authorities' establishment of the facts was proper and whether their evaluation of those facts was unbiased and objective. If the establishment of the facts was proper and the evaluation was unbiased and objective, even though the panel might have reached a different conclusion, the evaluation shall not be overturned;

(ii) the panel shall interpret the relevant provisions of the Agreement in accordance with customary rules of interpretation of public international law. Where the panel finds that a relevant provision of the Agreement admits of more than one permissible interpretation, the panel shall find the authorities' measure to be in conformity with the Agreement if it rests upon one of those permissible interpretations.

17.7 Confidential information provided to the panel shall not be disclosed without formal authorization from the person, body or authority providing such information. Where such information is requested from the panel but release of such information by the panel is not authorized, a non-confidential summary of the information, authorized by the person, body or authority providing the information, shall be provided.

Appendix I

Agreement on Implementation of Article VII of the General Agreement on Tariffs and Trade 1994

Article 19

Consultations and Dispute Settlement

1. Except as otherwise provided herein, the Dispute Settlement Understanding is applicable to consultations and the settlement of disputes under this Agreement.

2. If any Member considers that any benefit accruing to it, directly or indirectly, under this Agreement is being nullified or impaired, or that the achievement of any objective of this Agreement is being impeded, as a result of the actions of another Member or of other Members, it may, with a view to reaching a mutually satisfactory solution of this matter, request consultations with the Member or Members in question. Each Member shall afford sympathetic consideration to any request from another Member for consultations.

3. The Technical Committee shall provide, upon request, advice and assistance to Members engaged in consultations.

4. At the request of a party to the dispute, or on its own initiative, a panel established to examine a dispute relating to the provisions of this Agreement may request the Technical Committee to carry out an examination of any questions requiring technical consideration. The panel shall determine the terms of reference of the Technical Committee for the particular dispute and set a time period for receipt of the report of the Technical Committee. The panel shall take into consideration the report of the Technical Committee. In the event that the Technical Committee is unable to reach consensus on a matter referred to it pursuant to this paragraph, the panel should afford the parties to the dispute an opportunity to present their views on the matter to the panel.

5. Confidential information provided to the panel shall not be disclosed without formal authorization from the person, body or authority providing such information.

Where such information is requested from the panel but release of such information by the panel is not authorized, a non-confidential summary of this information, authorized by the person, body or authority providing the information, shall be provided.

ANNEX II

TECHNICAL COMMITTEE ON CUSTOMS VALUATION

2. The responsibilities of the Technical Committee shall include the following:

   (f) to carry out an examination of a matter referred to it by a panel under Article 19 of this Agreement;

3. The Technical Committee shall attempt to conclude its work on specific matters, especially those referred to it by Members, the Committee or a panel, in a reasonably short period of time. As provided in paragraph 4 of Article 19, a panel shall set a specific time period for receipt of a report of the Technical Committee and the Technical Committee shall provide its report within that period.

9. The Technical Committee shall meet as necessary but at least two times a year. The date of each meeting shall be fixed by the Technical Committee at its preceding session. The date of the meeting may be varied either at the request of any member of the Technical Committee concurred in by a simple majority of the members of the Technical Committee or, in cases requiring urgent attention, at the request of the Chairman. Notwithstanding the provisions in sentence 1 of this paragraph, the Technical Committee shall meet as necessary to consider matters referred to it by a panel under the provisions of Article 19 of this Agreement.

20. Representatives of a simple majority of the members of the Technical Committee shall constitute a quorum.

21. Each member of the Technical Committee shall have one vote. A decision of the Technical Committee shall be taken by a majority comprising at least two thirds of the members present. Regardless of the outcome of the vote on a particular matter, the Technical Committee shall be free to make a full report to the Committee and to the CCC on that matter indicating the different views expressed in the relevant discussions. Notwithstanding the above provisions of this paragraph, on matters referred to it by a panel, the Technical Committee shall take decisions by consensus. Where no agreement is reached in the Technical Committee on the question referred to it by a panel, the Technical Committee shall provide a report detailing the facts of the matter and indicating the views of the members.

Appendix J

Agreement on Subsidies and Countervailing Measures

Article 4

Remedies

4.1 Whenever a Member has reason to believe that a prohibited subsidy is being granted or maintained by another Member, such Member may request consultations with such other Member.

4.2 A request for consultations under paragraph 1 shall include a statement of available evidence with regard to the existence and nature of the subsidy in question.

4.3 Upon request for consultations under paragraph 1, the Member believed to be granting or maintaining the subsidy in question shall enter into such consultations as quickly as possible. The purpose of the consultations shall be to clarify the facts of the situation and to arrive at a mutually agreed solution.

4.4 If no mutually agreed solution has been reached within 30 days[1] of the request for consultations, any Member party to such consultations may refer the matter to the Dispute Settlement Body ("DSB") for the immediate establishment of a panel, unless the DSB decides by consensus not to establish a panel.

4.5 Upon its establishment, the panel may request the assistance of the Permanent Group of Experts[2] (referred to in this Agreement as the "PGE") with regard to whether the measure in question is a prohibited subsidy. If so requested, the PGE shall immediately review the evidence with regard to the existence and nature of the measure in question and shall provide an opportunity for the Member applying or maintaining the measure to demonstrate that the measure in question is not a prohibited subsidy. The

[1]Any time periods mentioned in this Article may be extended by mutual agreement.
[2]As established in Article 24.

PGE shall report its conclusions to the panel within a time-limit determined by the panel. The PGE's conclusions on the issue of whether or not the measure in question is a prohibited subsidy shall be accepted by the panel without modification.

4.6 The panel shall submit its final report to the parties to the dispute. The report shall be circulated to all Members within 90 days of the date of the composition and the establishment of the panel's terms of reference.

4.7 If the measure in question is found to be a prohibited subsidy, the panel shall recommend that the subsidizing Member withdraw the subsidy without delay. In this regard, the panel shall specify in its recommendation the time period within which the measure must be withdrawn.

4.8 Within 30 days of the issuance of the panel's report to all Members, the report shall be adopted by the DSB unless one of the parties to the dispute formally notifies the DSB of its decision to appeal or the DSB decides by consensus not to adopt the report.

4.9 Where a panel report is appealed, the Appellate Body shall issue its decision within 30 days from the date when the party to the dispute formally notifies its intention to appeal. When the Appellate Body considers that it cannot provide its report within 30 days, it shall inform the DSB in writing of the reasons for the delay together with an estimate of the period within which it will submit its report. In no case shall the proceedings exceed 60 days. The appellate report shall be adopted by the DSB and unconditionally accepted by the parties to the dispute unless the DSB decides by consensus not to adopt the appellate report within 20 days following its issuance to the Members.[3]

4.10 In the event the recommendation of the DSB is not followed within the time-period specified by the panel, which shall commence from the date of adoption of the panel's report or the Appellate Body's report, the DSB shall grant authorization to the complaining Member to take appropriate[4] countermeasures, unless the DSB decides by consensus to reject the request.

4.11 In the event a party to the dispute requests arbitration under paragraph 6 of Article 22 of the Dispute Settlement Understanding ("DSU"), the arbitrator shall determine whether the countermeasures are appropriate.[5]

---

[3]If a meeting of the DSB is not scheduled during this period, such a meeting shall be held for this purpose.

[4]This expression is not meant to allow countermeasures that are disproportionate in light of the fact that the subsidies dealt with under these provisions are prohibited.

[5]This expression is not meant to allow countermeasures that are disproportionate in light of the fact that the subsidies dealt with under these provisions are prohibited.

4.12 For purposes of disputes conducted pursuant to this Article, except for time-periods specifically prescribed in this Article, time-periods applicable under the DSU for the conduct of such disputes shall be half the time prescribed therein.

Article 27

Special and Differential Treatment of Developing Country Members

27.7 The provisions of Article 4 shall not apply to a developing country Member in the case of export subsidies which are in conformity with the provisions of paragraphs 2 through 5. The relevant provisions in such a case shall be those of Article 7.

PART III: ACTIONABLE SUBSIDIES

Article 6

Serious Prejudice

6.6 Each Member in the market of which serious prejudice is alleged to have arisen shall, subject to the provisions of paragraph 3 of Annex V, make available to the parties to a dispute arising under Article 7, and to the panel established pursuant to paragraph 4 of Article 7, all relevant information that can be obtained as to the changes in market shares of the parties to the dispute as well as concerning prices of the products involved.

Article 7

Remedies

7.1 Except as provided in Article 13 of the Agreement on Agriculture, whenever a Member has reason to believe that any subsidy referred to in Article 1, granted or maintained by another Member, results in injury to its domestic industry, nullification or impairment or serious prejudice, such Member may request consultations with such other Member.

7.2 A request for consultations under paragraph 1 shall include a statement of available evidence with regard to *(a)* the existence and nature of the subsidy in question, and *(b)* the injury caused to the domestic industry, or the nullification or impairment, or serious prejudice[6] caused to the interests of the Member requesting consultations.

7.3 Upon request for consultations under paragraph 1, the Member believed to be granting or maintaining the subsidy practice in question shall enter into such consultations as quickly as possible. The purpose of the consultations shall be to clarify the facts of the situation and to arrive at a mutually agreed solution.

7.4 If consultations do not result in a mutually agreed solution within 60 days[7], any Member party to such consultations may refer the matter to the DSB for the establishment of a panel, unless the DSB decides by consensus not to establish a panel. The composition of the panel and its terms of reference shall be established within 15 days from the date when it is established.

7.5 The panel shall review the matter and shall submit its final report to the parties to the dispute. The report shall be circulated to all Members within 120 days of the date of the composition and establishment of the panel's terms of reference.

7.6 Within 30 days of the issuance of the panel's report to all Members, the report shall be adopted by the DSB[8] unless one of the parties to the dispute formally notifies the DSB of its decision to appeal or the DSB decides by consensus not to adopt the report.

7.7 Where a panel report is appealed, the Appellate Body shall issue its decision within 60 days from the date when the party to the dispute formally notifies its intention to appeal. When the Appellate Body considers that it cannot provide its report within 60 days, it shall inform the DSB in writing of the reasons for the delay together with an estimate of the period within which it will submit its report. In no case shall the proceedings exceed 90 days. The appellate report shall be adopted by the DSB and unconditionally accepted by the parties to the dispute unless the DSB decides by consensus not to adopt the appellate report within 20 days following its issuance to the Members.[9]

7.8 Where a panel report or an Appellate Body report is adopted in which it is determined that any subsidy has resulted in adverse effects to the interests of another Mem-

---

[6]In the event that the request relates to a subsidy deemed to result in serious prejudice in terms of paragraph 1 of Article 6, the available evidence of serious prejudice may be limited to the available evidence as to whether the conditions of paragraph 1 of Article 6 have been met or not.

[7]Any time periods mentioned in this Article may be extended by mutual agreement.

[8]If a meeting of the DSB is not scheduled during this period, such a meeting shall be held for this purpose.

[9]If a meeting of the DSB is not scheduled during this period, such a meeting shall be held for this purpose.

ber within the meaning of Article 5, the Member granting or maintaining such subsidy shall take appropriate steps to remove the adverse effects or shall withdraw the subsidy.

7.9 In the event the Member has not taken appropriate steps to remove the adverse effects of the subsidy or withdraw the subsidy within six months from the date when the DSB adopts the panel report or the Appellate Body report, and in the absence of agreement on compensation, the DSB shall grant authorization to the complaining Member to take countermeasures, commensurate with the degree and nature of the adverse effects determined to exist, unless the DSB decides by consensus to reject the request.

7.10 In the event that a party to the dispute requests arbitration under paragraph 6 of Article 22 of the DSU, the arbitrator shall determine whether the countermeasures are commensurate with the degree and nature of the adverse effects determined to exist.

PART IV: NON-ACTIONABLE SUBSIDIES

Article 8

Identification of Non-Actionable Subsidies

8.5 Upon the request of a Member, the determination by the Committee referred to in paragraph 4, or a failure by the Committee to make such a determination, as well as the violation, in individual cases, of the conditions set out in a notified programme, shall be submitted to binding arbitration. The arbitration body shall present its conclusions to the Members within 120 days from the date when the matter was referred to the arbitration body. Except as otherwise provided in this paragraph, the DSU shall apply to arbitrations conducted under this paragraph.

ANNEX V

PROCEDURES FOR DEVELOPING INFORMATION CONCERNING SERIOUS PREJUDICE

1. Every Member shall cooperate in the development of evidence to be examined by a panel in procedures under paragraphs 4 through 6 of Article 7. The parties to the dispute and any third-country Member concerned shall notify to the DSB, as soon as the provisions of paragraph 4 of Article 7 have been invoked, the organization responsible for administration of this provision within its territory and the procedures to be used to comply with requests for information.

2. In cases where matters are referred to the DSB under paragraph 4 of Article 7, the DSB shall, upon request, initiate the procedure to obtain such information from the government of the subsidizing Member as necessary to establish the existence and amount of subsidization, the value of total sales of the subsidized firms, as well as information necessary to analyze the adverse effects caused by the subsidized product.[10] This process may include, where appropriate, presentation of questions to the government of the subsidizing Member and of the complaining Member to collect information, as well as to clarify and obtain elaboration of information available to the parties to a dispute through the notification procedures set forth in Part VII.[11]

3. In the case of effects in third-country markets, a party to a dispute may collect information, including through the use of questions to the government of the third-country Member, necessary to analyze adverse effects, which is not otherwise reasonably available from the complaining Member or the subsidizing Member. This requirement should be administered in such a way as not to impose an unreasonable burden on the third-country Member. In particular, such a Member is not expected to make a market or price analysis specially for that purpose. The information to be supplied is that which is already available or can be readily obtained by this Member (e.g. most recent statistics which have already been gathered by relevant statistical services but which have not yet been published, customs data concerning imports and declared values of the products concerned, etc.). However, if a party to a dispute undertakes a detailed market analysis at its own expense, the task of the person or firm conducting such an analysis shall be facilitated by the authorities of the third-country Member and such a person or firm shall be given access to all information which is not normally maintained confidential by the government.

4. The DSB shall designate a representative to serve the function of facilitating the information-gathering process. The sole purpose of the representative shall be to ensure the timely development of the information necessary to facilitate expeditious subsequent multilateral review of the dispute. In particular, the representative may suggest ways to most efficiently solicit necessary information as well as encourage the cooperation of the parties.

5. The information-gathering process outlined in paragraphs 2 through 4 shall be completed within 60 days of the date on which the matter has been referred to the DSB under paragraph 4 of Article 7. The information obtained during this process shall be submitted to the panel established by the DSB in accordance with the provisions of Part X. This information should include, *inter alia*, data concerning the amount of the sub-

---

[10]In cases where the existence of serious prejudice has to be demonstrated.

[11]The information-gathering process by the DSB shall take into account the need to protect information which is by nature confidential or which is provided on a confidential basis by any Member involved in this process.

sidy in question (and, where appropriate, the value of total sales of the subsidized firms), prices of the subsidized product, prices of the non-subsidized product, prices of other suppliers to the market, changes in the supply of the subsidized product to the market in question and changes in market shares. It should also include rebuttal evidence, as well as such supplemental information as the panel deems relevant in the course of reaching its conclusions.

6. If the subsidizing and/or third-country Member fail to cooperate in the information-gathering process, the complaining Member will present its case of serious prejudice, based on evidence available to it, together with facts and circumstances of the non-cooperation of the subsidizing and/or third-country Member. Where information is unavailable due to non-cooperation by the subsidizing and/or third-country Member, the panel may complete the record as necessary relying on best information otherwise available.

7. In making its determination, the panel should draw adverse inferences from instances of non-cooperation by any party involved in the information-gathering process.

8. In making a determination to use either best information available or adverse inferences, the panel shall consider the advice of the DSB representative nominated under paragraph 4 as to the reasonableness of any requests for information and the efforts made by parties to comply with these requests in a cooperative and timely manner.

9. Nothing in the information-gathering process shall limit the ability of the panel to seek such additional information it deems essential to a proper resolution to the dispute, and which was not adequately sought or developed during that process. However, ordinarily the panel should not request additional information to complete the record where the information would support a particular party's position and the absence of that information in the record is the result of unreasonable non-cooperation by that party in the information-gathering process.

Appendix K

Decision of 5 April 1966 on Procedures under Article XXIII (14S/18)

The CONTRACTING PARTIES,

Recognizing that the prompt settlement of situations in which a contracting party considers that any benefits accruing to it directly or indirectly from the General Agreement are being impaired by measures taken by another contracting party, is essential to the effective functioning of the General Agreement and the maintenance of a proper balance between the rights and obligations of all contracting parties;

Recognizing further that the existence of such a situation can cause severe damage to the trade and economic development of the less-developed contracting parties; and

Affirming their resolve to facilitate the solution of such situations while taking fully into account the need for safeguarding both the present and potential trade of less-developed contracting parties affected by such measures;

Decide that:

1. If consultations between a less-developed contracting party and a developed contracting party in regard to any matter falling under paragraph 1 of Article XXIII do not lead to a satisfactory settlement, the less-developed contracting party complaining of the measures may refer the matter which is the subject of consultations to the Director-General so that, acting in an *ex officio* capacity, he may use his good offices with a view to facilitating a solution.

2. To this effect the contracting parties concerned shall, at the request of the Director-General, promptly furnish all relevant information.

3. On receipt of this information, the Director-General shall consult with the contracting parties concerned and with such other contracting parties or inter-governmental organizations as he considers appropriate with a view to promoting a mutually acceptable solution.

4. After a period of two months from the commencement of the consultations referred to in paragraph 3 above, if no mutually satisfactory solution has been reached, the Director-General shall, at the request of one of the contracting parties concerned, bring the matter to the attention of the CONTRACTING PARTIES or the Council, to whom he shall submit a report on the action taken by him, together with all background information.

5. Upon receipt of the report, the CONTRACTING PARTIES or the Council shall forthwith appoint a panel of experts to examine the matter with a view to recommending appropriate solution. The members of the panel shall act on a personal capacity and shall be appointed in consultation with, and with the approval of, the contracting parties concerned.

6. In conducting its examination and having before it all the background information, the panel shall take due account of all the circumstances and considerations relating to the application of the measures complained of, and their impact on the trade and economic development of affected contracting parties.

7. The panel shall, within a period of sixty days from the date the matter was referred to it, submit its findings and recommendations to the CONTRACTING PARTIES or to the Council, for consideration and decision. Where the matter is referred to the Council, it may, in accordance with Rule 8 of the Intersessional Procedures adopted by the CONTRACTING PARTIES at their thirteenth session[1], address its recommendations directly to the interested contracting parties and concurrently report to the CONTRACTING PARTIES.

8. Within a period of ninety days from the date of the decision of the CONTRACTING PARTIES, or the Council, the contracting party to which a recommendation is directed shall report to the CONTRACTING PARTIES or the Council on the action taken by it in pursuance of the decision.

9. If on examination of this report it is found that a contracting party to which a recommendation has been directed has not complied in full with the relevant recommendation of the CONTRACTING PARTIES or the Council, and that any benefit accruing directly or indirectly under the General Agreement continues in consequence to be nullified or impaired, and that the circumstances are serious enough to justify such action, the CONTRACTING PARTIES may authorize the affected contracting party or parties to suspend, in regard to the contracting party causing the damage, application of any concession or any other obligation under the General Agreement whose suspension is considered warranted, taking account of the circumstances.

---

[1]7S/7.

10. In the event that a recommendation to a developed country by the CONTRACTING PARTIES is not applied within the time-limit prescribed in paragraph 8, the CONTRACTING PARTIES shall consider what measures, further to those undertaken under paragraph 9, should be taken to resolve the matter.

11. If consultations, held under paragraph 2 of Article XXXVII, relate to restrictions for which there is no authority under any provisions to the General Agreement, any of the parties to the consultations may, in the absence of a satisfactory solution, request that consultations be carried out by the CONTRACTING PARTIES pursuant to paragraph 2 of Article XXIII and in accordance with the procedures set out in the present decision, is being understood that a consultation held under paragraph 2 of Article XXXVII in respect of such restrictions will be considered by the CONTRACTING PARTIES as fulfilling the conditions of paragraph 1 of Article XXIII if the parties to the consultations so agree.

Appendix L

Improvements to the GATT Dispute Settlement Rules and Procedures

Decision of 12 April 1989
(L/6489)

G. *Adoption of Panel Reports*

1. In order to provide sufficient time for the members of the Council to consider panel reports, the reports shall not be considered for adoption by the Council until thirty days after they have been issued tot he contracting parties.

2. Contracting parties having objections to panel reports shall give written reasons to explain their objections for circulation at least ten days prior to the Council meeting at which the panel report will be considered.

3. The parties to a dispute shall have the right to participate fully in the consideration of the panel report by the Council, and their views shall be fully recorded. The practice of adopting panel reports by consensus shall be continued, without prejudice to the GATT provisions on decision-making which remain applicable. However, the delaying of the process of dispute settlement shall be avoided.

4. The period from the request under Article XXII:1 or Article XXIII:1 until the Council takes a decision on the panel report shall not, unless agreed to by the parties, exceed fifteen months. The provisions of this paragraph shall not affect the provisions of paragraph 6 of Section F(f).*

***

*This deals with the timing of the panel report and is not relevant to adoption and implementation.

I. Surveillance of Implementation of Recommendations and Rulings

1. Prompt compliance with recommendations or rulings of the CONTRACTING PARTIES under Article XXIII is essential in order to ensure effective resolution of disputes to the benefit of all contracting parties.

2. The contracting party concerned shall inform the Council of its intentions in respect of implementation of the recommendations or rulings. If it is impracticable to comply immediately with the recommendations or rulings, the contracting party concerned shall have a reasonable period of time in which to do so.

3. The Council shall monitor the implementation of recommendations or rulings adopted under Article XXIII:2. The issue of implementation of the recommendations or rulings may be raised at the Council by any contracting party at any time following their adoption. Unless the Council decides otherwise, the issue of implementation of the recommendations or rulings shall be on the agenda of the Council meeting after six months following their adoption and shall remain on the Council's agenda until the issue is resolved. At least ten days prior to each such Council meeting, the contracting party concerned shall provide the Council with a status report in writing of its progress in the implementation of the panel recommendations or rulings.

4. In cases brought by developing contracting parties, the Council shall consider what further action it might take which would be appropriate to the circumstances, in conformity with paragraphs 21 and 23 of the 1979 Understanding regarding Notification, Consultation, Dispute Settlement and Surveillance (BISD 26S/214).

Appendix M

Understanding Regarding Notification, Consultation, Dispute Settlment and Surveillance

Adopted on 28 November 1979
(L/4907)

21. Reports of panels and working parties should be given prompt consideration by the CONTRACTING PARTIES. The CONTRACTING PARTIES should take appropriate action on reports of panels and working parties within a reasonable period of time. If the case is one brought by a less-developed contracting party, such action should be taken in a specially convened meeting, if necessary. In such cases, in considering what appropriate action might be taken the CONTRACTING PARTIES shall take into account not only the trade coverage of measures complained of, but also their impact on the economy of less-developed contracting parties concerned.

***

23. If the matter is one which has been raised by a less-developed contracting party, the CONTRACTING PARTIES shall consider what further action they might take which would be appropriate to the circumstances.

Appendix N

Vienna Convention on the Law of Treaties

SIGNED AT VIENNA 23 May 1969
ENTRY INTO FORCE 27 January 1980

Article 31

General rule of interpretation

1. A treaty shall be interpreted in good faith in accordance with the ordinary meaning to be given to the terms of the treaty in their context and in the light of its object and purpose.

2. The context for the purpose of the interpretation of a treaty shall comprise, in addition to the text, including its preamble and annexes:

(a) any agreement relating to the treaty which was made between all the parties in connexion with the conclusion of the treaty;

(b) any instrument which was made by one or more parties in connexion with the conclusion of the treaty and accepted by the other parties as an instrument related to the treaty.

3. There shall be taken into account, together with the context:

(a) any subsequent agreement between the parties regarding the interpretation of the treaty or the application of its provisions;

(b) any subsequent practice in the application of the treaty which establishes the agreement of the parties regarding its interpretation;

(c) any relevant rules of international law applicable in the relations between the parties.

4. A special meaning shall be given to a term if it is established that the parties so intended.

Article 32

Supplementary means of interpretation

Recourse may be had to supplementary means of interpretation, including the preparatory work of the treaty and the circumstances of its conclusion, in order to confirm the meaning resulting from the application of article 31, or to determine the meaning when the interpretation according to article 31:

(a) leaves the meaning ambiguous or obscure; or

(b) leads to a result which is manifestly absurd or unreasonable.

Index

About the Authors

David Palmeter is a member of the law firm of Powell, Goldstein, Frazer & Murphy LLP, Washington, DC. He advises and represents governments and interested private parties in panel and appellate dispute settlement proceedings in the World Trade Organization.

Petros C. Mavroidis is Professor of Law at the University of Neuchâtel, Switzerland. He previously served in the Legal Affairs Division of GATT and subsequently the WTO, and was responsible for advising dispute settlement panels.

GPSR Compliance

The European Union's (EU) General Product Safety Regulation (GPSR) is a set of rules that requires consumer products to be safe and our obligations to ensure this.

If you have any concerns about our products, you can contact us on ProductSafety@springernature.com

In case Publisher is established outside the EU, the EU authorized representative is:

Springer Nature Customer Service Center GmbH
Europaplatz 3
69115 Heidelberg, Germany

The manufacturer's authorised representative in the EU is Springer
Nature Customer Service Centre GmbH, Europaplatz 3, 69115 Heidelberg,
Germany. If you have any concerns regarding our products, please
contact ProductSafety@springernature.com

Printed and bound by CPI Group (UK) Ltd, Croydon, CR0 4YY
30/09/2026
02225436-0007